Unity 3.x Game Development by Example
by Example
Beginner's Guide

A seat-of-your-pants manual for building fun, groovy little games quickly with Unity 3.x

Ryan Henson Creighton

[PACKT] PUBLISHING

BIRMINGHAM - MUMBAI

Unity 3.x Game Development by Example
Beginner's Guide

First edition: September 2010

Second edition: September 2011

Production Reference: 1160911

Livery Place
35 Livery Street
Birmingham B3 2PB, UK.

ISBN 978-1-84969-184-0

www.packtpub.com

Cover Image by Dan Cox (http://dancoxart.com/)

Credits

Author

Ryan Henson Creighton

Reviewer

Clifford Peters

Acquisition Editor

Wilson D'souza

Development Editor

Wilson D'souza

Technical Editor

Kavita Iyer

Project Coordinator

Jovita Pinto

Proofreader

Lisa Brady

Indexer

Monica Ajmera Mehta

Graphics

Nilesh Mohite

Production Coordinator

Arvindkumar Gupta

Cover Work

Arvindkumar Gupta

About the Author

Ryan Henson Creighton is a veteran game developer and the founder of Untold Entertainment Inc. (`http://www.untoldentertainment.com/blog`) where he creates games and applications. Untold Entertainment specializes in games for kids, teens, tweens, and preschoolers. Prior to founding Untold, Ryan worked as the Senior Game Developer at Canadian media conglomerate Corus Entertainment, creating advergames and original properties for YTV and Treehouse TV using Flash. Ryan is hard at work developing a suite of original products with Untold Entertainment, which includes Sissy's Magical Ponycorn Adventure, the game he authored with his five-year-old daughter Cassie. Ryan maintains one of the most active and enjoyable blogs in the industry. He is also the author of the book that you are currently reading.

When Ryan is not developing games, he's goofing off with his two little girls and his fun-loving wife in downtown Toronto.

Big thanks to Cheryl, Cassandra, and Isabel for their love, their support, and their cinnamon rolls. Thanks to Jean-Guy Niquet for introducing me to Unity; to Jim "McMajorSupporter" McGinley for help with the book outline and ongoing mentorship; to the technical reviewers and Packt staff for letting me leave a few jokes in the book; and to David Barnes, for having such a great sense of humor in the first place. Special thanks to Michael Garforth and friends from the #Unity3D IRC channel on Freenode. I also want to thank Mom, God, and all the usual suspects.

About the Reviewer

Clifford Peters is currently a college student pursuing a degree in Computer Science. He enjoys programming and has been doing so for the past 4 years. He enjoys using Unity and hopes to use it more in the future.

Clifford has also helped to review the books *Unity Game Development Essentials* and *Unity 3D Game Development Hotshot.*

www.PacktPub.com

Support files, eBooks, discount offers and more

You might want to visit www.PacktPub.com for support files and downloads related to your book.

Did you know that Packt offers eBook versions of every book published, with PDF and ePub files available? You can upgrade to the eBook version at www.PacktPub.com and as a print book customer, you are entitled to a discount on the eBook copy. Get in touch with us at service@packtpub.com for more details.

At www.PacktPub.com, you can also read a collection of free technical articles, sign up for a range of free newsletters and receive exclusive discounts and offers on Packt books and eBooks.

http://PacktLib.PacktPub.com

Do you need instant solutions to your IT questions? PacktLib is Packt's online digital book library. Here, you can access, read and search across Packt's entire library of books.

Why Subscribe?

- Fully searchable across every book published by Packt
- Copy and paste, print and bookmark content
- On demand and accessible via web browser

Free Access for Packt account holders

If you have an account with Packt at www.PacktPub.com, you can use this to access PacktLib today and view nine entirely free books. Simply use your login credentials for immediate access.

Table of Contents

Preface   1

Chapter 1: That's One Fancy Hammer!   9
Introducing Unity 3D   9
Unity takes over the world   10
Browser-based 3D? Welcome to the future   10
Time for action – Install the Unity Web Player   10
Welcome to Unity 3D!   11
  What can I build with Unity?   12
    FusionFall   12
  Completely hammered   13
  Should we try to build FusionFall?   13
  Another option   13
    Off-Road Velociraptor Safari   14
  I bent my Wooglie   15
    Big Fun Racing   16
    Diceworks   16
Walk before you can run (or double jump)   17
There's no such thing as "finished"   18
Stop! Hammer time   18
  Explore Bootcamp   19
The wonders of technology!   21
The Scene window   22
  The Game window   22
  The Hierarchy   23
    The Project panel   24
    The Inspector   25
    Heads up?   26
    Layers and layout dropdowns   28
    Playback controls   28
    Scene controls   29

Don't stop there—live a little!   29
Summary   31
   Big ambition, tiny games   31

Chapter 2: Let's Start with the Sky   33
That little lightbulb   34
The siren song of 3D   35
Features versus content   36
A game with no features   36
Mechanic versus skin   36
Trapped in your own skin   37
That singular piece of joy   37
One percent inspiration   37
Motherload   38
Heads up!   40
Artillery Live!   40
Pong   44
The mechanic that launched a thousand games   46
Toy or story   48
Redefining the sky   49
Summary   50
   Let's begin   50

Chapter 3: Game 1: Ticker Taker   51
Kick up a new Unity project   51
   Where did everything go?   52
'Tis volley   53
Keep the dream alive   54
Slash and burn!   54
The many faces of keep-up   55
Creating the ball and the hitter   55
Time for action – Creating the ball   55
A ball by any other name   57
Time for action – Renaming the ball   57
Origin story   58
   XYZ/RGB   59
Time for action – Moving the ball Into the "sky"   60
Time for action – Shrinking the ball   61
Time for action – Saving your scene   62
Time for action – Adding the paddle   62
   What is a mesh?   65
   Poly wanna crack your game performance?   67

Keeping yourself in the dark	68
Time for action – Adding a light	68
Time for action – Moving and rotating the light	69
Extra credit	72
Are you a luminary?	**72**
Who turned out the lights?	72
Darkness reigns	72
Time for action – Camera mania	73
Time for action – Test your game	73
Let's get physical	74
Time for action – Adding physics to your game	74
Understanding the gravity of the situation	75
More bounce to the ounce	76
Time for action – Make the ball bouncy	76
Summary	79
Following the script	79

Chapter 4: Code Comfort	**81**
What is code?	81
Time for action – Writing your first Unity script	81
A leap of faith	83
Lick it and stick it	84
Disappear Me!	84
It's all Greek to me	84
You'll never go hungry again	85
With great sandwich comes great responsibility	86
Examining the code	86
Time for action – Find the Mesh Renderer component	87
Time for action – Make the ball re-appear	88
Ding!	89
Time for action – Journey to the Unity Script Reference	89
The Renderer class	91
What's another word for "huh"?	94
It's been fun	95
Time for action – Unstick the script	95
Gone, but not forgotten	96
Why code?	96
Equip your baby bird	97
Time for action – Creating a new MouseFollow script	97
A capital idea	99
Animating with code	100

Time for action – Animating the paddle	100
Pick a word—(almost) any word	101
Screen coordinates versus world coordinates	102
Move the paddle	103
Worst. Game. Ever.	103
See the matrix	104
Time for action – Listening to the paddle	104
A tiny bit o' math	104
Tracking the numbers	105
Futzing with the numbers	106
Time for action – Logging the new number	106
She's A-Work!	107
Somebody get me a bucket	107
Time for action – Declaring a variable to store the screen midpoint	108
Using all three dees	110
Time for action – Following the Y position of the mouse	111
A keep-up game for robots	111
Once more into the breach	112
Time for action – Re-visiting the Unity Language Reference	112
Our work here is done	113
Time for action – Adding the sample code to your script	113
One final tweak	115
What's a quaternion?	115
Wait, what's a quaternion?	115
WHAT THE HECK IS A QUATERNION??	115
Educated guesses	116
More on Slerp	117
Right on target	117
Keep it up	119
Beyond the game mechanic	120
Chapter 5: Game #2: Robot Repair	**121**
You'll totally flip	122
A blank slate	123
You're making a scene	124
Time for action – Setting up two scenes	124
No right answer	125
Time for action – Preparing the GUI	126
The beat of your own drum	128
Time for action – Creating and linking a custom GUI skin	128
Time for action – Creating a button UI control	130

Want font?	134
Cover your assets	136
Time for action – Nix the mip-mapping	137
Front and center	138
Time for action – Centering the button	138
To the game!	140
Time for action – Adding both scenes to the Build List	141
Set the stage for robots	142
Time for action – Preparing the game scene	142
The game plan	143
Have some class!	144
Time for action – Storing the essentials	145
Start me up	147
Going loopy	148
The anatomy of a loop	148
To nest is best	149
Seeing is believing	150
Time for action – Creating an area to store the grid	151
Build that grid	151
Now you're playing with power!	154
Chapter 6: Game #2: Robot Repair Part 2	**155**
From zero to game in one chapter	155
Finding your center	157
Time for action – Centering the game grid vertically	157
Time for action – Centering the game grid horizontally	160
Down to the nitty griddy	162
Do the random card shuffle	162
Time for action – Preparing to build the deck	163
Let's break some robots	163
Time for action – Building the deck	164
Time for action – Modifying the img argument	167
What exactly is "this"?	169
Random reigns supreme	171
Second dragon down	172
Time to totally flip	172
Time for action – Making the cards two-sided	172
Time for action – Building the card-flipping function	174
Time for action – Building the card-flipping function	177
Pumpkin eater	179
Stabby McDragonpoker rides again	180

Game and match	**180**
Time for action – ID the cards	**180**
Time for action – Comparing the IDs	**181**
On to the final boss	**184**
Endgame	184
Time for action – Checking for victory	**184**
Endgame	187
Bring. It. On.	**188**

Chapter 7: Don't Be a Clock Blocker — 193

Apply pressure	**194**
Time for action – Preparing the clock script	**194**
Time for more action – Preparing the clock text	**195**
Still time for action – Changing the clock text color	**196**
Time for action rides again – Creating a font texture and material	**197**
Time for action – What's with the tiny font?	**200**
Time for action – Preparing the clock code	**201**
Time for action – Creating the countdown logic	**202**
Time for action – Displaying the time onscreen	**204**
Picture it	**207**
Time for action – Grabbing the picture clock graphics	**207**
Time for action – Flexing those GUI muscles	**209**
The incredible shrinking clock	**213**
Keep your fork—there's pie!	**214**
How they did it	**214**
Time for action – Rigging up the textures	**216**
Time for action – Writing the pie chart script	**217**
Time for action – Commencing operation pie clock	**220**
Time for action – Positioning and scaling the clock	**223**
Unfinished business	**225**

Chapter 8: Ticker Taker — 227

Welcome to Snoozeville	**227**
Model behavior	228
Time for action – Exploring the models	**229**
Time for action – Hands up!	**232**
Time for action – Changing the FBX import scale settings	**233**
Time for action – Making the mesh colliders convex	**234**
Time for action – Making the hands and tray follow the mouse	**235**
Time for action – Get your heart on	**236**
Time for action – Ditch the ball and paddle	**239**
Time for action – Material witness	**240**

This just in: this game blows   244
Time for action – Multiple erections   244
Time for action – Creating a font texture   247
Time for action – Creating the HeartBounce script   248
Time for action – Tagging the tray   248
Time for action –Tweak the bounce   251
Time for action – Keeping track of the bounces   252
Time for action – Adding the lose condition   254
Time for action – Adding the Play Again button   256
   Ticker taken   258

Chapter 9: Game #3: The Break-Up   **259**
Time for action – Bombs away!   261
Time for action – Poke those particles   264
Time for action – Creating a spark material   266
Time for action – Prefabulous   269
Time for action – Lights, camera, apartment   272
Time for action – Adding the character   273
Time for action – Registering the animations   274
Time for action – Scripting the character   275
Time for action – Opening the pod bay door, Hal   278
Time for action – Collision-enable the character   278
Time for action – Re-prefab the prefab   279
Time for action – Apocalypse now?   280
Time for action – Go boom   281
Time for action – The point of impact   284
Time for action – Hook up the explosion   285
Summary   286

Chapter 10: Game #3: The Break-Up Part 2   **287**
Time for action – Amass some glass   287
Time for action – Creating a Particle System   288
Time for action – Making it edgier!   291
Time for action – Containing the explosion   292
Time for action – Let's get lazy   293
Very variable?   296
Terminal velocity is a myth—bombs fall faster   296
Time for action – Tagging the objects   297
Time for action – Writing the collision detection code   299
Time for action – Animation interrupts   300
Time for action – Adding facial explosions   301
Time for action – Making some noise   302

Time for action – Adding sounds to the FallingObjectScript	303
What's the catch?	305
Time for action – Mixing it up a bit	306
Summary	310

Chapter 11: Game #4: Shoot the Moon — 311

Time for action – Duplicating your game project	312
Time for action – Spacing this sucker up a bit	313
Time for action – Enter the hero	318
Time for action – It's a hit!	320
Time for action – Bring on the bad guys	323
Time for action – Do some housekeeping	324
Time for action – Fixing the fall	325
Time for action – Tweak the hero	327
Time for action – Give up the func	330
Time for action – Itchy trigger finger	332
Time for action – Futurize the bullet	333
Time for action – Building Halo	334
Time for action – Fire!	337
Time for action – Code do-si-do	339
Time for action – The maaagic of aaaarguments	341
Time for action – Adding the most important part of any space shooter	342
Last year's model	344
Summary	345
More hospitality	345

Chapter 12: Action! — 347

Open heart surgery	347
Time for action – Haul in the hallway	348
Time for action – Meet me at camera two	350
Time for action – Adjusting the Main Camera	351
Time for action – Deck the halls	352
Time for action – Turn on the lights	353
Time for action – Setting up the camera rig	361
Time for action – Animating the bouncer	362
Time for action – I like to move it, move it	364
Time for action – Animating the runner	367
Time for action – How to "handle" Nurse Slipperfoot	369
Time for action – You spin me right round	370
Time for action – Deploying your game	373
Time to grow	375
Beyond the book	376

Appendix: References   **377**

  Online resources   **377**

  Offline resources   **378**

  Free development tools   **379**

    Graphics   379

    Sound   379

  Content sites   **380**

  Game portals   **380**

Index   **381**

Preface

Beginner game developers are wonderfully optimistic, passionate, and ambitious. But that ambition is often dangerous! Too often, budding indie developers and hobbyists bite off more than they can chew. Some of the most popular games in recent memory—*Doodle Jump*, *Angry Birds*, and *Canabalt*, to name a few—have been fun, simple games that have delighted players and delivered big profits to their creators. This is the perfect climate for new game developers to succeed by creating simple games with Unity.

This book starts you off on the right foot, emphasizing small, simple game ideas and playable projects that you can actually finish. The complexity of the games increases gradually as we progress through the chapters. The chosen examples help you learn a wide variety of game development techniques. With this understanding of Unity and bite-sized bits of programming, you can make your own mark in the game industry by finishing fun, simple games.

Unity 3.x Game Development by Example shows you how to build crucial game elements that you can reuse and re-skin in many different games, using the phenomenal (and free!) Unity 3D game engine. It initiates you into indie game culture by teaching you how to make your own small, simple games using Unity 3D and some gentle, easy-to-understand code. It will help you turn a rudimentary keep-up game into a madcap race through hospital hallways to rush a still-beating heart to the transplant ward, program a complete 2D game using Unity's user interface controls, put a dramatic love story spin on a simple catch game, and turn that around into a classic space shooter game with spectacular explosions and "pew" sounds! By the time you're finished, you'll have learned to develop a number of important pieces to create your own games that focus in on that small, singular piece of joy that makes games fun.

What this book covers

Chapter 1, *That's One Fancy Hammer!*, introduces you to Unity 3D—an amazing game engine that enables you to create games and deploy them to a number of different devices, including (at the time of writing) the Web, PCs, iOS platforms, Android devices, and marketplaces on all current generation consoles. You'll play a number of browser-based Unity 3D games to get a sense of what the engine can handle, from a massively-multiplayer online game all the way down to a simple kart racer. You'll download and install your own copy of Unity 3D, and atmospheric Angry Bots demo that ships with the product.

Chapter 2, *Let's Start with the Sky*, explores the difference between a game's skin and its mechanic. Using examples from video game history, including *Worms*, *Mario Tennis*, and *Scorched Earth*, we'll uncover the small, singular piece of joy upon which more complicated and impressive games are based. By concentrating on the building blocks of video games, we'll learn how to distil an unwieldy behemoth of a game concept down to a manageable starter project.

Chapter 3, *Game #1: Ticker Taker*, puts you in the pilot seat of your first Unity 3D game project. We'll explore the Unity environment and learn how to create and place primitives, add components like physic materials and rigidbodies, and make a ball bounce on a paddle using Unity's built-in physics engine without even breaking a sweat.

Chapter 4, *Code Comfort*, continues the keep-up game project by gently introducing scripting. Just by writing a few simple, thoroughly-explained lines of code, you can make the paddle follow the mouse around the screen to add some interactivity to the game. This chapter includes a crash course in game scripting that will renew your excitement for programming where high school computer classes may have failed you.

Chapter 5, *Game#2: Robot Repair*, introduces an often-overlooked aspect of game development: "front-of-house" user interface design—the buttons, logos, screens, dials, bars, and sliders that sit in front of your game—is a complete discipline unto itself. Unity 3D includes a very meaty Graphical User Interface system that allows you to create controls and fiddly bits to usher your players through your game. We'll explore this system, and start building a complete two-dimensional game with it! By the end of this chapter, you'll be halfway to completing *Robot Repair*, a colorful matching game with a twist.

Chapter 6, *Game#2: Robot Repair Part 2*, picks up where the last chapter left off. We'll add interactivity to our GUI-based game, and add important tools to our game development tool belt, including drawing random numbers and limiting player control. When you're finished with this chapter, you'll have a completely playable game using only the Unity GUI system, and you'll have enough initial knowledge to explore the system yourself to create new control schemes for your games.

Chapter 7, Don't be a Clock Blocker, is a standalone chapter that shows you how to build three different game clocks: a number-based clock, a depleting bar clock, and a cool pie wedge clock, all of which use the same underlying code. You can then add one of these clocks to any of the game projects in this book, or reuse the code in a game of your own.

Chapter 8, Ticker Taker, revisits the keep-up game from earlier chapters and replaces the simple primitives with 3D models. You'll learn how to create materials and apply them to models that you import from external art packages. You'll also learn how to detect collisions between Game Objects, and how to print score results to the screen. By the end of this chapter, you'll be well on your way to building *Ticker Taker*—a game where you bounce a still-beating human heart on a hospital dinner tray in a mad dash for the transplant ward!

Chapter 9, Game#3: The Break-Up is a wild ride through Unity's built-in particle system that enables you to create effects like smoke, fire, water, explosions, and magic. We'll learn how to add sparks and explosions to a 3D bomb model, and how to use scripting to play and stop animations on a 3D character. You'll need to know this stuff to complete *The Break-Up*—a catch game that has you grabbing falling beer steins and dodging explosives tossed out the window by your jilted girlfriend.

Chapter 10, Game#3: The Break-Up Part 2, completes *The Break-Up* game from the previous chapter. You'll learn how to reuse scripts on multiple Game Objects, and how to build prefabs, which enable you to modify a whole army of objects with a single click. You'll also learn to add sound effects to your games for a much more engaging experience.

Chapter 11, Game #4: Shoot the Moon, fulfills the promise of *Chapter 2* by taking you through a re-skin exercise on *The Break-Up*. By swapping out a few models, changing the background, and adding a shooting mechanic, you'll turn a game about catching beer steins on terra firma into an action-packed space shooter! In this chapter, you'll learn how to set up a two-camera composite shot, how to use code to animate Game Objects, and how to re-jig your code to save time and effort.

Chapter 12, Action!, takes you triumphantly back to *Ticker Taker* for the coup de grace: a bouncing camera rig built with Unity's built-in animation system that flies through a model of a hospital interior. By using the two-camera composite from *The Break-Up*, you'll create the illusion that the player is actually running through the hospital bouncing a heart on a tin tray. The chapter ends with a refresher on bundling your project and deploying it to the Web so that your millions of adoring fans can finally experience your masterpiece.

Appendix, References, is packed with great Unity-related websites, resources, free game development tools and more. Don't miss it!

What you need for this book

You'll need to be in possession of a sturdy hat, a desk chair equipped with a seatbelt, and an array of delicious snack foods that won't get these pages all cheesy (if you're reading the e-book version, you're all set). Early chapters walk you through downloading and installing Unity 3D (`http://unity3d.com/unity/download/`). A list of resources and links to additional software can be found in the appendix.

Who this book is for

If you've ever wanted to develop games, but have never felt "smart" enough to deal with complex programming, this book is for you. It's also a great kick-start for developers coming from other tools like Flash, Unreal Engine, and Game Maker Pro.

Conventions

In this book, you will find several headings appearing frequently.

To give clear instructions of how to complete a procedure or task, we use:

Time for action – heading

1. Action 1

2. Action 2

3. Action 3

Instructions often need some extra explanation so that they make sense, so they are followed with:

What just happened?

This heading explains the working of tasks or instructions that you have just completed.

You will also find some other learning aids in the book, including:

Pop quiz – heading

These are short multiple choice questions intended to help you test your own understanding.

Have a go hero – heading

These set practical challenges and give you ideas for experimenting with what you have learned.

You will also find a number of styles of text that distinguish between different kinds of information. Here are some examples of these styles, and an explanation of their meaning.

Code words in text are shown as follows: "The result is that the first time the `Update` function is called the paddle appears to jump out of the way to two units along the X-axis."

A block of code is set as follows:

```
function Update () {
    renderer.enabled = false;
}
```

When we wish to draw your attention to a particular part of a code block, the relevant lines or items are set in bold:

```
GUI.BeginGroup (new Rect (Screen.width - clockBG.width - gap,
  gap, clockBG.width, clockBG.height));
GUI.DrawTexture (Rect (0,0, clockBG.width, clockBG.height),
    clockBG);
GUI.EndGroup ();
```

New terms and **important words** are shown in bold. Words that you see on the screen, in menus or dialog boxes for example, appear in the text like this: "A new script is added to the **Project** panel. Name it **MouseFollow**".

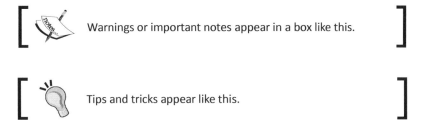

Warnings or important notes appear in a box like this.

Tips and tricks appear like this.

Reader feedback

Feedback from our readers is always welcome. Let us know what you think about this book—what you liked or may have disliked. Reader feedback is important for us to develop titles that you really get the most out of.

To send us general feedback, simply send an e-mail to feedback@packtpub.com, and mention the book title via the subject of your message.

If there is a book that you need and would like to see us publish, please send us a note in the **SUGGEST A TITLE** form on www.packtpub.com or e-mail suggest@packtpub.com.

If there is a topic that you have expertise in and you are interested in either writing or contributing to a book, see our author guide on www.packtpub.com/authors.

Customer support

Now that you are the proud owner of a Packt book, we have a number of things to help you to get the most from your purchase.

Downloading the example code

You can download the example code files for all Packt books you have purchased from your account at http://www.PacktPub.com. If you purchased this book elsewhere, you can visit http://www.PacktPub.com/support and register to have the files e-mailed directly to you.

Errata

Although we have taken every care to ensure the accuracy of our content, mistakes do happen. If you find a mistake in one of our books—maybe a mistake in the text or the code—we would be grateful if you would report this to us. By doing so, you can save other readers from frustration and help us improve subsequent versions of this book. If you find any errata, please report them by visiting http://www.packtpub.com/support, selecting your book, clicking on the **errata submission form** link, and entering the details of your errata. Once your errata are verified, your submission will be accepted and the errata will be uploaded on our website, or added to any list of existing errata, under the Errata section of that title. Any existing errata can be viewed by selecting your title from http://www.packtpub.com/support.

Piracy

Piracy of copyright material on the Internet is an ongoing problem across all media. At Packt, we take the protection of our copyright and licenses very seriously. If you come across any illegal copies of our works, in any form, on the Internet, please provide us with the location address or website name immediately so that we can pursue a remedy.

Please contact us at copyright@packtpub.com with a link to the suspected pirated material.

We appreciate your help in protecting our authors, and our ability to bring you valuable content.

Questions

You can contact us at questions@packtpub.com if you are having a problem with any aspect of the book, and we will do our best to address it.

1
That's One Fancy Hammer!

Technology is a tool. It helps us accomplish amazing things, hopefully more quickly, more easily, and more amazingly if we hadn't used the tool. Before we had newfangled steam-powered hammering machines, we had hammers. And before we had hammers, we had the painful process of smacking a nail into a board with our bare hands. Technology is all about making our lives better, easier, and less painful.

Introducing Unity 3D

Unity 3D is a relatively new piece of technology that strives to make life better and easier for game developers. Unity is a game engine or a game authoring tool that enables creative folk like you to build video games.

By using Unity, you can build video games more quickly and easily than ever before. In the past, building games required an enormous stack of punch cards, a computer that filled a whole room, and a burnt sacrificial offering to an ancient God named Fortran. Today, instead of spanking nails into boards with your palm, you have Unity. Consider it your hammer—a new piece of technology for your creative tool belt.

Unity takes over the world

Throughout this book, we'll be distilling our game development dreams down to small, bite-sized nuggets instead of launching into any sweepingly epic open-world games. The idea here is to focus on something you can actually finish instead of getting bogged down in an impossibly ambitious opus. This book will teach you to build four games, each of which focus on a small, simple gameplay mechanic. You'll learn how to build discrete pieces of functionality that you can apply to each project, filling the games out to make them complete experiences. When you're finished, you can publish these games on the Web, a Mac, or a PC.

The team behind Unity 3D is constantly working on packages and export options for other platforms. At the time of writing, Unity could additionally create games that can be played on the iPhone, iPod, iPad, Android devices, Xbox Live Arcade, PS3, and Nintendo's WiiWare service. Each of these tools is add-on functionality to the core Unity package, and comes at an additional cost. As we're focusing on what we can do without breaking the bank, we'll stick to the core Unity 3D program for the remainder of this book.

With the initial skills that you learn in this book, you'll be able to expand your knowledge and start building more and more complex projects. The key is to start with something you can finish, and then for each new project that you build, to add small pieces of functionality that challenge you and expand your knowledge. Any successful plan for world domination begins by drawing a territorial border in your backyard; consider this book your backyard.

Browser-based 3D? Welcome to the future

One of Unity's most astonishing capabilities is that it can deliver a full 3D game experience right inside your web browser. It does this with the Unity Web Player—a free plugin that embeds and runs Unity content on the Web.

Time for action – Install the Unity Web Player

Before you dive into the world of Unity games, download the Unity Web Player. In much the same way that Flash player runs Flash-created content, the Unity Web Player is a plugin that runs Unity-created content in your web browser.

1. Go to `http://unity3D.com`.

2. Click on the button on the main page to install the Unity Web Player.

3. Follow all of the onscreen prompts until the Web Player has finished installing.

4. The process is only slightly more involved on a Mac. You have to download and run a .dmg file, and then enter your administrator password to install the plugin, but it's relatively quick and painless.

Welcome to Unity 3D!

Now that you've installed the Web Player, you can view the content created with the Unity 3D authoring tool in your browser.

What can I build with Unity?

In order to fully appreciate how fancy this new hammer is, let's take a look at some projects that other people have created with Unity. While these games may be completely out of our reach at the moment, let's find out how game developers have pushed this amazing tool to its very limits.

FusionFall

The first stop on our whirlwind Unity tour is FusionFall—a **Massively Multiplayer Online Role-Playing Game (MMORPG)**. You can find it at `fusionfall.com`. You may need to register to play, but it's definitely worth the extra effort!

FusionFall was commissioned by the Cartoon Network television franchise, and takes place in a re-imagined, anime-style world where popular Cartoon Network characters are all grown up. Darker and more sophisticated versions of the *Powerpuff Girls*, *Dexter*, *Foster* and his imaginary friends, and the kids from *Codename: Kids Next Door* run around battling a slimy green alien menace.

Completely hammered

FusionFall is a very big and very expensive high-profile game that helped draw a lot of attention to the then-unknown Unity game engine when the game was released. As a tech demo, it's one of the very best showcases of what your new technological hammer can really do! FusionFall has real-time multiplayer networking, chat, quests, combat, inventory, NPCs (non-player characters), basic AI (artificial intelligence), name generation, avatar creation, and costumes. And that's just a highlight of the game's feature set. This game packs a lot of depth.

Should we try to build FusionFall?

At this point, you might be thinking to yourself: "Heck YES! FusionFall is exactly the kind of game I want to create with Unity, and this book is going to show me how!"

Unfortunately, a step-by-step guide in creating a game of the size and scope of FusionFall would likely require its own flatbed truck to transport, and you'd need a few friends to help you turn each enormous page. It would take you the rest of your life to read, and on your deathbed, you'd finally realize the grave error that you had made in ordering it online in the first place, despite having qualified for free shipping.

Here's why: check out the game credits link on the Fusion `http://fusionfall. cartoonnetwork.com/game/credits.php`.

This page lists all of the people involved in bringing the game to life. Cartoon Network enlisted the help of an experienced Korean MMO developer called Grigon Entertainment. There are over 80 names on that credits list! Clearly, only two courses of action are available to you:

1. Build a cloning machine and make 79 copies of yourself. Send each of those copies to school to study various disciplines, including marketing, server programming, and 3D animation. Then spend a year building the game with your clones. Keep track of who's who by using a sophisticated armband system.

2. Give up now because you'll never make the game of your dreams.

Another option

Before you do something rash and abandon game development for farming, let's take another look at this. FusionFall is very impressive, and it might look a lot like the game that you've always dreamed of making. This book is not about crushing your dreams. It's about dialing down your expectations, putting those dreams in an airtight jar, and taking baby steps. Confucius said: "A journey of a thousand miles begins with a single step." I don't know much about the man's hobbies, but if he was into video games, he might have said something similar about them—creating a game with a thousand awesome features begins by creating a single, less feature-rich game.

So, let's put the FusionFall dream in an airtight jar and come back to it when we're ready. We'll take a look at some smaller Unity 3D game examples and talk about what it took to build them.

Off-Road Velociraptor Safari

No tour of Unity 3D games would be complete without a trip to `Blurst.com`—the game portal owned and operated by indie game developer Flashbang Studios. In addition to hosting games by other indie game developers, Flashbang has packed Blurst with its own slate of kooky content, including Off-Road Velociraptor Safari.

In Off-Road Velociraptor Safari, you play a dinosaur in a pith helmet and a monocle driving a jeep equipped with a deadly spiked ball on a chain (just like in the archaeology textbooks). Your goal is to spin around in your jeep doing tricks and murdering your fellow dinosaurs (obviously).

For many indie game developers and reviewers, Off-Road Velociraptor Safari was their first introduction to Unity. Some reviewers said that they were stunned that a fully 3D game could play in the browser. Other reviewers were a little bummed that the game was sluggish on slower computers. We'll talk about optimization a little later, but it's not too early to keep performance in mind as you start out.

Fewer features, more promise

If you play Off-Road Velociraptor Safari and some of the other games on the Blurst site, you'll get a better sense of what you can do with Unity without a team of experienced Korean MMO developers. The game has 3D models, physics (code that controls how things move around somewhat realistically), collisions (code that detects when things hit each other), music, and sound effects. Just like FusionFall, the game can be played in the browser with the Unity Web Player plugin. Flashbang Studios also sells downloadable versions of its games, demonstrating that Unity can produce standalone executable game files too.

Maybe we should build Off-Road Velociraptor Safari?

Right then! We can't create FusionFall just yet, but we can surely create a tiny game like Off-Road Velociraptor Safari, right? Well... no. Again, this book isn't about crushing your game development dreams. But the fact remains that Off-Road Velociraptor Safari took five supremely talented and experienced guys eight weeks to build on full-time hours, and they've been tweaking and improving it ever since. Even a game like this, which may seem quite small in comparison to a full-blown MMO game like FusionFall, is a daunting challenge for a solo developer. Put it in a jar up on the shelf, and let's take a look at something you'll have more success with.

I bent my Wooglie

Wooglie.com is a Unity game portal hosted by M2H Game Studio in the Netherlands. One glance at the front page will tell you that it's a far different portal than Blurst.com. Many of the Wooglie games are rough around the edges, and lack the sophistication and the slick professional sheen of the games on Blurst. But here is where we'll make our start with Unity. This is exactly where you need to begin as a new game developer, or as someone approaching a new piece of technology like Unity.

Play through a selection of games on Wooglie. I'll highlight a few of them for your interest:

Big Fun Racing

Big Fun Racing is a simple but effective game where you zip around collecting coins in a toy truck. It features a number of different levels and unlockable vehicles. The game designer sunk a few months into the game in his off-hours; with a little help from outsource artists to create the vehicle models.

Diceworks

Diceworks is a very simple, well-polished game designed for the iPhone in Unity 3D. We won't be covering any iPhone development, but it's good to know that your Unity content can be deployed to a number of other devices and platforms, including Apple iOS, Android, and the Nintendo Wii. These add-on versions of the software cost an additional fee, but you can deploy your games to the Web, to the Mac, and to your PC for free using the indie version of Unity.

Diceworks was created by one artist and one programmer working together as a team. It's rare to find a single person who possesses both programming and artistic talent simultaneously; scientists say that these disciplines are split between two different lobes in our brains, and we tend to favor one or the other. The artist-programmer pairing that produced Diceworks is a common setup in game development. What's your own brain telling you? Are you more comfy with visuals or logic? Art or programming? Once you discover the answer, it's not a bad plan to find someone to make up the other half of your brain so that your game handles both areas competently.

At any event, with Diceworks we're definitely getting closer to the scope and scale that you can manage on your own as you start out with Unity.

It's also interesting to note that Diceworks is a 2D game created in a 3D engine. The third "D" is largely missing, and all of the game elements appear to exist on a flat plane. Nixing that extra dimension when you're just starting out isn't a half bad idea. Adding depth to your game brings a whole new dimension of difficulty to your designs, and it will be easier to get up and running with Unity by focusing on the X and Y axes, and leaving the Z-axis in one of those dream jars. With a few sturdy working game examples under your belt, it won't be long before you can take that jar with Z axis down off the shelf and pop it open. The games that we'll be building in this book will stick to a two-dimensional plane, using three-dimensional models. Even so, certain games have taken this concept and ran with it. For example, the *New Super Mario Bros. Wii* locked its 3D characters to a 2D plane and wound up an extremely complex and satisfying platformer.

Walk before you can run (or double jump)

A common mistake that new game developers make is biting off more than they can chew. Even experienced game developers make this mistake when they get really excited about a project, or when they approach a new technology and expect to be immediately proficient at using it. The real danger here is that you'll sit down and try to create your dream—let's say it's a sword and sorcery RPG epic that combines all the best parts of Diablo, ChuChu Rocket!, and Microsoft Excel. When you've sunk days and weeks and months into it and it still looks nothing like the game you envisioned, you give up. You figure that since you failed at creating your dream game, you were never really cut out to be a game developer to begin with.

You owe it to yourself to start small! Rome wasn't built in a day, and neither was your dream kart racing game starring famous figures from Roman history. By taking smaller steps, you can experience success with a number of smaller games. Then you can take what you learn and add to it, slowly building your expertise until you're in a position to take that dream game jar off the shelf.

For now, let's keep our dream shelf fully stocked, and turn our attention to something small and achievable. By the end of this book, you'll have a collection of working games that started out simply, and grew more and more complex as you got smarter. My hope is that once you finish the book, you'll be well-equipped to dream up new incremental features for your games, and to hunt down the resources you need to fill the gaps in your new-found knowledge.

In *Chapter 2*, we'll go into detail about where you should start when you're deciding what kind of game to create. We'll also see some real-world examples of games that began as simple, effective ideas and later grew into enormously complex and feature-rich titles. From small acorns, mighty multiplayer oak tree games grow.

There's no such thing as "finished"

We'll be learning a lot about iteration throughout this book. Some game developers who produce content for fixed media such as game disks and cartridges are used to producing a gold master—the final build of the game—and calling it a day. One of the joys of deploying games to the Web is that they're never truly finished. You can continue tweaking your web games and modifying them until you end up with a far more fun and polished game than you started with.

Flashbang Studios constantly modified and improved upon Off-Road Velociraptor Safari even years after they were "finished" - three years afterward, in fact! The team addressed critics' initial concerns about sluggish performance by relentlessly tweaking the game and improving upon its performance.

Likewise, we'll be creating some games that are really raw and unfinished at first. But as we learn more about how to program the crucial bits and pieces common to many games, we'll keep revisiting our rough, early games to add those pieces and improve them.

Stop! Hammer time

Now that you've seen some of what Unity can do, it's time to download the program and kick the tires! Unity indie version is available for the low price of **free** (at the time of writing) from the Unity 3D website.

1. Go to `http://unity3D.com`.
2. Click on the **Download Now** button.
3. Download the latest version of the Unity 3D authoring tool for your platform—Mac or PC. If you are given the option, make sure to download the sample project along with the program.

4. Follow all the onscreen prompts until the Unity authoring tool has finished installing.

5. Launch Unity!

Explore Bootcamp

After a quick registration process, Unity is ready to go. With any luck, the **AngryBots Demo** will automatically open. If it doesn't, and you're faced with a dialog asking you to open a project, you can find the **AngryBots Demo** here by default:

Max OS:

```
/Users/Unity/
```

Windows XP:

```
C:\Documents and Settings\All Users\Documents\Unity Projects\
AngryBots
```

Or

```
C:\Documents and Settings\All Users\Shared Documents\Unity Projects\
AngryBots
```

Windows 7/Vista:

```
C:\Users\Public\Documents\Unity Projects\AngryBots
```

If you thought you'd be a rebel and you unchecked the sample projects box when you downloaded Unity, you may find yourself re-downloading Unity to get the **AngryBots Demo**. You can pull down other sample learning projects such as the **AngryBots Demo** from the Unity website:

```
http://unity3d.com/support/resources/example-projects/
```

 As the Unity Technologies team improves the software, they launch new and more impressive demos to show off what Unity can do. If you're reading this book, and your copy of Unity 3D launches a different demo project, don't freak out—everything we're about to discuss can be generally applied to most demos.

When the **AngryBots Demo** first opens, you should see a splash screen referring you to different tutorial resources and language guides. How helpful! Now close it. (Don't worry; it'll be there next time, unless you uncheck the **Show at Startup** checkbox). If you checked the box but you'd really like to see that **Welcome Screen** again, look in the menus under **Help | Welcome Screen**.

Go to **Window | Layouts | 2 by 3** menu to see the different panels that we are about to tour.

To try out the demo, click on the **Play** button at the top-center of the screen.

You can walk around the **AngryBots Demo** using the *WASD* keys on your keyboard. Hold down the main mouse button to fire your boomstick at the aggravated automatons. When you're finished exploring, press the *Esc* key to pause the game and regain mouse control. Then click on the **Play** button again to end the demo.

The wonders of technology!

Unity contains terrain tools that let you model your level right inside the software. It contains a readymade **First Person Controller Prefab** object you can plunk into the world with automatic *WASD* keyboard controls that will allow you to explore the terrain, or you can replace the AngryBots hero with your own character to build a third-person game. Unity automatically takes care of the rendering (drawing), collisions, physics, and sound effects. That's one fancy hammer!

Wide-open worlds with Will

If you'd like to learn how to sculpt your own terrain in Unity, and to add 3D models, sounds, and interactivity to create a simple but functional 3D open-world game, check out, *Unity 3.x Game Development Essentials*, Will Goldstone, *Packt Publishing*.

Much of what you see in the **AngryBots Demo** can't be built directly in Unity. Most of the assets were created with other software; Unity is the program you use to put everything together and to make it interactive. The demo contains special models, such as the airlocks, which were imported from 3D software packages like 3D Studio Max, Maya, or Blender. Certain elements, such as robot enemies, have scripts attached to them. **Scripts** are lists of instructions that tell the items in the game world how to behave. Throughout the book, we'll learn how to import 3D models and to write scripts to control them.

Let's take a quick look around the Unity interface and note a few points of interest.

The Scene window

The **Scene** window is where you can position your **Game Objects** and move them around. This window has various controls to change its level of detail. Use these controls to toggle lighting on and off, and to display the window contents with textures, wireframes, or a combination of both. You can use the colorful gizmo in the top-right corner to constrain the view to the X, Y, and Z axes to view the top and sides of your scene. Click on the white box in the middle to return to perspective view. This window also features a search field. Try clicking on the gizmo's green Y cone to view the **AngryBots Demo** from above, and then type rock into the search field. Every object with "rock" in its name lights up, while the rest of the scene fades to grayscale. Press the tiny **x** button to clear the search field.

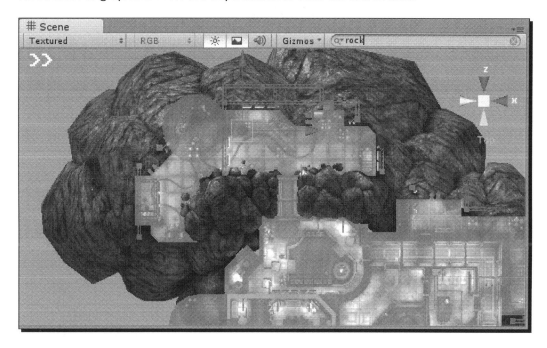

The Game window

The **Game** window shows you what your players will see. When you click on the **Play** button to test your game (as you just did with the **AngryBots Demo**) the results of your efforts play out in this window. Toggle the **Maximize on Play** button to test your game in full-screen mode.

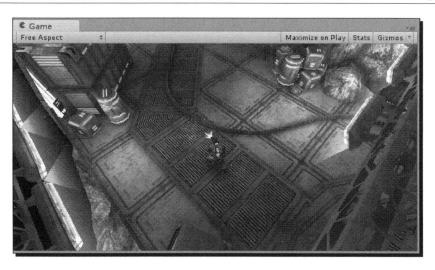

The Hierarchy

The **Hierarchy** panel lists all of the **Game Objects** in your **Scene**. **Game Objects**—cameras, lights, models, and prefabs—are the things that make up your game. They can be "tangible" things like the airlock doors and the cannisters in the **AngryBots Demo**. They can also include intangible things, which only you as the game developer get to see and play with, such as the cameras, the lights, and colliders, which are special invisible shapes that tell the game engine when two **Game Objects** are touching.

The **AngryBots Demo Hierarchy** contains **Game Objects** for the cannisters, the tables, the airlocks and the computer terminals, to name a few. It also lists the **Player**, a very complicated **Game Object** that controls how the hero moves and collides with his environment. The player character has a camera following him. That camera is our eye into the game world. The demo lists a collection called **Environment (sounds)**—a series of **Game Objects** that determine what the player hears when he walks through different parts of the level (such as torrential rain outside, and the droning equipment hum when he moves indoors). So, **Game Objects** can include touchy-feely "physical" objects such as cannisters and airlocks, as well as behind-the-scenes intangible things such as lights, cameras, and actions (scripts).

Click on a **Game Object** in the **Hierarchy** panel, and then hover your mouse over the **Scene** window. Press the *F* key on your keyboard, and the **Scene** window will automatically pan and zoom directly to that object. Alternatively, you can go to **Edit | Frame Selected**, which can be more reliable than using the keyboard shortcut. (I like to think of the *F* as standing for *Focus* to help me remember what this shortcut does.)

The Project panel

The **Project** panel lists all of the elements that you'll use to create **Game Objects** in your project. For example, look for the mech_bot in the Objects/Enemies folder. The **AngryBots Demo** EnemyMech **Game Object** is made up of a series of meshes that represent the mech's shape, a material to depict its "skin" or coloring, and an animation to describe its movement. All of these types of goodies are listed in the **Project** panel.

The **Project** panel displays the contents of a special folder on your computer's operating system called Assets. Unity automatically creates the Assets folder for you when you create a new project. If you drag a compatible file, like a 3D model, a sound effect, or an image into the **Project** panel, Unity copies it to the Assets folder behind the scenes, and displays it in the **Project** panel.

> **Don't mess with the Assets folder!**
>
> Unity stores metadata about the folder, and by moving stuff around or deleting things through your operating system, you may break your project. If you need to make changes, make them right inside Unity in the **Project** panel.

The Inspector

The **Inspector** is a context-sensitive panel, which means that it changes depending on what you select elsewhere in Unity. This is where you can adjust the position, rotation, and scale of **Game Objects** listed in the **Hierarchy** panel. The **Inspector** can also display controls to configure components that add functionality to **Game Objects**. Between the three main panels in Unity (**Hierarchy**, **Project**, and **Inspector**), the **Inspector** is where you'll likely spend most of your time because that's where you'll be tweaking and fiddling with every aspect of the elements that comprise your game projects.

The preceding screenshot of the **Inspector** shows the components attached to the **Player Game Object** in the **AngryBots Demo**: a number of scripts (including **Free Movement Motor** and **Player Move Controller**), a Rigidbody component, a Capsule Collider, and others. To see the same content on your computer, click to open the **Player Game Object** in the **Hierarchy** panel.

Heads up?

Let's use the **Inspector** panel to make a quick change to the orientation of the character. We'll begin the demo with the hero standing on his head (which is a sure-fire way to make those bots even angrier, by the way).

We can use the **Inspector** panel to change the rotation of the player. Follow these steps:

1. In the **Hierarchy** panel, click to select the **Player Game Object**.

2. Click on the **Rotate** button, which looks like two arrows sniffing each others' behinds.

A globe appears around the bottom of the **Player Game Object**. The red X-axis rotator handle encircles the player's body. Clicking and dragging it rotates the player model as if he were standing in a very dodgy canoe. The blue Z-axis rotator handle rotates the player as if there was an invisible pin running through his ankles. If we click-and-drag that handle, the player rotates to either fall flat on his face, or flat on his back, like he's got space sickness. And the green Y-axis rotator handle runs around the player like a hula hoop.

Dragging this handle around makes the player spin to face different directions. The **Player Game Object** can get pretty hairy; in order to isolate the rotation controls, type **player** into the **Scene** window's search field to exclude all other **Game Objects**. (Remember that you can bring the selected **Game Object** into view by pressing the *F* key when your mouse cursor is within the Scene view.)

3. You can click-and-drag the red X-axis arrow to turn the player upside down, but a better method is to change the X-axis rotation in the **Inspector** panel. Expand the gray arrow next to **Transform** in the **Inspector** panel if it's not already open, and change the **X** value under **Rotation** to **180**. The player flips upside down.

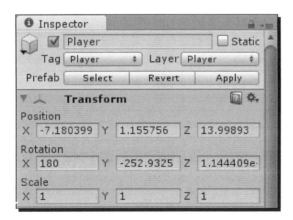

4. Now, when you click on **Play** to test the game, the player will break-dance his way around the **AngryBots Demo**, electric boogaloo-style. The robots are freaking out, thinking "ERROR! DOES NOT COMPUTE!" Way to keep them on their mechanical toes.

Layers and layout dropdowns

Above the **Inspector** panel, you'll see the **Layers** and **Layout** dropdowns. **Game Objects** can be grouped into layers, somewhat like in Photoshop or Flash. Unity stores a few commonly used layouts in the **Layout** dropdown (mine is set to the "2 by 3" configuration). You can also save and load your own custom layouts.

Playback controls

These three buttons help you test your game and control playback. As you've seen, the **Play** button starts and stops your game. The **Pause** button works as expected—it pauses your game so that you can make changes to it on the fly. The third button is a **Step-Through** control; use it to advance frame-by-frame through your game so that you can more tightly control what's going on.

Changes you make while testing don't stick!

One of the more surprising features of Unity is that you can make changes to **Game Objects** and variables on the fly while you're testing your game. But it's important to know that the changes you make during testing will not "stick". Once you stop testing your game, the changes that you made during testing will revert to the state they were in before you clicked on the **Play** button. It's disheartening to make a number of changes to your game, only to realize that the **Play** button was on the entire time, and your changes will be lost. One way to avoid this problem is to toggle the **Maximize on Play** button in the **Game** window so that you'll be more aware of when you're testing and when you're not.

Scene controls

At the top-left of your screen, you'll see four controls that help you move around your **Scene**, and position **Game Objects** within it. These controls are mapped to the *Q, W, E,* and *R* keys on your keyboard. From left to right, they are:

- ◆ **The Hand tool (Q):** Use it to click-and-drag around your scene. Hold down the *Alt* key on your keyboard to rotate the view. Hold down the *Ctrl* key (Windows) or the *Command/control* key (Apple) to zoom in and out. Your mouse wheel will also zoom the scene. Hold down the *Shift* key to pan, zoom, and rotate in larger increments to speed things up. This is a way for you to navigate around the game world. It doesn't actually impact the way the player sees the game. To modify the **Game** view, you need to use the **Move** or **Rotate** tools to modify the **Camera** position.

- ◆ **The Move tool (W):** This tool lets you move the **Game Objects** around your scene. You can either drag the object(s) around by the X, or Y, or Z-axis handles, or by the square in the center for freeform movement. Holding down the *Ctrl* key or *Command* key (Apple) will snap movement to set grid increments. Hold down *Shift* at the same time to snap objects to the "floor".

- ◆ **Rotate tool (E):** Use it to spin your objects around using a neat spherical gizmo. The red, green, and blue lines map to the X, Y, and Z axes.

- ◆ **Scale tool (R):** This tool works much the same as the **Move** and **Rotate** tools. Use it to make your **Game Objects** larger or smaller. Dragging an X, Y, or Z handle will non-uniformly scale (squash and stretch) the object, while dragging the gray cube in the center will uniformly scale it.

Don't stop there—live a little!

We've glanced briefly at the key elements of the Unity interface, but there's no need to stop poking around. Far beyond the scope of this book, there is a wealth of menu options, buttons, and controls that we haven't covered. Why not explore those menus or start randomly clicking on things that you don't yet understand? Now is the time to safely break stuff. You didn't work hard to create the **AngryBots Demo**, so why not mess around with it a little bit?

Here are some things to try:

◆ Select some of the **Game Objects** in the **Hierarchy** panel and move them around in the **Scene** window using the **Scene** controls. What happens when you put an airlock in the middle of the sky? Can the player still pass through? What if you put the cannisters or the computers over the player's head before the game starts? Do they fall, or do they hover? Can you remove objects to help the player career off the edge of the balcony? What happens when he does?

◆ Randomly right-click in the three different panels and read through the context menu options to see what you're getting yourself into.

◆ Poke around in the **Game Object | Create Other** menu. There's a whole list of interesting things that you can add to this scene without even touching the 3D modeling program.

◆ What happens when you delete the lights from the scene? Or the camera? Can you add another camera? More lights? How does that affect the **Scene**?

◆ Can you move the player to another part of the demo to change your starting position?

◆ Can you replace the audio files to make the gun "moo" whenever you fire it?

◆ Download a picture of kittens from the Internet and see if you can wrap it around a boulder model. Kittens rock! You can pull the kitties into your project using the **Assets | Import New Asset** option in the menu.

A tuner's paradise

The Unity 3D interface is designed to be customized. Not only can you define your own custom window layouts, but you can even write custom scripts to make certain buttons and panels appear inside Unity to speed up your workflow. That kind of thing is well beyond the scope of this book, but if you're the kind of person who really likes to get under the hood, you'll be happy to know that you can tweak Unity 3D to your heart's content—maybe add a few racing stripes and install an enormous pair of subwoofers in the back?

Summary

Chapter 1 was all about getting a feel for what Unity can do and for what the program interface had to offer. Here's what we found out:

- Massive 80 person teams, all the way down to tiny one or two person teams are using Unity to create fun games.

- By thinking small, we'll have more success in learning Unity and producing fully functional games instead of huge but half-baked abandoned projects.

- Different flavors of Unity help us deploy our games to different platforms. By using the free indie version, we can deploy to the Web, the Mac, and PC platforms.

- The Unity interface has controls and panels that let us visually compose our game assets, and test games on the fly right inside the program!

I hope you've taken some time to thoroughly vandalize the **Bootcamp Demo**. If you save the file by clicking on **File | Save Project**, you'll have a perma-upside-down space marine in your demo. If you want to return to a pristine **AngryBots Demo** later to wreak more havoc, don't bother saving the hilarious (but meaningless) changes we've made in this chapter.

Big ambition, tiny games

Now that we've trashed this joint, let's take a quick trip through some game design theory. In the next chapter, we'll figure out the scope and scale of a game that a solo, beginner developer should actually tackle. Crack your knuckles and put on your favorite hat because you're about to dip yourself in awesome sauce.

2

Let's Start with the Sky

So, you've downloaded and cracked the seal on a fresh copy of Unity.
You've seen some examples of what other people have done with the game
engine, and you've taken a whirlwind tour of the interface. You can clear out
*the AngryBots Demo project by clicking on **File | New Project** in the menu.*
After choosing a folder for the new project (you can call it "Intro"), Unity may
close down completely and start up again. Once it does, you're left staring at a
3D plane.

Click the little landscape button at the top-middle of the **Scene** view to see this plane. It
stretches on forever in all directions—seemingly infinitely to either side of you, ahead of you,
behind you, straight down to the deepest depths, and straight up to the sky. It's time to build
a game, right? But how do you start? Where do you start?

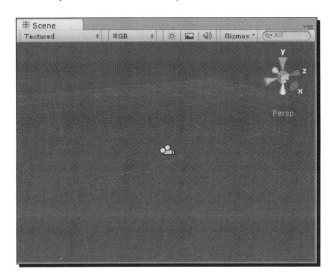

That little lightbulb

The idea's the thing. Every game starts with an idea—that little lightbulb above your head that flicks on all of a sudden and makes you say "aha!" If you've gone as far as picking up a book on Unity, you probably have at least one game idea floating around in your noggin. If you're like me, you really have *10,000* game ideas floating around in your head, all clamoring for your attention. "Build me! Build me!" Which of these ideas should you go ahead with?

The quality that defines a successful game developer is not the number of ideas he has. The guy with ten game ideas is equally as valuable as the girl with 500 game ideas. They're both essentially worthless! A game developer develops games. The one thing that separates you from success is not the number of ideas you've had or the number of projects you've started and abandoned. It's the games you've finished that count. To put it another way: he who executes, wins. Don't worry about getting it right just yet; worry about getting it done.

And what's with all this pressure to make your first game good, anyway? Before he directed *Titanic* and *Avatar*, James Cameron worked on the sequel to *Piranha*—a zero-budget, B-movie schlockfest about murderous fish. Don't worry—you'll be the game world's answer to Cameron some day. But for now, let's finish the fish.

The siren song of 3D

The biggest barrier to your success as a Unity game developer is finishing a project. The idea stage that you enter when you sit staring at that endless 3D plane is crucial to you overcoming that barrier. If you choose the right idea, you will have a much better shot at finishing. Choose the wrong idea, and you might crash and burn. Then you'll probably go back to school and study to be an accountant. Starting in game development and ending in accounting is your worst case scenario. Let's avoid that at all costs.

Before you even begin, the odds are stacked against you. That endless 3D plane is calling you, begging you to start a project that's way over your head. You may begin thinking of the other 3D games you've played: gritty, wide-open "sandbox" games like *Crackdown* or *Grand Theft Auto*; tightly-controlled platformer games with lots of exploration and interesting challenges like *Super Mario 64*; sweeping, epic role-playing games like *Fable* or *Fallout 3*. All of these games have a few things in common: an animated character or first-person camera moving around in a physics-based environment; a rich and detailed 3D world with maps, quests, non-player characters, and pick-ups; and teams of hundreds of people burning through multimillion dollar budgets.

Odds are that you're not reading this book with 99 of your closest, wealthiest friends who all want to help you build your game. You need to ignore the dizzying and endless scope that eternal 3D plane implies, and foster the creativity and resourcefulness that will get you from point A to point B; that is, from an idea to a finished game.

Features versus content

Another trap that fledgling game developers fall into is reducing the scope of their ideas in ways that still prove the project impossible. For example, they'll say: "I don't want to set my sights too high, so I'm going to make a game like *Gran Turismo*, except with fewer cars," or "I want to make *Diablo* with smaller levels," or "I'm going to build *World of Warcraft* with fewer classes and about half the items."

To understand why this approach is so dangerous is to understand a little more about how games are put together. The two issues here are **features** and **content**. All things being equal, a game with 50 levels has more **content** than a game with five levels. The 50-level game has ten times more content, but both games have the same feature: levels. A role-playing game with 12 character classes has more **content** than a game with three character classes, but they both have the same **feature**: character classes.

So, while you may recognize that it's more work to build additional content for a game, try to peer behind the curtain and recognize the number of features that go into a game. Every feature that your game supports takes more work, and sometimes it's easier to build 20 different enemies for a game than to actually build the enemies feature.

A game with no features

We see how it can be dangerous and self-defeating to choose a game with many features and reduce the amount of content in that game. And, because some features are so time-consuming to develop, it's also dangerous to choose a fully featured game and start stripping features to reduce the scope of our project.

A much better approach, and one that you'll have much more success with, is to start with a game that has zero features, and then add them slowly, one by one. Using this approach, you can decide when your game is good enough to unleash on your players, and any additional features you had planned can go into the sequel. This is a winning approach that will see you through many small victories, and many finished games!

Mechanic versus skin

One skill that may help you finish is recognizing the difference between **mechanic** and **skin**. Your game's mechanic is how it physically functions. The very best games contain a simple mechanic that's easy to learn, hard to master, and compelling enough to keep a player interested. The mechanic in *Tetris* is to move and rotate falling blocks into place to create one or more solid lines. The mechanic in many golf games is to simulate swinging a golf club by moving the controller's thumbstick around or tapping a button when the "Power" and "Accuracy" meters are at the right level. The mechanic in *Breakout* is to move a paddle back and forth to bounce a ball into a wall of fragile bricks.

A game's **skin** is how it looks and sounds. It's the animated cutscenes that establish a story. It's the theme that you choose for your game. Imagine a game where you've programmed an object to follow the mouse cursor. There are "bad" objects on the screen that you must avoid, and "good" objects on the screen that you must collect. That's the game mechanic. The game skin could be practically anything. The player object could be a mouse collecting "good" cheese objects and avoiding "bad" rat objects. Or it could be a spaceship collecting space gold and avoiding black holes. Or it could be a fountain pen collecting verbs and avoiding conjunctive pronouns. As they say, "the sky's the limit!"

Trapped in your own skin

The advantage that you gain by separating mechanic from skin is that you can shuck off video game conventions and free yourself to develop anything you want. If you think, "I'd like to create a space-themed strategy game", and you think back to all of the space-themed strategy games that you've played, you might think of 4X games like *Alpha Centauri* or *Master of Orion*—they both pit you in a massive quest to conquer the universe. They are *huge* games that you likely won't finish alone. So, you start trimming them down for sanity's sake—"I'll just build *Master of Orion* with fewer planets," or "I'll just build *Alpha Centauri* with fewer features." Now you've unwittingly fallen into that self-defeating trap. Your project is still too huge. You eventually abandon all hope. A few years later, you're an accountant wondering what might have been.

That singular piece of joy

Instead of going down that doomed copycat road, start asking yourself questions about the outer space theme and the strategy mechanic. What's fun about each of them? Which moments in a game like *Master of Orion* really turn your crank? Do you like mining a planet for resources and buying new stuff? Do you like the thrill of discovering a new planet? Or maybe building an armada of spaceships and conquering enemies really get you excited?

Distill your game down to that one thing—that **singular piece of joy**. Create that one joyful experience for your player, and nail it. That's your game. Everything else is just feature creep.

One percent inspiration

The Internet is packed with small, simple, and free-to-play games that offer the cheap thrill of a singular piece of joy. Let's analyze some of these games to see what we can learn. For each example, we'll identify:

- ◆ The core game mechanic—that singular piece of joy
- ◆ The skin

- ◆ The feature set
- ◆ Possible additional features
- ◆ Alternate skin ideas

These games require the Flash Player plugin, which you probably already have. If, for some weird reason, your computer's been living under a digital rock and you need to install it, browse to `http://get.adobe.com/flashplayer/` and follow the instructions there.

Motherload

Motherload by XGen Studios (`http://www.xgenstudios.com/play/motherload`) distills a complicated 4X game, like *Master of Orion*, down to two joy-inducing tasks: mining for resources and shopping for stuff.

The core mechanic: Pilot your vehicle by using the arrow keys—dig, fly, and avoid long falls—with a finite fuel source. There's only one real "level" in the game, and it stretches down your screen for a loooong time. Your drill-enabled vehicle can only dig down so deep and dig up so many pieces of ore before having to return to the surface to sell off the goods and clear some cargo space. The trick is to dig up and sell enough ore to upgrade your ship so that it can dig deeper, carry more loot, and survive longer falls. The initial goal is to rack up ludicrous cash, but a story eventually develops that adds meaning to your loot-lust. This mechanic is similar to the much simpler game *Lunar Lander*, where the player must gently land a spacecraft on a single non-scrolling screen with limited fuel. You can look at *Motherload* as either a dramatically toned-down *Master of Orion* or a trumped-up *Lunar Lander*!

The skin: A quasi-cartoony space mine with a layer of grit and grime over it. The player character is a futuristic mining vehicle. The only non-player character is a human being (... or is he?).

The feature set:

♦ Vehicle control
♦ Vehicle upgrades (which include both vehicle and terrain strengths and attributes)
♦ Shops
♦ Diggable terrain
♦ Scrollable story or Dialog windows
♦ Save game
♦ Front-of-house features

Front-of-house

We'll be looking at front-of-house game wrappers later on. They include things like the title screen, instructions screen, pause screen, and win or lose screens, and are an essential part of your finished game. The best part is that if you build them well, you can reuse a lot of your work for every new game that you create!

Possible additional features: Sequel features for *Motherload* could include:

♦ Switching between vehicle types
♦ Mining on different planets
♦ Managing multiple vehicles at the same time
♦ A character mode where you get out and run around as a little guy, as in *Blaster Master*.

Alternatively, the sequel could just add new content: more ship upgrades, more ore types, and a larger play area, more story sequences, more sound effects and music tracks, and so on. This is what game reviewers can derisively call a **MOTS (more-of-the-same)** sequel. These days, you can get away with it by calling it an "expansion pack".

Stretch your skills

We're looking way down the road here, but if you create a sequel for your game, be sure to add at least one new feature. And, because you'll still be learning Unity, make sure that developing the new feature requires a skill that you don't already have. In this way, each game that you create will stretch your capabilities farther and wider, until you're an unstoppable Unity pro.

Heads up!

Pay close attention to a game's **Head-up display (HUD)**. Video game HUDs contain graphical elements that usually don't make sense within the context of the game world, but they provide vital information to the player. A great example is the heart health meter in any *Zelda* game, or the energy bar in any fighting game. The *Motherload* HUD includes draining fuel and hull bars. It displays dynamic money and depth tallies. Three clickable elements lead the player to the **Inventory**, **Options**, and **Instructions** screens. Finally, a piece of text lets the player know that there are more shops to be found past the borders of the viewable game area.

Unity has great features for building game HUDs. Every HUD item type that you see in *Motherload*—the graphical bar, the dynamic (changeable) text, the clickable icons, and the flashing helper text—can all be built in the Unity game engine. Skip ahead to *Chapter 4, Code Comfort* if you're dying to try it!

Artillery Live!

Artillery Live! (`http://www.gamebrew.com/game/artillery-live/play`) is one of the many, many iterations of the classic artillery game mechanic, which is nearly as old as video games themselves. It was also built in Flash, but there's no reason it couldn't be built in Unity using 3D tank models and some awesome exploding particle effects.

The core mechanic: Artillery games share a familiar mechanic where the player sets the trajectory and power of his shot to demolish the enemy tanks. This version also has a wind speed feature that affects the way the tank shells travel through the air. Over time and in other incarnations, the game mechanic evolved into a pull-back-and-release experience, mimicking a slingshot. Other versions have the gun turret automatically angling towards the mouse, and the player holds down the mouse button to power up his shot.

The skin: The Gamebrew version is a classic tanks-and-mountains affair, holding true to the very first artillery games developed by game development pioneers in the 1970s. These games transformed from text-only titles to primitively illustrated games with pixelated tanks. An obvious alternate skin is to replace the tank with a man holding a bow and arrow (refer to the *Bowman* series of online games).

Among the more interesting artillery skins in recent memory are the *Worms* series, which replaces tanks with teams of anthropomorphic annelids bent on heavily armed destruction, and *GunBound*, an online multiplayer game where players pilot giant vehicles and mount into battle. In addition to tanks, *GunBound* throws animals and mythical creatures into the mix.

The feature set: In addition to the core mechanic, the front-of-house features, and computer-controlled players, the Gamebrew version of artillery offers turn-based multiplayer gameplay. Multiplayer games are a huge topic and deserve a book of their own. Unity does have features to enable multiplayer play. Unity interfaces nicely with out-of-the-box socket server solutions like SmartFoxServer or ElectroServer, or any server you decide to write on your own. But multiplayer is outside the scope of this book. If you've never programmed a multiplayer game before, you should know that they come with a universe of headaches all of their own! You're definitely better off tackling single-player games if you're just starting out.

The skinny on multiplayer: More and more gaming is moving from the lonely, isolated hobby of teenage boys in their moms' basements to a pastime that people enjoy in groups, either in person or virtually. Any time you move beyond a single-player experience, you're spending more time, money, and brain power to build the game. Here's a list of multiplayer features in order from the most expensive or difficult to least:

◆ **Multiplayer, different computers, real-time**: Think of an action game like *Quake* where everyone's running around and shooting all at once. Real time is the most expensive to develop because you need to make sure all the computers "see" the same thing at once. What if the computer drops a connection or is slower than the rest?

◆ **Multiplayer, different computers, turn-based, synchronous**: *Boggle*, *Battleship*, and various card and parlor games fit into this category. You don't have to worry about the computers constantly sending and receiving the right messages multiple times per second, so it's a little more forgiving.

◆ **Multiplayer, different computers, turn-based, asynchronous**: Instead of people playing at the same time, their latest turn is sent via a Facebook message or an e-mail. Enabling players to grow old and die between moves really takes the messaging pressure off. The *Scrabble*-like *Words With Friends* is a great example.

◆ **Multiplayer, human versus computer**: This is a costly option because you have to write code to make the computer player "intelligent" enough to defeat a human player. The difficulty in doing this changes depending on the type of game. It's easier to program artificial intelligence for a game like *Connect Four* than *Chess*.

◆ **Multiplayer, same computer, human versus human**: This is the easiest to do. There's no complicated messaging going back and forth between computers, and you don't have to write artificial intelligence for a computer player. Regardless, it's still more effort to build than a strictly single-player game and it's dubious if people actually crowd around a single computer playing games in this way. (Devices like the iPad may make this style of play more likely.)

Possible additional features: The *Worms* series did a great job of iterating on the artillery concept by adding a slew of additional features:

◆ Weapons inventories (including the standard issue bazooka, and the not-so-standard-issue *Super Sheep* and *Holy Hand Grenade*)

◆ Limited or collectible ammo

◆ Team-based play with turn time limits

◆ Environmental extras such as land mines, oil barrels, and cargo drops

◆ Moving and jumping

◆ Physics-based platforming with the ninja rope

◆ Cutscenes

- ◆ Nameable characters
- ◆ Single-player levels
- ◆ Unlockable extras

The *Worms* series is an excellent example of how you can take a simple, fun mechanic, skin it creatively, and go nuts with a bevy of brilliant features. But, the most important thing is to start by building artillery, not Worms.

Bang for your buck

By far, the Holy Grail of feature development is finding features that are fast and cheap to build, but that give players the most pleasure. Being able to name your team of worms provided untold entertainment. I remember spending a lot of time with one version of the game creating my own custom sound effects for the worms to say whenever they'd blow stuff up. It wasn't too tough a feature for the developers to build, and I almost spent more time customizing my team than I did playing the game!

Build a game, buy a house?

If you think that players only notice the big ideas and the big games with hundreds of people working on them, artillery offers you a re-education! iPhone developer Ethan Nicholas released a version of artillery on the iPhone and, to date, has earned $600, 000 on his game. It's definitely possible to be small and successful.

Pong

Seriously, *Pong*? Yes, *Pong*. The British Academy of Film and Television Arts hosts an online version of the classic game (`http://www.bafta.org/awards/video-games/play-pong-online,678,BA.html`). The original *Pong* is credited with kickstarting the commercial video game industry that we know today.

The mechanic: *Pong* takes its name from **ping pong**—a real-world activity where two players use paddles to bounce a ball at each other across a table with a tiny net. Ping pong was adapted from tennis, after people finally realized that all that running around was too much effort.

Some real-world activities lend themselves very well to video game mechanics. Not quite 50 years old, the video game industry is still very much in its infancy. There is an enormous wealth of fun stuff in the physical world (like playing ping pong or blowing up tanks) that's waiting to be adapted to a terrific video game mechanic. Are you clever enough to find one of those undiscovered mechanics and build the next *Pong*?

The skin: Like many early games, *Pong* obviously leaves a lot to be desired. Video game skins of tennis and ping pong have come a very long way, and can be radically diverse. Compare the ultra-realistic treatment of ping pong in *Rockstar Games presents Table Tennis* with the all-out insanity of Nintendo's *Mario Tennis* games, which add spinning stars and carnivorous plants to the playing field.

In both cases, be aware of the HUD elements. All three games—*Pong*, *Table Tennis*, and *Mario Power Tennis*—display a dynamic (changeable) piece of text on the screen to show score data. *Table Tennis* also has player names, an exertion meter, and little circles that display how many games each player has won. Look at the positioning of those elements. In all cases, and in our *Motherload* example, these HUD elements are displayed at the top of the screen.

The feature set: As *Pong* evolved, the feature set became far richer. Satisfied that the simple mechanic of hitting a virtual ball back and forth was enough to hang a game on, both Rockstar Games and Nintendo were able to blow out *Pong* with feature sets so juicy that the games' *Pong* origins were barely recognizable. By implementing tennis-style scoring, they made these games much more like tennis with very little effort. Both games add tournaments, rankings, and different player characters with varying skill sets. *Mario Power Tennis* adds about 30 new features involving mushrooms. *Pong* is a true testament to the level of complexity a simple, strong game mechanic can aspire to. But, again, if you want to make a fully-featured game like *Table Tennis* or *Mario Power Tennis*, the key is to start with a simple game like *Pong*.

The mechanic that launched a thousand games

The *Pong* game mechanic is so simple and so effective that its impact can be felt far and wide throughout the annals of video game history.

From *Pong*, we get *Breakout*. The iteration here is to turn *Pong* into a single-player game like real-world handball or squash, with the addition of a breakable brick wall. *Breakout* introduces stages or levels to the *Pong* concept, each with a different configuration of bricks.

Arkanoid iterates on *Breakout* by changing the skin to a sci-fi theme. The paddle becomes a spaceship. *Arkanoid* adds a few new features, most importantly power-ups that come in the form of capsules that are released when the ball smashes into the bricks. When the player catches the capsules with the spaceship, the game rules get bent. The spaceship can become longer. It can become sticky so that the player can catch the ball and plan the next shot. My favorite *Arkanoid* power-up is the red capsule marked "L"; it enables the spaceship to fire laser beams to destroy the bricks!

The *Pong* legacy brings us all the way to the present day, with *Peggle* by **PopCap Games**. *Peggle* combines a few different game mechanics: the brick-smashing and ball-bouncing of *Breakout*, the angular aiming of *Bust-A-Move* or *Puzzle Bobble*, and the random insanity of real-world pachinko games. To jazz up the skin, PopCap adds cartoon unicorns and gophers, and in one of the most talked-about payoffs in video game history, *Peggle* rewards players with an absolutely over-the-top slow-motion winning shot while blaring the climax of Beethoven's *9th Symphony*!

Peggle teaches us some important lessons:

◆ A few small twists on a timeless mechanic will still sell. *Peggle* has been downloaded over 50 million times!

◆ Small games and large games can play nicely together. Famed MMORPG **World of Warcraft (WoW)** is embedded with a special version of *Peggle*, along with another blockbuster PopCap Games hit, *Bejewelled*. WoW players can use *Peggle* to decide how to distribute loot among the party members, which is probably more fun than flipping a coin.

◆ You stand to reach a broader audience if you package your game with friendly, well-illustrated unicorns and gophers instead of dark and brooding axe-wielding superwarriors named "Kane" or "Glorg".

◆ Music and sound play a crucial role in your design. They can make the game.

Have a go hero – Redesign your favorite games

What if *you* were in charge of creating sequels to some very well-known games? Sequels to *Pac-Man* added 3D mazes, jumping, and a red bow to the main character's head. Is that what you would have done? Take a look at this list of popular games and think about which gameplay features you might add if you were in charge of the sequel:

◆ *Pac-Man*

◆ *Tetris*

◆ *Wolfenstein 3D*

◆ *Wii Sports – Boxing*

◆ *Chess*

◆ *Space Invaders*

Toy or story

The approach that we're taking to your initial idea phase is not an approach that comes naturally. Usually, new game developers want to start with setting, story, and character, as if writing a book. That's how we've always been taught to begin a creative project. As there's often so much overlap between narrative forms like books, movies, and TV shows, it's tempting to start there. "My game is about a dark, brooding superwarrior named Kane Glorg who doesn't know who his parents are, so he travels the wasted landscape with his two-handed axe and his vicious battle sloth, slicing through hordes of evil slime demons in his ultimate quest to punch Satan in the face."

The take-away from this chapter is that all that stuff is window dressing. When you're just starting out - and unless you're building an explicitly narrative game like a graphic or textbased adventure - story, setting, or character will be the end point, not the start point. Too many would-be game developers get caught up in the epic implications of their story design instead of worrying about what's most important: does my game have a fun, simple mechanic that players will enjoy?

When you're designing a game, you're not creating a narrative. You're creating a toy, which can be wrapped like a sausage roll in flaky layers of delicious storytelling, character arcs, and twist endings, but you need to start with the toy. You need to start with that small, singular piece of joy that puts a smile on your player's face. As Shigeru Miyamoto, the man who created *Mario*, *Donkey Kong*, and *Zelda*, said in his 2007 keynote at the Game Developers Conference, start by imagining your player having fun with your game, and work backwards from there.

Shopping for ideas

One great place to find inspiration for games is your local toy store. Ignore the toy skins, like the high-seas adventure of *Lego Pirates* sets, and focus on the *mechanic*: building. Ignore the giant fire-breathing scorpion head skin on that *Hot Wheels* track set, and think about the mechanic: the fun, physical way the little cars fly over the ramps. And be sure to investigate the small, simple toys in the end aisles, in the nickel bins, and inside those chocolate eggs and bags of caramel popcorn. You're bound to find game mechanic ideas there.

Pop Quiz – Finding that singular piece of joy

What follows is a list of video games that are all based on a real-world physical game mechanic. In some cases, they're based on a physical game, and in other cases, they're based on goofing around. Can you identify the singular piece of joy from which these games take their cue? The answers are written on a folded piece of paper that I've hidden underneath your chair.

- **Super Monkey Ball**: Tilt the level to guide a sphere along ramps, spirals, and treacherously thin platforms suspended above a bottomless void.

- **Metal Gear Solid**: *Hide* behind crates and other pieces of cover while heavily armed guards *seek* you.

- **Boom Blox**: Throw a ball at a stack of blocks that have different physical properties to knock them all down or to make them explode.

- **Katamari Damacy**: Roll a ball around in random detritus scattered around the level and watch it grow ever larger. Roll up a writhing junk wad of sufficient size to reach the goal.

- **Dance Dance Revolution**: Light up a series of scrolling arrows by stepping on their corresponding buttons on a flat input pad. The button presses are timed to the beat of a backing soundtrack.

Redefining the sky

The sky's the limit, and Unity starts us off with an endless sky. But, through this chapter, we've seen that that endless sky can actually trap us into an ambitious concept that we'll have no chance of completing. So, let's redefine the sky. Instead of wondering how big and complex your game can be, think about the endless array of simple interactions and moments of joy our world contains. Throwing and catching a ball, knocking a pile of stuff over, feeding an animal, growing a plant—the world is packed with simple, effective interactions that ignite our most primitive, most basic Joy Cortexes, which is a neurological term that I've entirely invented just now.

If you want to discover one of these joy-producing real-world moments, study a child. Because games are all about play, the simple things that amuse and delight children and babies are the stuff of award-winning games. What is *Metal Gear Solid* if not a complex game of hide and seek? *Rock Band* and *Guitar Hero* are digital versions of all those times you played air guitar and pretended to be a rock star in front of the mirror with your bedroom door closed. Have you ever rolled snow into giant balls to build a snowman? *Katamari Damacy* is the video game expression of that joy-producing activity.

Summary

In case you ever need to answer a multiple-choice quiz on this chapter, here's a quick rundown of what we've learned:

- Big game ideas are the enemy! Consider thinking small and building slowly to achieve big success.

- By cutting features from your game ideas, you can whittle your design down to a more manageable size than by cutting content.

- A game's mechanic is distinct from its skin. A single, strong game mechanic can support a myriad of different skins through a whole host of great games.

- Start taking notice of the front-of-house aspects and HUDs in the games that you play. You'll be building your own a few chapters from now!

Let's begin

For the rest of this book, we're going to ignore the epic implications of that endless Big Sky Country 3D plane in the Unity **Scene** view. We're going to focus on small, simple, and fun game mechanics. Once you close the back cover of this book, you can take those simple concepts and iterate on them, even blowing them out to ambitious fully-featured crazy-fests like *Master of Orion* or *Mario Power Tennis*. But, stick to the strategy that will make you successful throughout—start at zero, discover that singular piece of joy, and iterate until your game is finished.

3
Game 1: Ticker Taker

So far, we've taken a look at what other developers, large and small, are doing with Unity. We talked about what it's going to take for you as a small developer to succeed—to finish a fully functional game. Now it's time to roll up your sleeves, tie up your inner procrastinator and lock it in the trunk of your car, and start learning to build a game with Unity.

Here's what we're gonna do:

◆ Come up with a game idea

◆ Distil it down to that small, singular piece of joy

◆ Start building the game in Unity using placeholder objects

◆ Add lighting to the scene

◆ Tie into Unity's built-in physics engine

◆ Modify a **GameObject** using components to bend it to your steely will

Let's get cracking!

Kick up a new Unity project

Let's get to that crucial decision-making stage where we're staring at a wide-open 3D frontier in an empty project file.

1. Open Unity 3D. The last project you had opened should appear. (This might be the **AngryBots Demo** from *Chapter 1, That's One Fancy Hammer*!).

2. In the menu, click on **File | New Project...**.

3. Under **Project Location**, type in or browse to the folder where you want your project created. It's a good idea to create a new folder somewhere on your computer where you'll be able to find it again, and name it something that makes sense. I created a folder on my desktop called `Unity Games`, and created my new project in an empty folder called `Chapter1Game`.

4. Unity gives us the option to import a bunch of useful premade goodies into our new project. Select the `Character Controller.unityPackage` file checkbox to import it as shown in the following screenshot:

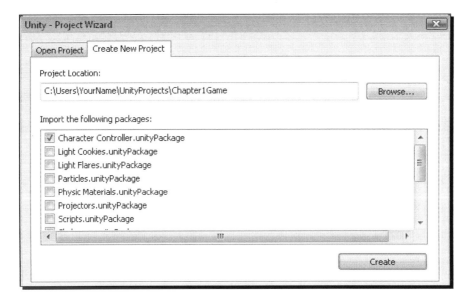

5. Next, click on the **Create** button. Unity will briefly close and restart. After importing the assets we selected, the program will open.

6. Close the **Welcome to Unity** start screen if it's open. You'll find yourself staring face-to-face with that wide-open 3D plane.

Where did everything go?

If you're staring at nothing but a 3D plane in the **Scene** view, Unity has pulled a switcheroo on you. To get back to a layout like the one you saw in the **AngryBots Demo**, choose **2 by 3** from the **Layout** drop-down at the top-right of the screen. Note that there are other choices here, and that Unity enables you to save and restore your own custom layouts.

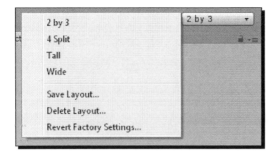

'Tis volley

What kind of game are we going to make? Well, let's pretend that you are totally pumped up about volleyball (work with me here). All you can think about night and day is volleyball. You dream about it at bedtime. You play it every chance you get. So, when it comes to making your first game in Unity, there's no question: you *have* to make a volleyball game.

Let's back away from that idea a little and, using what we learned in *Chapter 2, Let's Start with the Sky*, evaluate the difficulty level of a volleyball game. Volleyball features two teams of six players on either side of a net. A server hits a ball with his hands over the net, and the teams compete to keep the ball in the air, hitting it back and forth over the net. The rally ends when:

◆ One team lets the ball hit the floor

◆ The ball goes out of bounds

◆ An angry puma bursts onto the court and starts chewing on the star player

The first team to score 25 points wins the set. A match is best-of-five. Then there are a number of rules that govern how often and in what way a player may hit the ball (hint: no grabsies).

Hopefully, it's clear that volleyball is a BIG game with lots of rules and a heaping helping of complexity. Multiple teams mean that you have four options:

◆ Two-player, same computer, both players share the keyboard and mouse to compete against each other

◆ One-player, same computer, so, you'd have to program AI—artificial intelligence—to enable the computer to play against a human

◆ Two-player, different computers

◆ Multiple players, multiple computers, where every human player controls a team volleyball team member

We saw in the last chapter that these multiplayer options can add significant layers of complexity to a simple game. Right out of the gate, the challenge is daunting. In addition to providing for two teams, having multiple players on each team means that you have to program a way for the player to switch between different characters. And who knows *how* you're ever gonna animate that puma?

Keep the dream alive

All this results in the simple mathematic equation: **You + volleyball game = badIdea^10**. That's a bad idea to the power of ten, which (mathematically) makes it an exponentially bad idea.

But, volleyball is your passion. Does that mean you can never follow your dreams and make the kinds of games you'd always hoped to build? Of course not! Let's see if we can distil the game of volleyball down to its barest essentials—to that small, singular piece of joy.

Slash and burn!

If you want to finish a game, you need to cut the complexity and the features. Get out your red pen and/or machete, and follow along:

1. Scrap the sets and the best-of-five match structure.

2. Kibosh the teams.

3. Jettison the multiple players.

4. Ditch the net.

5. Nix the referee and the spectators.

    What do we have? Just a person with a ball, looking kind of lonely. Hmm. That person might be a little tricky to model, texture, rig, and animate. Let's keep slashing.

6. Next, trash the player.

Now where are we? We have a ball, floating in midair; a ball that can't hit the floor. So, we need something simple to hit the ball with. A human character is too complicated, so let's just say it's a surface. We'll have some kind of thing that we can bounce the ball on.

The many faces of keep-up

You know what? This game is starting to sound a lot like keep-up. You might have played that as a kid with a balloon that couldn't hit the ground. Or you might have played it in a circle of hippies and called it Hacky Sack or footbag. You might have played it in a soccer drill by bouncing the ball on different parts of your body. You may even have played it by taking something scalding hot out of the oven, calling it "Ow! Ow! Ow! It burns! Get me an oven mitt already! OW!"

Keep-up looks a whole lot like Pong or Breakout from *Chapter 2, Let's Start with the Sky*. You have an object to keep up and an object to keep it up with. The innovation is a little bit of physics—in this case, gravity, which is the force that constantly pulls the object toward the ground. It's simple, it's effective, and your players will instantly get it. It distills volleyball down to that singular piece of joy. It's what volleyball was meant to be, before Johnny McBuzzkill came along and added all of those formalized rules and unflattering shorts. And, because little kids play and enjoy keep-up, you know that you're tapping into some primal, intuitive game mechanic that will stand the test of time.

Keep-up sounds like a *great* first project for learning Unity. Let's do it! Let's build a keep-up game!

Creating the ball and the hitter

For now, we'll use Unity's built-in 3D primitives to create our Game objects. Aside from the terrain editor, Unity doesn't have any great modeling tools built in. You'll need a piece of 3D software for that. Let's see what we can manage with what Unity gives us. Add a built-in **GameObject** to the **Scene**:

Time for action – Creating the ball

Add a built-in **GameObject** to the **Scene**.

1. In the menu, click on **GameObject**.

2. Point to **Create Other** and then click on **Sphere**.

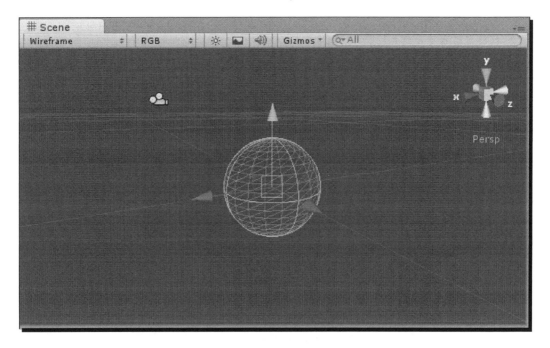

What just happened – that's all there is to it?

Well, yeah, actually! Unity has a number of prebuilt simple 3D models, also known as **primitives**, which we can use to get started. You've just created a built-in **Game** object with four components on it. Look at the **Inspector** panel to see what those components are:

- ◆ **Transform**: This determines how a **Game Object** is positioned, rotated, and scaled (made big or small) in your **Scene**.

- ◆ **Mesh Filter**: This component takes a mesh, which is the stuff our **Game Object** is made from, and runs it through the **Mesh Renderer**.

- ◆ **Sphere Collider**: This is a sphere-shaped boundary on our **Game Object** that helps Unity figure out when instances of **Game Object Colliders** touch, overlap, or stop touching.

- ◆ **Mesh Renderer**: This component enables the player to see our meshes. Without it, meshes don't get drawn or rendered to the screen.

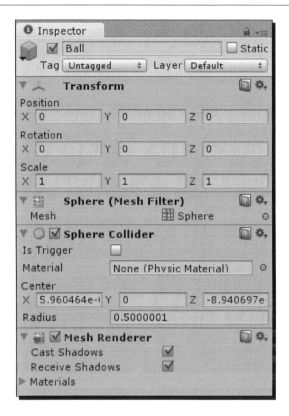

We'll get a better understanding of what exactly a **Mesh** is when we add the **Paddle** to the **Scene** a few steps from now.

A ball by any other name

Let's make a few changes to our ball. We should rename it and move it up into the "air" so that it has some place to fall from.

Time for action – Renaming the ball

1. In the **Hierarchy** panel, find the **Game Object** below **Main Camera** called **Sphere**.

    To rename the **Sphere**, you can either right-click/alternate-click on it and click on **Rename**, or press *F2* on the keyboard if you're on a PC. Mac users can press the *Return* or *Enter* key to rename the **Sphere**. You can also rename a **Game Object** by selecting it and typing a new name into the field at the top of the **Inspector** panel.

2. Rename the **Game Object** as **Ball**.

Your project can fill up fast with generically named **Game Objects** and other assorted things, so let's stay on top of our project by naming **Game Objects** as we create them.

Origin story

The center of your game world is called the **origin**. The origin is the magical place in 3D space where everything begins. 3D space is divided up by X, Y, and Z axes. If you remember your Cartesian grid from grade school, or if you've ever seen a bar or line graph, the X-axis runs one way (usually horizontally), and the Y-axis runs perpendicular to it (usually vertically). 3D is like taking a second piece of paper and sticking it at right angles to your graph so that you have a third axis firing straight up at your face from your desk, and down into the floor in the opposite direction.

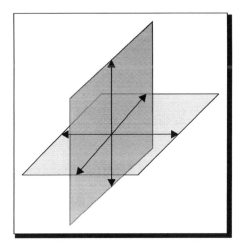

The orientation (the way the X, Y, and Z axes are positioned) varies from program to program. Unity has a Y-up orientation. The X and Z axes run perpendicular to each other on the "floor". If you hold your arms out like a scarecrow, your arms are the X axis, and the Z axis runs through your belly button. The Y axis runs straight up into the sky, and straight down to the center of the Earth where there are probably goblins or some such creatures.

Let's get a better look at that ball. To orbit around the **Scene** view, hold down the *Alt* or *Option* key on your keyboard (depending on whether you're using a PC or a Mac) and press and hold the left mouse button. If the ball is centered near the origin, you should notice that the "ground" plane slices right through it. That's because the ball's transform ("registration" or "pivot point" in other software) is at its center. Half the ball is above ground, half the ball is below. If the ball's X, Y and Z position values are all zero, the center of the ball is at the origin, where the three 3D planes converge. It's entirely likely that your ball is floating around somewhere else in the **Scene**. Let's fix that right now.

Disoriented?

If you ever get lost orbiting, panning, and zooming around the **Scene** view, remember that you can reorient yourself by clicking on the gizmo at the top-right of the **Scene** view. Click on the green **Y** cone to view the scene from the top-down. Click the red **X** cone to view the scene from the right. Clicking on the blue **Z** cone focuses us at the front of the **Scene**. Click the gray box in the middle of the gizmo to return to a perspective view. If you want to completely reverse your view, you can click on the white cone sitting opposite to your orientation—doing this will flip the view around so that you're looking at things from the opposite angle. The label beneath the cone tells you which view you're currently using.

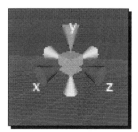

XYZ/RGB

If you've ever listened to your science or art teacher drone on about color spectrum of light, you might have noticed that X, Y, and Z map onto Red, Green, and Blue. Red, Green, and Blue are the primary colors of light, and are always listed in that order. If you're visually-oriented, it might help you to know that X is Red, Y is Green, and Z is Blue when you're looking at any depiction of axes in Unity. Most often, your selected axis turns yellow when you hover over or select it.

Time for action – Moving the ball Into the "sky"

We want the ball to start somewhere in the "sky" (the area above the "ground" plane) so that it will have somewhere to fall from.

1. Make sure that the **Ball Game Object** is selected. Click on it in the **Hierarchy** panel.

2. See the control gizmo poking out from the center of the ball? You can either click-and-drag the green Y-axis to move the ball up, or type a new Y position for it in the **Inspector** panel. As we want to stay on the same page together, let's type it. Look in the **Inspector** panel and find the **Y** field—it's next to **Position** in the **Transform** component of the **Ball**.

3. Change the **Y** position from **0** to **2**.

4. Press the *Enter* key to commit this change.

5. Your ball may not have begun life at the origin. Make sure that the values for its **X** and **Z** position are at **0**.

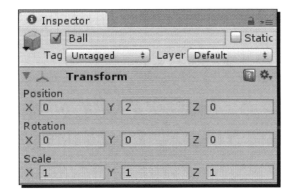

6. The **Ball Game Object** should now be hovering two units above the ground plane, which is a marvelous height from where any self-respecting ball can endeavor to fall.

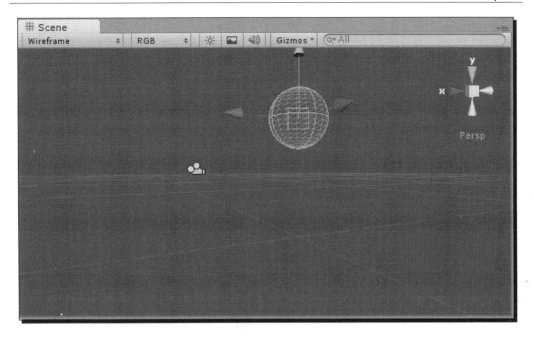

Time for action – Shrinking the ball

The units in our 3D world are arbitrary. When you're working on your game, it may help to ascribe real-world measurements to these units. Perhaps one unit equals one foot or one meter? If you're building a real-time strategy game where the scale is much larger, maybe one unit equals one mile or one kilometer? The **Ball** that we've just created is a little large for our purposes, so let's shrink it down a touch.

1. With the **Ball** still selected type **0.4** for the **X**, **Y**, and **Z** scale values in the **Transform Component** of the **Ball**.

2. Press *Tab* to move the carat to each new field, and press *Enter* after typing in each field to commit the change.

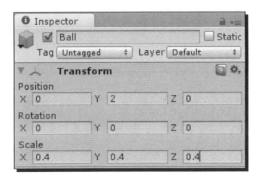

The **Ball** should shrink down to 0.4, or 40% of its original size. Note that if you enter 0.4 only into one or two of the three **Scale** fields, you'll accidentally create a weird-looking egg or an ovoid-shaped ball.

Time for action – Saving your scene

A computer teacher of mine once gave me sage advice: save often, cry seldom. Throughout the book, I won't pester you to save your project in every other paragraph—that's up to you and how comfortable you feel with your dodgy power cable and the fact that you're reading this book during a lightning storm. At the very least, let's learn how to save the **Scene** that we're working on. Save frequency is up to you from this point on!

1. Click on **File | Save** or **Save Scene As** in the menu. You're asking Unity to save the current named **Scene**, but there really is no named **Scene** for it to save yet. Let's fix that.

2. In the resulting dialog, type a name for your **Scene**. I chose to call mine **Game**.

3. Click on the **Save** button. Unity actually creates a **Scene** asset in the **Project** panel called **Game**. You know that it's a **Scene** because it has a Unity 3D icon next to it.

4. Now that you've named your **Scene**, you can quickly save changes at any point by pressing *Ctrl* or *Command + S,* or by clicking **File | Save Scene** in the menu. Clicking **File | Save Project** will do a blanket save across your entire project.

Time for action – Adding the paddle

We'll borrow a term from Pong to name our hittable surface "paddle". The paddle will be the thing the player uses to bounce the ball and keep it up in the air. We can build the paddle using Unity's built-in **Cube** primitive, like we did with the **Sphere**.

1. In the menu, choose **Game Object | Create Other | Cube**.

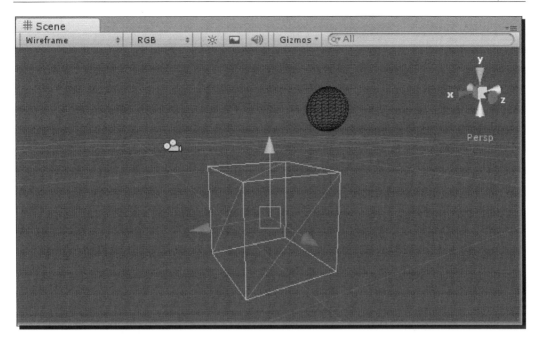

Now, according to **Hierarchy**, we have three instances of **GameObject** in our **Scene**: the **Ball**, a **Cube**, and the **Main Camera**. Let's rename our **Cube** to remind us what it will do in the game.

2. If the **Cube** is not selected, click on its name in the **Hierarchy** panel.

Rename it **Paddle**.

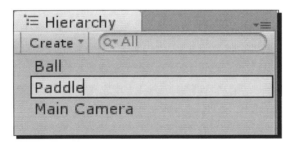

Now, we should make the **Paddle** more paddle-like by changing the **Scale** properties of the **Transform** component.

4. Make sure that the **Paddle** is still selected in the **Hierarchy** panel.

5. In the **Inspector** panel, change the **X Scale** value of the **Paddle** to **1.1**.

6. Change the **Y Scale** value of the **Paddle** to **0.04**. Make sure the **Position** values are zeroed out to move the **Paddle** to the origin.

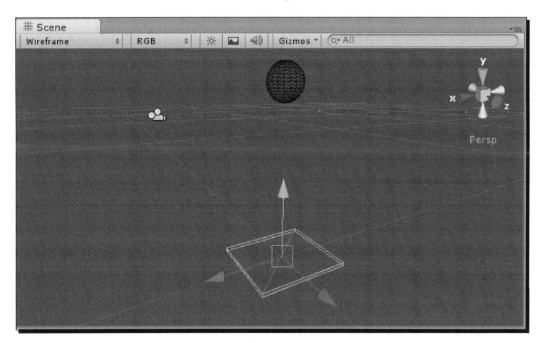

Ah, that's better! The **Paddle** looks like a thin, flat, smackable surface—perfect for whacking around our **Ball**.

What is a mesh?

Although technology is constantly changing, most often a piece of 3D artwork comprises three types of pieces: vertices, edges, and faces. A vertex is a point in 3D space. The **Paddle** that we just added has eight vertices (points)—one on each corner. In these illustrations, we'll depict a cube mesh to make this easier to grasp.

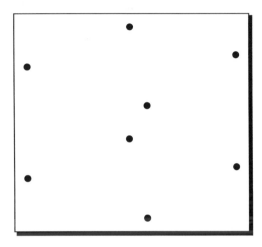

Edges connect the dots—building lines between the vertices. Our **Paddle** has 12 visible edges: four along the top, four along the bottom, and four edges at each corner connecting the top and bottom.

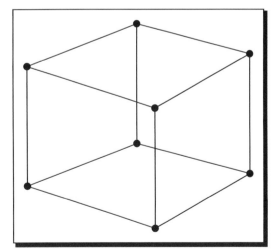

Faces are surfaces that are drawn between (usually) three vertices. Our **Paddle** has six faces, like a die. Edges help define where one face ends and another begins.

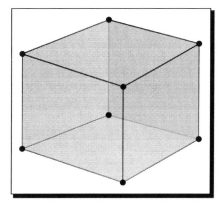

Each face in our **Paddle** actually has a hidden edge splitting it up into two triangles. So, the **Paddle** is made up of 6 x 2 = 12 triangles.

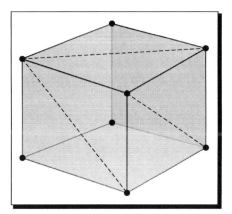

3D models, then, are made up of three-sided (or sometimes four or more-sided) surfaces. A multisided shape is called a **polygon**. When you hear someone say **polygon count**, he's talking about the number of triangles that make up a 3D model. The fewer the polygons, the less work the computer needs to do to render, or draw, the model. That's why you may have heard that game artists need to produce low-polygon (or low-poly) count models, while film and teevee artists are free to produce high-poly count models. In film or teevee, a shot only has to be rendered once before it's committed to a frame of the movie forever. But, video game engines such as Unity have to constantly draw and redraw models on the fly. The fewer the polygons, the faster the game will potentially run.

A low-polygon model looks more crude and roughly-hewn than a high-polygon model. As video games are built for better and faster systems, the models start featuring higher-polygon counts. Compare the character models in a game like *Half-Life* with the higher-polygon count models in the game's sequel, which required a faster computer to run it. The difference is clear!

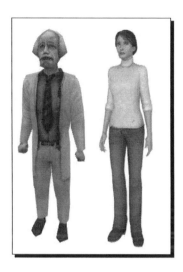

Poly wanna crack your game performance?

The number of polygons that Unity can handle in a single **Scene** really depends on the hardware that's running your game. Unity games are hardware-accelerated—the faster the machine that runs your game, the more polygons you can push. The best thing to do is to build your models with as few polygons as you can get away with, without making your game a giant cube-fest (unless you're making *Minecraft*, in which case, more power to you). Decide on a minimum system specification, then test early and often on that minimally-powered system to ensure that your game actually runs!

Of course, it entirely depends on your game, but you might try staying between 1,500 and 4,000 triangles per mesh to keep things humming.

Keep in mind that a number of factors beyond polygon count determine how quickly or slowly your game runs. Learning how to put together a lean, mean, and optimized game is something you'll learn over time as you gain experience as a game developer.

When you bring a 3D model into Unity from another program (as you'll be doing later in this book), Unity converts the model's whatever-gons into triangles. When you read about model architecture in Unity, "triangles" is the term that will crop up most often.

Keeping yourself in the dark

If you've kept an eye on the **Game** view, which is what the player sees, you've noticed that the **Mesh Game Objects** in our **Scene** are a dark, dreary gray color. Would you believe me if I told you they're actually closer to white?

Just like on a real movie or teevee set, 3D scenes require lights to illuminate objects. The lights aren't actually "real" objects (like our **Ball** and **Paddle** meshes) they're virtual objects in 3D space that determine whether the faces on a mesh will appear bright or dark. The computer figures this out for us based on the kind of light we use, the way we position and rotate it, and the settings we give it.

So, while you can move a light around your scene just like the **Ball** or the **Paddle**, there's no actual geometry or triangles comprising the light. Lights aren't made of triangles, they're made of data. In Unity, as in many 3D programs, lights are represented in the **Scene** view by icons (or as Unity calls them—"gizmos"), with lines indicating their direction or their area of influence.

Time for action – Adding a light

Let's add one of these virtual lights to our **Scene** so that we can see our objects a bit better.

1. In the **Scene** view frame, click the **Wireframe** button and switch to **Textured** rendering. Then click on the little light icon (it looks like a sun) a few buttons over to see the effects of our (as-yet-non-existent) lighting. Your ball and paddle should look as dreary and dark gray as they do in the **Game** view.

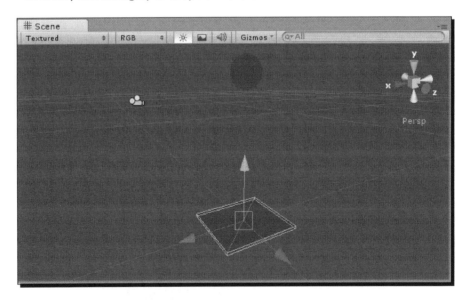

2. In the menu, click on **Game Object | Create Other**. The three types of lights that Unity supports are listed there: point light, spotlight, and directional light.

3. Choose **Directional Light**.

A new directional light is added to the **Scene**. The icon also looks like a little yellow sun. When the light is selected (as it is now), a tube of yellow rays shoot out from it. This tube shows us which way the light is pointing.

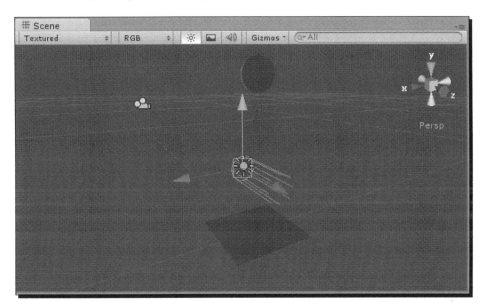

Notice that one side of your ball is now lit, and the objects in the **Game** view have brightened up.

Time for action – Moving and rotating the light

This new light is kind of in the way, and a big chunk of our ball isn't properly lit. Let's fix that.

1. Ensure that the **Directional Light** is still selected. If you deselected it, click on the **Directional Light** label in the **Hierarchy** panel.

2. In the **Inspector** panel, change the light's position to move it up and out of the way. Enter **0** for the **X** position, **4** for the **Y** position, and **-4** for the **Z** position. Moving a **Directional Light** like this does not alter its intensity, but we're just making sure it's within reach in the **Scene** view.

3. Rotate the light so that it shines down on the objects. Enter a value of **44** for the light's **X Rotation** in the **Inspector** panel.

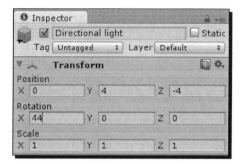

4. Now, the light is casting its sunny rays a bit more pleasantly on our **Scene**.

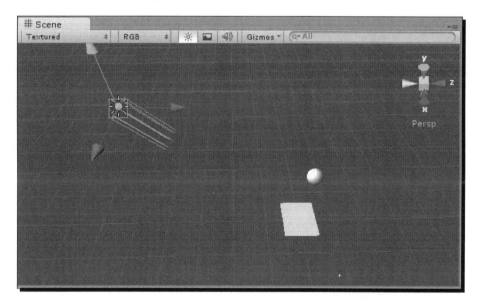

Have a go hero – Let there be (additional) light

If you're feeling adventurous, now's a great time to get a better feel for these virtual lights. Switch to the *rotate* mode by using the controls at the top-left of the screen, or press the *E* key on your keyboard. You can freely rotate the light around to see how it affects your objects.

Switch to *move* mode by clicking on the **Move** icon or by pressing *W* on the keyboard. Click on the **Transform** gizmo to move the light around the scene. How does moving the light affect the way your objects appear?

Kill the light by pressing *Delete* on the keyboard (*Command + Delete* if you're on a Mac). Add one of the other two types of lights—a spotlight or a point light—by clicking on **GameObject | Create Other** and choosing another light. You can also change an existing light's type in the **Type** drop-down in the **Inspector** panel. What's the difference between the light you chose and the directional light? Move the new light all around to get a sense of how each light type treats your objects slightly differently.

Here are the differences between the lights in a nutshell:

- **Directional light**: This light can travel an infinite distance and illuminate everything in the **Scene**. This kind of light works like the sun. As we've seen, it doesn't matter how large or small a directional light is, or where you place it in the **Scene**—only by rotating it can we determine which surfaces it illuminates.

- **Point light**: These lights start at a point in 3D space and shine all around like a light bulb. Unlike directional lights, point lights have a range—anything outside of that range doesn't get lit.

- **Spotlight**: Spotlights are cone-shaped. They have a range *and* a direction. Objects outside a spotlight's cone don't get lit by that light.

- **Ambient**: This is the default type of lighting that you see in your **Scene**, without adding any light **Game Objects**. Ambient lighting is the most efficient, but it's also the most boring. You can crank the level of ambient lighting in your **Scene** up and down by fiddling with the render settings (**Edit | Render Settings**). Try clicking on the **Ambient Light** swatch to cast a creepy, bright green glow over your entire **Scene.**

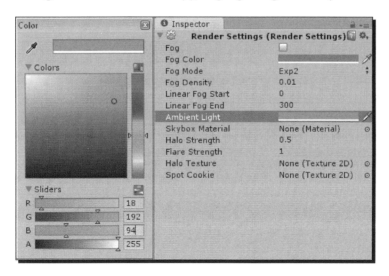

Extra credit

If this lighting stuff really revs you up, check out all of the settings and things to fiddle with within the **Inspector** panel when you select a light. You can get more information on what these and any other **Component** settings do by clicking on the blue book icon with the question mark on it in each **Component** section in the **Inspector** panel.

Are you a luminary?

Unity takes care of the science behind lighting our scenes, but arranging the lights is an art. On many 3D animated movies and teevee shows, as well as on large game development teams, there's often at least one person dedicated to lighting the scene, just as there are lighting specialists on real-world film sets. Virtual lights are built to mimic the properties of real-world lights. Lighting, like modeling, can be an entirely unique discipline in the world of 3D gaming.

When you're finished exploring lights, follow the steps mentioned previously to restore your directional light, or just press *Ctrl + Z* or *Command + Z* on the keyboard to undo everything back to when you started messing around.

Who turned out the lights?

When you light a scene with multiple lights, it can be tricky to see which light is affecting which area. To turn a light off, select the light in the **Hierarchy** panel. Then, uncheck the checkbox at the top of the **Inspector** panel. Poof! The light is gone, but not forgotten. Check the checkbox again to make it reappear.

In fact, you can turn any **GameObject** on and off by using this checkbox. It's a handy way to isolate things in your **Scene** without deleting your hard work.

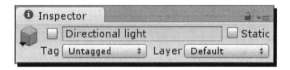

Darkness reigns

If you're working on a particularly grim game and you want to be able to see what's going on in your **Scene**, toggle the internal lighting by pressing the sunny little button at the top of your **Scene** view. When it's lit, your light **Game Objects** take over. When it's unlit, internal lighting hits your meshes so that you can see what's what.

Time for action – Camera mania

If you had a good time playing with all the light settings, you're going to lose your mind when you check out the camera! Cameras in 3D programs are simulations of how the light rays bend around from a single perspective point. 3D cameras can simulate many different lenses, focal lengths, and effects. For now, we're just going to ensure that our camera is adjusted properly so that we're all on the same page, but don't be afraid to goof around with the camera controls if you're dying to get into some trouble.

1. In the **Hierarchy** panel, click to select the **Main Camera Game Object**. You'll notice you get a cool little **Camera Preview** picture-in-picture to show you what the camera "sees".

2. In the **Inspector** panel, adjust the camera's position to X:0 Y:1 Z:-2.5. The paddle and ball should now be nicely framed in the **Game** view as shown in the following screenshot:

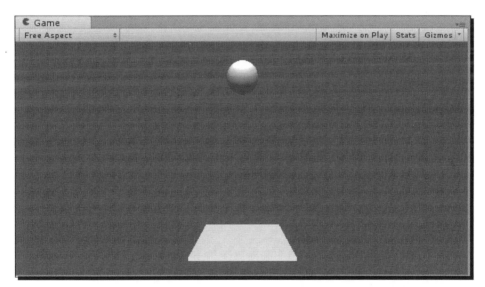

Time for action – Test your game

We have a well-lit and nicely-framed **Scene** containing a **Ball** and a **Paddle**. The **Ball** is poised in midair, ready to fall. Everything looks good. Let's test our game to see what happens next.

1. Click on the **Play** button to test your game.

Ack! That was anti-climactic. The **Ball** is just sort of sitting there, waiting to fall, and the **Paddle's** not moving. Somewhere in the distance, a slow, sad strain of violin music plays.

But, not to worry! We're one step away from making something amazing happen. Press the **Play** button again to stop testing the game.

The pitfalls of Play

Remember that when you're testing your game with the **Play** button activated, you can still make changes to your **Scene**, but these changes don't get saved! When you stop testing, everything will go back to the way it once was, like Cinderella after the royal ball. To make it very clear that you're in this potentially confusing game-testing mode, click on the **Maximize on Play** button at the top of the **Game** window. Now, whenever you test your game, the window will fill the screen to prevent you from absentmindedly messing with stuff.

Let's get physical

I wanted you to test your game at this point, even though nothing happened, to pinpoint that magic moment when Unity becomes awesome. If you're already having a good time, you ain't seen nothin' yet!

Time for action – Adding physics to your game

Let's tap into Unity's built-in physics engine by adding a **Rigidbody** component to the **Ball**.

1. Select the **Ball** in the **Hierarchy** panel.

2. In the menu, choose **Component | Physics | Rigidbody**.

3. A **Rigidbody** component is added to the **Ball**. You can see it in the list of the components of the **Ball Game Object** in the **Inspector** panel.

4. Make sure that the **Rigidbody** component's **Use Gravity** checkbox is checked in the **Inspector** panel.

5. Click on **Play** to test your game.

6. Click on **Play** again when you've recovered from how awesome that was.

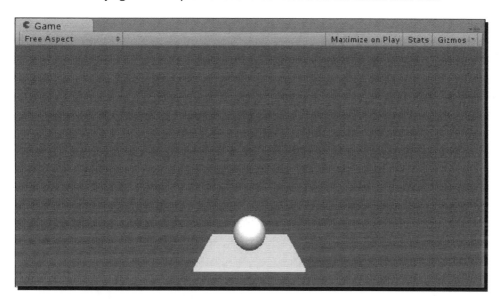

No way! When you tested your game, you should have seen your **Ball** plummet straight down and land on the **Paddle**. How cool was that? If you answered "especially cool", give yourself ten points.

Understanding the gravity of the situation

Unity's built-in physics engine is ready for you to hook into it, but it will ignore your **Game Objects** unless you opt in by adding a component like **Rigidbody** to your **Game Object**. **Rigidbody** is so-named to differentiate it from **soft body dynamics**, which are calculations that actually distort and deform your meshes. Soft bodies like cloth are partially supported in Unity 3, after numerous developers requested the feature. You can view and vote on upcoming Unity features here: `http://feedback.unity3d.com/forums/15792-unity`

Rigidbody dynamics treat all of our objects as if they're made of wood, steel, or very stale cake. Collider components tell Unity when **Game Objects** crash into each other. As both our **Ball** and our **Paddle** already have sphere and cube-shaped colliders surrounding their meshes, the missing link is the **Rigidbody** component. By adding a **Rigidbody** component to the **Ball**, we include the **Ball** in Unity's physics calculations. The result is hot ball-on-paddle action.

More bounce to the ounce

The **Ball** hits the **Paddle** and comes to a dead stop. Pretty cool for such a small effort, but it won't do for a keep-up game. We need to get that **Ball** bouncing!

Select the **Ball** and take a close look at its **Sphere Collider** component in the **Inspector** panel. One of the parameters, or options, is called **Material**. Next to that, we see the label **None (Physic Material)** (this text may be slightly cut off—to see the whole label, click-and-drag the left edge of the **Inspector** panel to increase its width.) There's a small black arrow next to the label that means it's a drop-down list. What hidden wonders await us in that list?

Time for action – Make the ball bouncy

1. Let's import a new package with certain goodies we'll need to make the ball bounce. In the menu, click on **Assets | Import Package | Physic Materials**, then click on the **Import** button. A bunch of **Physic Materials** (whatever *they* are) get added to our **Project** panel.

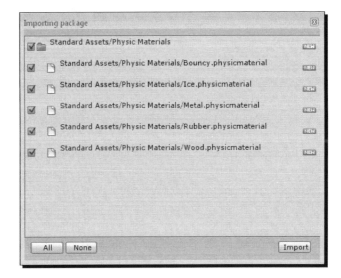

2. Make sure that the **Ball** is selected.

3. In the **Inspector** panel, find the **Sphere Collider** component of the **Ball**. If it is closed, click on the gray triangular arrow to expand it so that you can get at its goodies.

4. Find the **Material** parameter of the **Sphere Collider**.

5. Click on the small black circle next to the label that reads **None (Physic Material)**.

6. Choose **Bouncy** from the list.

7. Test your game by clicking on the **Play** button.

8. When you finally snap out of it, click on **Play** again to escape the mesmerizing results.

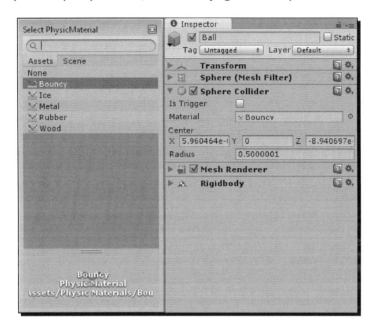

The **Physic Materials** package that we just imported includes a number of useful prebuilt physic materials. These special materials change what happens when a collider hits another collider. We chose the one called **Bouncy**, and lo and behold, when the **Ball** game object's **Sphere Collider** hits the **Cube Collider** of the **Paddle**, it reacts like a bouncy ball should. At our current phase of human technological progress, this is as close to a **Make Game** button as you're gonna get!

Have a go hero – DIY physic materials

Unity's **Standard Assets** package provided us with a **Bouncy Physic Material** to use, but we could just as easily have created our own. If you want to create your own **Physic Material** from scratch, right-click on a blank area of the **Project** panel, and then select **Create | Physic Material**. Alternatively, you can click-and-hold the mouse button on the **Create** button at the top of the **Project** panel and choose **Physic Material**.

A new **Physic Material** called (appropriately enough) **New Physic Material** appears in the **Project** panel. You can rename it the same way you renamed the **Ball** and **Paddle** game objects. **Call it BouncyBall**.

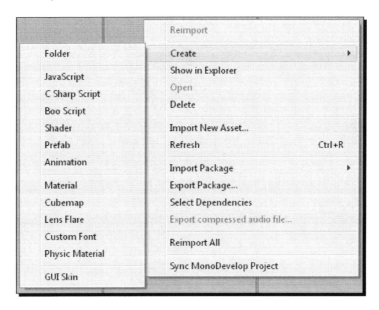

Click to select the **Physic Material**. Its parameters are listed in the **Inspector** panel. If you're desperate to know what everything does, click on the blue book icon with the question mark on it, and prepare to be bored to tears by talk of anisotropic friction. YAWN! What you really want to do is change the **Bouncyness** to **1**, and set the **Bounce Combine** to **Maximum**. Or choose your own settings if you just want to see what they do.

Select the **Ball** again. Find where the **Sphere Collider Component's Material** parameter is set to that built-in **Bouncy Physic Material**, and then drag-and-drop your **BouncyBall Physic Material** into the slot where the built-in **Bouncy** one is. Alternatively, you can choose your **BouncyBall Physic Material** from the menu. The **Bouncy Physic Material** is swapped for your own custom-created **BouncyBall Physic Material**.

What a drag!

We'll be pulling that same drag-and-drop maneuver again and again as we use Unity. If you weren't feeling up to trying those last steps, don't worry; you'll get plenty of chances to drag stuff around the interface as we build more games.

Test the game by clicking on the **Play** button. The paddle is flat, the ball is bouncy, and everything seems right with the world! We haven't programmed any interactivity yet, but try moving and rotating the paddle around while the game is running using the Unity tools to get a sense of how the ball might react when we rig up mouse control in the next chapter. (You'll have to deselect **Maximize on Play** to gain access to your tools to try this out in the **Scene** view.)

Summary

In this chapter, we started to put the Unity 3D engine through its paces.

We learned how to:

♦ Add built-in **Game Objects** to our **Scene**

♦ Position, rotate, and scale those **Game Objects**

♦ Add lighting to the **Scene** to brighten things up

♦ Add **Rigidbody** components to our **Game Objects** to tie into Unity's physics calculations

♦ Create **Physic Materials**

♦ Customize **Collider** components to make **Game Objects** become bouncy

We took an impossibly complex game idea and hacked it down to its fun, naked essentials. We explored the origin point—the center of our game's universe. We learned about the building blocks of 3D construction: vertices, edges, and faces. We talked about how polygon counts can affect game performance. We laughed, we cried. It was profound.

Following the script

What we have so far is not a game, but a very dull movie about the best keep-up player in the world who never, ever drops the ball. One key thing that distinguishes movies from games is popcorn. Also, games are interactive. We need to introduce interactivity to our game so that the player can move that paddle around.

We do this by writing a **Script**. Just like in the movies, where everyone follows a list of stage cues, lines, and notes to put the finished product together, **Game Objects** in Unity can follow **Scripts** to determine what to do. **Scripts** are essentially lists of instructions for people, or **Game Objects**, to follow. In the next chapter, we'll learn how to add **Scripts** to our **Game Objects** to add interactivity to our game.

4
Code Comfort

We've reached the precipice: we're staring at a game that doesn't do much and WON'T do much more unless we write some code. If you're brand new to this stuff, code is scary—or, rather, the idea of code is scary. Will you have to type a bunch of ones and zeroes, or cryptic punctuation along thousands of monotonous line numbers? If you have ever tried developing a game or if you have ever been taught to program using some ancient language in a high school computer course, code might have been the thing to undo you. But, here you are giving it one more crack at the bat. The world NEEDS a three-dimensional keep-up game, by cracky! It's time to show the world what you're made of.

What is code?

Code is just a series of instructions that you give to Unity to make it do stuff. We write lines (sentences) of code describing what we want to accomplish; these lines are called **statements**. Unity reads these statements and carries out our instructions. In Unity, you usually take a set of instructions and "stick" it to a **GameObject**. From now on, we'll use Unity's terminology **Script** to describe a collection of code statements.

Time for action – Writing your first Unity script

Let's open our keep-up game project from the previous chapter, if it's not open already. We will write a really simple script and stick it to our **Ball Game Object**.

In the **Project** panel, right-click on an empty chunk of space and choose **Create | JavaScript**. Alternatively, you can click on **Assets | Create | JavaScript** in the menu at the top of the screen, or use the **Create** button at the top of the **Project** panel. A new script is added to the **Project** panel, inviting you to type a name for it. Name the script as "DisappearMe". It's also a good idea to use the same **Create** menu to make a folder and name it "Scripts", then drag your new DisappearMe script into it to keep your **Project** panel organized.

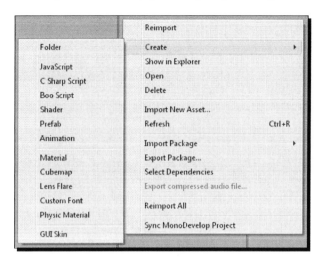

A brand new window opens up. This is Unity's default script editor, called Monodevelop. Its main panel looks a lot like a basic text editor because that's all that scripts really are—plain old boring text.

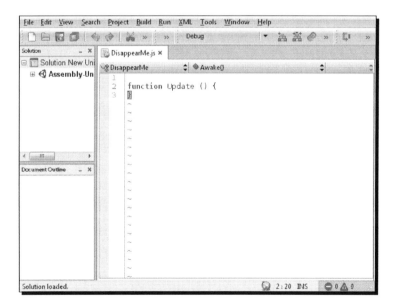

Rolling your own

If you have your own favorite script editor, you can configure Unity to launch it instead. But, for the remainder of the book, we'll use the default editor.

A leap of faith

The first piece of code (the first lines of our script) looks like this:

```
function Update () {
}
```

Click to place your cursor after the first curly bracket, and press the *Enter* key to make some space between the top and bottom curly braces. Press the *Tab* key to indent, to make your code look pretty, if the editor doesn't automatically do it for you. Then, type a single line of code so that your script looks like this:

```
function Update () {
    renderer.enabled = false;
}
```

Downloading the example code

You can download the example code files for all Packt books you have purchased from your account at http://www.PacktPub.com. If you purchased this book elsewhere, you can visit http://www.PacktPub.com/support and register to have the files e-mailed directly to you.

You will notice that as you type each word in this line of code, entire drop-down lists pop open with a dizzying list of strange-looking options. This is called **Code Hinting**, and while it may seem annoying when you first encounter it, you'll be erecting a shrine to it by the time you have finished this book. Code hinting brings a programming language's entire dictionary to your fingertips, saving you the hassle of looking things up or misspelling special keywords.

A little asterisk ("star") appears next to your script's name whenever you have unsaved changes. Save your script by pressing *Ctrl + S* or *Command + S* on the keyboard, or by choosing **File | Save** from the menu. For the remainder of this book, we'll assume that you've saved any modifications that you've made to your scripts before trying them out.

Lick it and stick it

Return to Unity. You should still see your **DisappearMe** script in the **Project** panel. In order to attach it to the ball, drag-and-drop the file over the **Ball Game Object** in the **Hierarchy** panel. If drag-and-drop isn't your thing, you can also select the **Ball Game Object**, and choose **Component | Scripts | Disappear Me** from the menu. Once you do this, it may not look as if anything happened. To confirm that you did it correctly, click on the **Ball**. At the bottom of the **Inspector** panel where components of the **Ball** are listed, you should see your **DisappearMe** script.

Disappear Me!

Uncheck the **Maximize on Play** button in the **Game** view to experience the full effect of your script. (Cue circus music) And now, ladies and gentlemen, thrill to the astounding spectacle that you have created with a single line of code! Click on the **Play** button to test your game, and watch with amazement as your **Ball** disappears!

What just happened?

A good magician never reveals his tricks, but let's break down that piece of code we wrote to see what's going on behind the scenes.

It's all Greek to me

First, we created a JavaScript script. Unity scripts are written in three languages that are somewhat like English: JavaScript, C#, and Boo. You may have already dabbled in JavaScript if you've tried your hand at web development. Unity's version of JavaScript (called "UnityScript") is a bit different because it talks about Unity-related things and runs much faster than your father's JavaScript.

In this book, we'll use JavaScript because it's the simplest of the three languages to learn. For this reason, many of the online Unity scripting tutorials you'll find are also written in JavaScript.

Stay sharp

JavaScript may be the best learning language for Unity beginners, but if you end up getting serious about developing games with this software, consider learning C#. It's much closer to a "real" programming environment, and it gives you certain organizational advantages that you won't get with JavaScript.

The first thing that we did was to write a line of code between two curly braces. I like to think of curly braces as delicious sandwich buns that group code together. The single lines of code are like the thin layers of salami or tomato in the sandwich. Above the curly braces is the description, or declaration, of the sandwich. It's like saying: *We are now going to make a hoagie*—top sandwich bun, yummy ingredients, bottom sandwich bun.

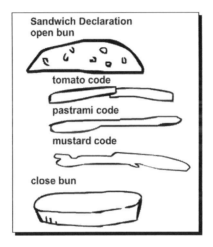

In more technical, less sandwich terms, the area grouped by the buns is called a **statement block**. The layers between the buns are called statements. And the type of sandwich we're making, the *Update* sandwich, is known as a **function**.

You'll never go hungry again

A function is a piece of the script that can be executed, or called, over and over again. It's like having a sandwich that you can eat as many times as you want. We use functions to organize our code, and to house lines of code that we may need more than once.

The function we used is called `Update`. Just as there's an ongoing physics process in the background of our game that we can tap into to make our ball move and bounce, there's an ongoing `Update` loop as well. `Update` is eaten (or called) again and again and again while our game runs. Any script lines, or statements, that we put inside the `Update` function tap into that loop.

Notice the way the `Update` function is declared. On a restaurant menu, we might declare that our Street-Fightin' Hoagie is a scrumptious offering of mile-high pastrami with lettuce, tomatoes, bacon, and cucumbers, topped with a fried egg and slathered with mustard. We can declare a function much more simply. It starts with the word `function`, and adds the function name and a pair of round brackets. If our hoagie was a JavaScript function, it might look like this:

```
function Hoagie() {
}
```

With great sandwich comes great responsibility

There are a few rules and "best practices" to follow when declaring functions.

- ◆ Your function name should start with a capital letter.

- ◆ You must never start a function with a number or some weirdo character like the Rod of Asclepius or you will get an error. An error is a written notice that Unity sends you when something you typed doesn't work or doesn't make sense.

- ◆ You can press the *Enter* key to drop the top sandwich bun down a line. Some programmers (like me) prefer writing code this way so that they can see the open or closed sandwich buns lined up, but other programmers prefer code that doesn't spread out too much.

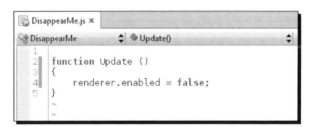

- ◆ In this book, we'll use both approaches just to keep you on your toes.

Examining the code

Let's look closely at the line of code that we wrote:

```
renderer.enabled = false;
```

The semicolon at the end of the line is like the period at the end of a sentence. Nearly all single-line statements must end in a semicolon or the code might break. When code breaks, Unity uses a special popped-up window called the **console** to tell us about it. When you have code that throws an error, we say there is a bug in your code.

Semi-confusing

So why doesn't the function declaration have a semicolon? Why don't the curly braces each have one? It's because they're a different beast. They're not a single line of code—they're more like a house where code lives. If you start seeing the declaration and statement block as one complete thing instead of three different things, you'll be well on your way to getting past the confusing bracket hurdle that many new programmers face.

In order to understand the rest of that line, you need to realize that there is a LOT of code going on behind the scenes that you can't see. It looks like a bunch of pretty pictures to you and me, but the Unity team had to write code to make it look that way. Behind each instance of your **GameObject**, and behind the Unity program itself, there are thousands of lines of code telling your computer what to show you.

Renderer is one such piece of code. When you set the `enabled` property of your ball's renderer to `false`, you're saying that you don't want Unity to draw the triangles in the mesh that makes up your ball.

Time for action – Find the Mesh Renderer component

Does renderer sound familiar to you? We already saw a component called **Mesh Renderer** when we created our **Paddle** and **Ball** Game Objects. If you don't remember, have a look at the following steps:

1. Select the **Ball**, if you haven't already.

2. Look in the list of the components of the **Ball** in the **Inspector** panel. There should be one component there called **Mesh Renderer**.

3. If you see only the name of the component, click on the gray arrow next to the component name to expand the component.

Aha! What do we have here? Something called **Mesh Renderer**—it has a checkmark next to it. What happens if you click to uncheck that checkbox?

Go on—try it!

The ball disappeared. No surprises there. We saw something similar happen when we clicked on the checkmark beside an entire **Game Object** in the last chapter.

But, I wonder, does this **Mesh Renderer** component have anything to do with the "renderer" we talked about in our **DisappearMe** script? Checking that checkbox certainly seemed to have the same effect as running a script that said `renderer.enabled = false;`.

Let's be bold here. We need to figure this out. We'll leave the checkbox unchecked and modify our script to get a solid answer.

Time for action – Make the ball re-appear

1. Double-click on the **DisappearMe** script. **MonoDevelop** will open up and display the script.

2. Change the word `false` to `true`.

3. Save the script.

4. Click on the **Play** button to test your game.

   Your script should look like this:

   ```
   function Update () {
       renderer.enabled = true;
   }
   ```

Bingo! The **Ball** started out invisible and then magically appeared. That means that the **Mesh Renderer** component and the renderer that we referred to in our script are the same thing. And the checkbox in the **Inspector** panel is actually the `enabled` property in checkbox form—instead of `true` and `false`, it shows us checked and unchecked states! In fact, you can even keep an eye on the checkbox when you click on **Play** and see it change states. That tingling sensation means it's working.

Ding!

Hopefully, a little lightbulb has appeared above your head at this point. You may be wondering what *else* you see in that **Inspector** panel that you can get your grubby mitts on through code. Let's take a quick glance at what else is in that **Mesh Renderer** component:

- A checkbox labeled **Cast Shadows** (this is a Unity Pro feature)
- Another checkbox labeled **Receive Shadows**
- Something a little more complicated involving **Materials**

Unless you're some kind of whiz kid, it's unlikely that you'll figure out how to fiddle with this stuff on your own. Let's take a trip to the Unity Language Reference to see what it tells us about the **Renderer** class.

Time for action – Journey to the Unity Script Reference

The **Unity Script Reference** is like a dictionary that contains every single word of Unity JavaScript we'll ever need. It's organized extremely well, is searchable, and has hyperlinks to related sections. Look *that* up in your Funk and Wagnalls.

1. Make sure that the **Ball** is still selected.

2. Find the **Mesh Renderer** component of the **Ball** in the **Inspector** panel.

3. Click on the blue book icon with the question mark on it to open the manual.

Your default browser should open, and the **Mesh Renderer** page of the Unity manual will load. Note that you're not viewing this information online. These are HTML files stored locally on your computer that Unity displays in your browser. You can find this same Unity manual online at this address: `http://unity3d.com/support/documentation/Manual/index.html`.

The manual tells you how to work with the things that you see in the Unity interface. The page you're looking at now tells you everything you always wanted to know about the **Mesh Renderer** component. Click on the **Scripting** button at the top-right of the page; the Unity Script Reference should appear.

As we want to explore the **Renderer** class, type the word **Renderer** into the search field at the top-left of the page. (My browser asked me to enable ActiveX controls to view the page; yours might do the same). Click on the link to the Renderer class at the top of the resulting list.

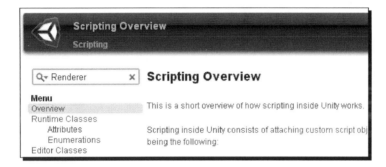

The Renderer class

The **Renderer** class lists a bunch of stuff that might look like so much gibberish to you. It has these lists:

- Variables
- Messages sent
- Inherited variables
- Inherited functions
- Inherited class functions

From that list, the only familiar word might be "functions", which we just learned are reusable bundles of code (or endlessly eatable sandwiches, if you prefer). As we write more code in this chapter, we'll come to understand what variables are. For now, focus on the things listed under the **Variables** section.

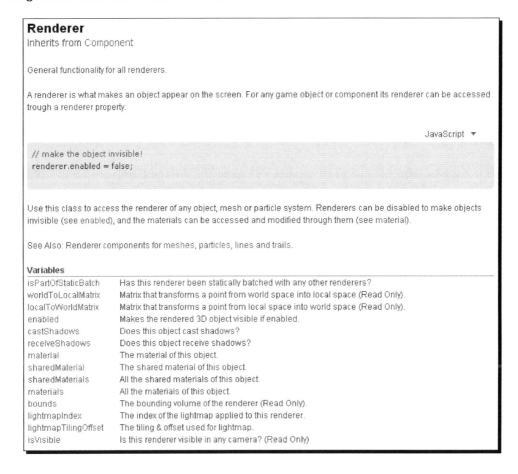

One of the variables is called `enabled`. Do you remember when you wrote `renderer. enabled = false;`? You've already used a variable, perhaps without knowing it. And, check it out—some of the other things that we noticed in the **Mesh Renderer** component are listed here. There are variables called `castShadows` and `receiveShadows`, which we saw as checkboxes in the **Inspector** panel. There are also some material-related variables. At the bottom of the list, there's a variable called `isVisible`, which appears to do something different than the `enabled` variable.

Have a go hero - Pulling the wings off of flies

If you were the type of kid who disassembled your parents' clock radio, or got up close and personal with the insects in your backyard to see what made them tick, this is your time to shine. The Language Reference is your gateway to every special reserved word ("keyword") in the Unity language. Try clicking on the `enabled` variable in that list. The resulting page not only repeats the explanation of the variable, but it also provides an example of how you might use that variable in code. You can even use the drop-down lists on the right to see the C# and Boo translations. (Go ahead check them out! Fortune favors the bold.)

Renderer.enabled

var **enabled** : bool

Description
Makes the rendered 3D object visible if enabled.

JavaScript ▼

```
// make the object invisible
renderer.enabled = false;
```

another example:

JavaScript ▼

```
// Toggle the Object's visibility each second.

// make the object visible
renderer.enabled = true;

function Update () {
    // Find out whether current second is odd or even
    var seconds : int = Time.time;
    var oddeven = (seconds % 2) == 0;
    // Enable renderer accordingly
    renderer.enabled = oddeven;
}
```

If you're wired a certain way, you've already thrown this book down and are eagerly scouring the Language Reference looking for code you can mess around with. That's okay. We'll be here when you get back. If you are still a little wary of this foreign language and would like a little more guidance using it, read on.

What's another word for "huh"?

Perhaps the most challenging thing about using a language reference as a beginner is that you don't know what you don't know. The language is searchable to the tiniest detail, but if you don't know Unity's particular word for something, you'll still be lost. It's like not knowing how to spell a certain word. You can look it up in a dictionary, but if you don't know how to spell it, you might have trouble looking it up!

If you can't find what you're looking for, your best plan of attack is to bust out the synonyms. Try typing in any word you can think of that's related to what you want to do. If you want to hide or show something, try searching words such as visible, visibility, visual, see, show, appearance, draw, render, hide, disappear, and vanish! Even if it's a long shot, try "POOF!" You never know.

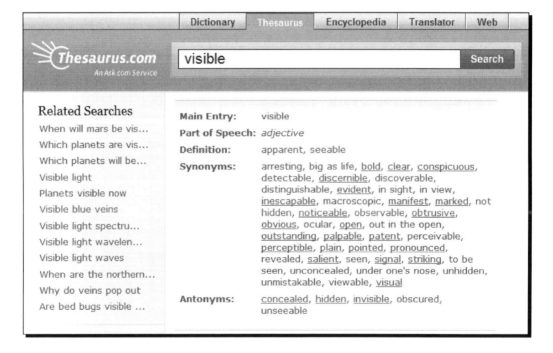

If you've exhausted your vocabulary and you still come up short, you can randomly click on words in the documentation and read about what they do. Another approach is to start scouring the Internet for Unity tutorials. Many developers like to share their code to help beginners like you learn new things. You might not understand what all this code does, but in grazing through it, you could find a line of code that looks like it might do what you're trying to do. Copy it, paste it into your own script, and start playing around. If it breaks your game, then good! You might think that you're not learning anything, but you are: you're learning how to **not** break your game. One final resource is chat channels, which you can find by using an Internet Relay Chat client, but as a Unity n00b (new user), you have to be careful and respectful of the way you speak to real people who know far more than you do. In most chat channels, there's very little love for new users who don't exhaust existing online resources before asking a question.

Be sure to check the appendix at the back of this book for a great list of Unity resources.

It's been fun

Our first attempt at scripting has been a laugh and a half, but we're no closer to making that paddle work in our keep-up game than when we started. Let's undo some of the work we did and get started on a script that's crucial to our game.

Time for action – Unstick the script

Let's remove the script from the **Ball** and recheck the **Mesh Renderer** component to make sure everything's back to normal.

1. Make sure that the **Ball** is still selected.

2. Find the **Mesh Renderer** component of the **Ball** in the **Inspector** panel, and make sure that the component is checked. The **Ball** should reappear in your **Scene** view.

3. Find the **DisappearMe** script at the bottom of the **Inspector** panel.

4. Right-click on the name of the component, and click on **Remove Component**. On a Mac, you can *Control* + click, or click the little black gear icon and choose **Remove Component** from the drop-down menu. Now, the script is no longer associated with your **Game Object**.

Gone, but not forgotten

It's just as important to learn how to remove a script from a **GameObject** as it is to learn about adding one. Note that we could also have unchecked the checkbox in the **DisappearMe** script component to temporarily disable it.

The **DisappearMe** script is no longer acting on the **Ball**, but we haven't deleted it. You should still be able to see it in the **Project** panel. To delete it, click on the script and press the *Delete* key on your keyboard, or *Command* + *Backspace* if you're on a Mac. If you want to keep the script around to remember what you did in this chapter, leave it.

A Script for all seasons

You may already have guessed that the **DisappearMe** script is not exclusive to the **Ball Game Object**. You can drag-and-drop the script on top of the **Ball**, the **Paddle**, or any other **Game Object** in your **Scene**. As long as that **Game Object** has a renderer component, the script will work.

Why code?

We'll write our next script armed with some juicy knowledge. We know that **Game** objects are backed by code. Some of that code is invisible to us, and we can tap into it only through scripting. Other code is exposed to us in the **Inspector** panel in the form of components with a GUI (like checkboxes and drop-down menus) on top.

You may already wonder why, when Unity gives us such a friendly and easy-to-use checkbox to click, we would ever want to bother writing code to do something. It's because the controls you fiddle with while you build your game are no good to you while your game is actually running.

Imagine you want a **Game Object** to suddenly appear in response to something your player does while playing your game. What if your player can grab a power-up that displays a second paddle on the screen? In that case, that checkbox is useless to you. Your player isn't going to enjoy your game inside the Unity 3D program, and it's silly to suggest that you'll be there sitting on his lap to click that checkbox whenever he collects the double paddle power-up. You need to write code to tell Unity what to do when you're not there anymore. It's like equipping a baby bird with all the skills it needs to survive in the world, and then booting it out of the nest. No one's going to be around to click that checkbox for you, baby bird.

Equip your baby bird

Let's teach Unity what to do when we're not around, and the player wants to move the paddle to bounce the ball. Make sure that the **Mesh Renderer** component of your **Ball** is enabled (checked). We're going to create a brand new script and attach it to the paddle.

Time for action – Creating a new MouseFollow script

1. In the **Project** panel, right-click/alternate click on an empty chunk of space and choose **Create | JavaScript**. Alternatively, you can click on **Assets | Create | JavaScript** in the menu at the top of the screen, or use the **Create** button at the top of the **Project** panel.

2. A new script is added to the **Project** panel. Name it MouseFollow.

3. Drag-and-drop your new **MouseFollow** script onto your **Paddle Game Object**.

4. Double-click to open the script in MonoDevelop. Just as before, we're going to add a single, simple line of code inside the curly braces (sandwich buns) of the Update function (sandwich):

```
function Update () {
    transform.position.x = 2;
}
```

5. Save the script and click on **Play** to test your game. Like pulling the chair out from beneath someone when he tries to sit down, your **Paddle** should act like a total jerk, and pop out of the way to let your **Ball** plummet to its doom. Not cool, **Paddle**.

   Not cool.

What just happened?

Just as we saw with the **Mesh Renderer** component, the **Transform** is also a component of your **GameObject**. It's the first attached component on the list in the **Inspector** when you select your **Paddle**. As we learned in *Chapter 3, Game #1: Ticker Taker*, the **Transform** component decides how the **GameObject** is positioned, rotated, and scaled (made larger or smaller).

In the Unity environment, the **Transform** component of our **Paddle** was set to position **0** in the X-axis. But, we changed this with our line of code, setting the x property of the paddle's transform to 2. The result is that the first time the Update function is called, the paddle appears to jump out of the way to two units along the X-axis.

The thought may have already struck you: if you can control the x position of the **Paddle**, you can probably also control its z and y positions just as easily. And if position is available to you, rotation and scale can't be far behind! But, which keywords should you use to change these properties? rotation and scale are two good guesses, but we'd rather be sure.

To satisfy your curiosity, let's hit the Unity Script Reference again; this time, we'll take a shortcut. Highlight the word transform in your script and press *Ctrl + '* on your keyboard, or *Command + '* on a Mac (that's the apostrophe character). You'll zip directly to the Script Reference with a list of hits as if you'd searched for "transform" in the search field. Note that you're taken to the online documentation, rather than the local copy that the blue book icon showed you. Click on the Transform class at the top of the list to see the wonders that await you.

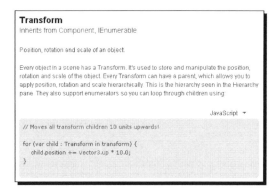

A capital idea

The transform component is listed as **Transform** with an uppercase **T**. When we refer to it in code, we use a lowercase "t". In the Language Reference, it has an uppercase "T" again. But, if you've already made the mistake of using an uppercase "T" in your code, Unity threw you an error in the console window. What gives? Unity's language is case sensitive, which means that a word with a capital letter is treated as a completely different thing than the same word with a small letter. So, "transform" and "Transform" are as different from each other as the words "night" and "day".

Capital "T" `Transform` is a class. A **class** is like a blueprint that you use to make other things. You might implement power-ups in your keep-up game. Your capital "P" `Powerup` class describes what a power-up should look like and how it should behave. You might create a new power-up using your `Powerup` class, and label it "powerup" with a small "p". The "P" `Powerup` contains the instructions for building something, and "p" power-up is the name you gave to the thing you built with that blueprint.

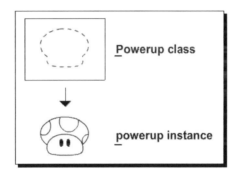

So, in this case, capital "T" `Transform` is the class, or blueprint, that describes how a transform works. Small "t" `transform` is the name our **GameObject** gives to its transform, which was built using the `Transform` blueprint. This upper-case class/lower-case instance is a coding convention, but so is not shouting at the dinner table; we'll follow the convention to keep things civil.

Here are a few more examples to help you understand:

- `Car` is the class (blueprint). We use it to make a new car instance, which we call "car" (small "c").

- `House` is the class (blueprint). We use it to build a new house instance, which we call "house" (small "h").

We can use these classes to create multiple copies, or instances, of the thing. The `Car` class could stamp out many things, which we could call "car1", "car2", and "car3". We could also call those things "sedan", "convertible", and "suv". In Unity-land, the developers decided to call the thing that was created with the `Transform` class "transform". It could just as easily have been called "pinkElephant", but "transform" makes more sense.

Animating with code

We talked about how the `Update` function is called again and again by Unity. We're about to see what that really means by making a slight adjustment to our code.

Time for action – Animating the paddle

1. Jump back into your `MouseFollow` script if you're not there already by double-clicking on it in the **Project** panel.

2. Change the line of code in the `Update` function ever so slightly so that it reads as follows:

```
function Update () {
    transform.position.x += 0.2;
}
```

The changes are very subtle. We added a plus sign (+) before the equals sign (=), and we made the number smaller by adding a zero and a decimal place in front of it, changing it from `2` to `0.2`.

Save the script and test your game. The `Paddle` should scoot out of the way, and fly straight off the right-edge of the screen!

What just happened - what witchcraft is this?

We made the `2` smaller, because the **Paddle** would have just rocketed off the screen in a twinkling and we may not have seen it. However, there's a tiny bit of code magic going on in that `+=` bit.

By changing the `transform.position.x` property with `+=` instead of `=`, we're saying that we want to add `0.2` to the x property. As the `Update` function is called again and again, the x position constantly increases. Let's follow the logic:

- The first time `Update` is called, x is 0. We add 0.2, and the **Paddle** moves to 0.2.

- The second time `Update` is called, x is 0.2. We add 0.2, and the **Paddle** moves to 0.4.

◆ Every time `Update` is called, the **Paddle's** x position increases. We get a real sense of how often the `Update` function is called by how quickly the **Paddle** moves across the screen in tiny 0.2 increments.

Any excuse to work less

`+=` is a bit of programmer shorthand. It's the same as typing:

```
transform.position.x = transform.position.x + 0.2;
```

But that's *way* more typing, and the less you have to type the better. Excessive typing kills 80% of computer programmers before their 40th birthday. I just made that stat up, so it's probably off by a few percentage points.

What just happened – why didn't the paddle animate before?

When we wrote the line `transform.x = 2`, the **Paddle** just jumped into position; it didn't go anywhere, like it does now. Why is that?

The `Update` function is still getting called multiple times. But, each time, it's putting the **Paddle** at two units on the X-axis. The value of x changes on every `Update`, but it changes to the same thing. So, once the **Paddle** is in position, it doesn't appear to move.

With our new modified line of code, the **Paddle's** x position is changing by 0.2 every time the `Update` function is called, so the **Paddle** moves across the screen.

An important part of being a beginner programmer is keeping a positive attitude. You should start with the assumption that what you want to do **can** be done—anything is possible. We now know how to set the position of the paddle. With your positive, can-do attitude, you might imagine that to get the paddle moving around with the mouse, you could find the position of the mouse, and set the `transform.position.x` property to match.

But, what *words* do you need to use to get the position of the mouse? For the answer, let's dive back into the Unity Language Reference.

Pick a word—(almost) any word

We're going to put the Language Reference through some serious stress testing here. We're going to arm ourselves with every synonym for "mouse" we can think of. Here's a list that I painstakingly brainstormed: mouse, screen position, cursor, pointer, input device, small rodent, two-button, aim, point. One of those *has* to do the trick. And, if we come up empty-handed, we're going to hit those online tutorials *hard* until we find our answer.

Go ahead, fire up the Unity Language Reference and type **mouse** into the **Search** field. Scour the resulting list. We will *not* back down. We will *not* take "no" for an... oh, hello, what's this?

Midway down the list, there's this entry:

Input.mousePosition

The current mouse position in pixel coordinates.

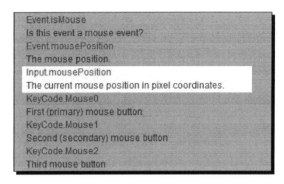

Well, uh... ahem. That was easy. I guess we won't be needing this synonyms list then.

Screen coordinates versus world coordinates

Click on the `Input.mousePosition` entry and check out the resulting page. The Language Reference tells us that we have a new origin to deal with. Unity treats our screen like a flat, 2D plane, with (0, 0)—the origin—in the bottom-left corner of the screen like a bar graph from fourth grade.

Input.mousePosition

static var **mousePosition** : Vector3

Description
The current mouse position in pixel coordinates. (Read Only)

The bottom-left of the screen or window is at (0, 0). The top-right of the screen or window is at (Screen.width, Screen.height).

JavaScript ▼

```
var particle : GameObject;
function Update () {
    if (Input.GetButtonDown ("Fire1")) {
        // Construct a ray from the current mouse coordinates
        var ray : Ray = Camera.main.ScreenPointToRay (Input.mousePosition);
        if (Physics.Raycast (ray)) {
            // Create a particle if hit
            Instantiate (particle, transform.position, transform.rotation);
        }
    }
}
```

We have a code example here, but it looks a little hairy. What's a `Physics.Raycast`? I have no idea. And how do we get the x, y, and z values for `Input.mousePosition`?

The answer is a tiny bit sneaky. Look at the top of the screen where it tells us that `Input.mousePosition` is a `Vector3`. What's a `Vector3`? I dunno. Click on it. Ah, the resulting page tells us that a `Vector3` has `x`, `y`, and `z` properties along with a slew of other useful stuff. That shall do nicely.

Vector3
Struct

Representation of 3D vectors and points.

This structure is used throughout Unity to pass 3D positions and directions around. It also contains functions for doing common vector operations.

Besides the functions listed below, other classes can be used to manipulate vectors and points as well. For example the Quaternion and the Matrix4x4 classes are useful for rotating or transforming vectors and points.

Variables

x	X component of the vector.
y	Y component of the vector.
z	Z component of the vector.
this [int index]	Access the x, y, z components using [0], [1], [2] respectively.
normalized	Returns this vector with a magnitude of 1 (Read Only).
magnitude	Returns the length of this vector (Read Only).
sqrMagnitude	Returns the squared length of this vector (Read Only).

Move the paddle

We are ready to rock. If we just set the paddle's `x` position to the mouse's screen position by using `Input.mousePosition`, we should be able to use the mouse to move the paddle. Change your line of code so that it looks like this:

```
transform.position.x = Input.mousePosition.x;
```

Save your script and try it out.

Worst. Game. Ever.

It may look like nothing actually happened. Your paddle is gone. Super. Obviously, controlling the paddle with the mouse isn't so simple.

But, don't despair. Try placing your mouse at the left edge of the screen, and then move it very, very slowly. You should see your paddle pass across the screen. You'll notice that even the tiniest horizontal movement of your mouse sends the paddle rocketing off into Never Neverland. This will not do.

See the matrix

We need to figure out what kind of numbers our mouse is throwing out. We can do this by using the Debug.Log() function. Whatever information we ask Debug.Log() to display will show up at the bottom of the screen while we test our game.

Time for action – Listening to the paddle

1. Add this line of code beneath the existing line of code:

```
Debug.Log(Input.mousePosition.x);
```

2. Your entire script should look like this:

```
function Update () {
    transform.position.x = Input.mousePosition.x;
    Debug.Log(Input.mousePosition.x);
}
```

3. Save and test your game.

Look at the very bottom of the screen for the results of your Debug.Log() statement. As you move the mouse cursor left and right, you'll see this number changing. It goes from 0 when your mouse is at the left edge, and rapidly increases. The upper limit depends on your monitor resolution; on my screen, Input.mousePosition.x maxes out at 1279! Earlier, a value of 2 put the paddle nearly all the way off the screen. With Debug.Log() reporting these crazy big numbers, we can see why our code behaves the way it does.

A tiny bit o' math

This code's not going to work. Our paddle moves only to the right, along the positive X-axis, because we're working only with positive numbers. We need some negative numbers in there so that the paddle will move to the left at some point. However, at what point?

Hmm... what if we take half of the screen's width and subtract it from Input. mousePosition.x? What does that do for us?

A quick trip to the Unity Language Reference tells us how to find the width of the screen in pixels. Let's divide that number by two and subtract it from the mouse position.

Change the Debug.Log() function call to look like this:

```
Debug.Log(Input.mousePosition.x - Screen.width/2);
```

Save and test. Watch the bottom of the screen for the result.

Tracking the numbers

When the mouse cursor is near the left edge of the screen, you get negative numbers. When it's closer to the right edge, you get positive numbers. And, if you try to position your cursor at exactly the halfway point, you get zero. This makes sense. We know that when the mouse is at the left edge, `Input.mousePosition.x` is zero. If we subtract half of the screen width from zero (on my monitor, that's 640 pixels), we get **-640** at the left edge instead.

We'll use what are called **hardcoded numbers** through this next bit. Later on, we'll start asking Unity to dynamically determine the screen width for us. My screen is 1280 pixels wide, so I'm using 640 to represent half of its width. Your mileage may vary! Common screen widths are 800, 1024, 1152, 1280, 1600, or 1920. If you're not sure how wide your display is, click on the drop-down beneath the **Game** tab and choose **Standalone** instead of **Free Aspect**. In brackets next to the word "Standalone", you'll see your monitor screen width.

When the mouse is in the middle of the screen, `Input.mousePosition.x` is 640. It's at the halfway point. If we subtract half the screen width (640 in my case), we get zero.

When the mouse position is at the right edge of the screen, `Input.mousePosition.x` is almost at 1280 on my 1280-pixel-wide display (again, your mileage may vary). Subtract half the `Screen.width` and we get 640. **-640** at the left edge, **0** in the middle, and **640** at the right edge.

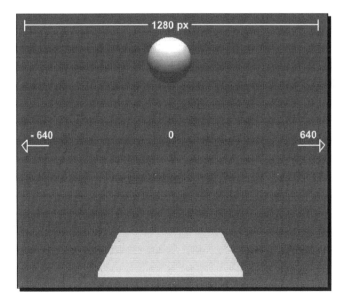

Futzing with the numbers

This is promising, but we already know that these numbers are still too big. If we move the paddle to 640 units along the X-axis, it's going to wind up in Timbuktu. We've got a good positive or negative number scale going—we just need to shrink that number down somehow. Let's try dividing our number by half of the screen's width.

Time for action – Logging the new number

1. Change your `Debug.Log()` call so that it looks like this:

```
Debug.Log( (Input.mousePosition.x -Screen.width/2) /

(Screen.width/2) );
```

Ack! So many brackets! We use those brackets because we want the division and subtraction stuff to happen in the right sequence. You may remember order of operations from algebra class. **BEDMAS**: evaluate the Brackets first, then the Exponents, then Division and Multiplication, and finally, Addition and Subtraction.

To wrap your brain around it, here's what we're doing, in pseudocode:

(first thing)/(second thing)

We're dividing something by something else. The first thing is the -640 to 640 number range that we cooked up. The second thing is `Screen.width/2` (the screen's midpoint). We wrap all of that in a tasty `Debug.Log()` shell:

Debug.Log((first thing)/(second thing));

> **Pseudocode** is fake code that will not work if you type it into a script. We're just using it to better understand the real code that we're writing. Some programmers use pseudocode to type their thoughts out with English words to help them puzzle through a problem. Then, they go back over the pseudocode and translate it into a language that the computer will understand—JavaScript, C#, and so on.

Now, we really have something. If you save and test and move the mouse cursor around, you'll see that as you get closer to the left edge of the screen, you get closer to -1. And, as you get closer to the right edge, you approach 1. In the middle, it's zero.

Copy or rewrite the chunk of code from the `Debug.Log()` statement to the line above so that it now reads:

```
transform.position.x = (Input.mousePosition.x -Screen.width/2) /

    (Screen.width/2);
```

Save and test your file.

She's A-Work!

THAT'S what we're after. The paddle moves at a reasonable rate along with the mouse, and now we can actually bounce the ball around a little. Success! To get more than just a straight vertical bounce, try clipping the ball with the edge of the paddle. The ball should bounce off the screen at an erratic angle. Game over!

Click on the **Play** button again to stop testing your game.

Somebody get me a bucket

A common programmer mantra is "duplication is evil". The idea is that any time you type the same thing twice you could be wasting time and effort. Remember that the less typing we do, the less likely we are to drop dead from the programmer illness I totally fabricated. The less duplication we do, the less "maintenance" we have to do if something goes wrong later—correcting one chunk of code is easier than correcting multiple duplicated chunks. But the rule for beginners is this: make it work first—then make it elegant.

Notice that we have some duplication in this line:

```
transform.position.x = Input.mousePosition.x - Screen.width/2)/

    (Screen.width/2);
```

We've typed `Screen.width/2` twice. That won't do! For starters, typing makes my hands tired. What's more, we're forcing the computer to do that complicated math calculation twice. Why not do the calculation once and ask the computer to remember the result? Then, any time we want to talk about the screen's midpoint, we can ask the computer to retrieve the result.

We do this by creating a variable. A *variable* is a reserved storage locker in memory. I like to think of it as a bucket that can hold one thing. Just as we saw with functions, variables are created by declaring them.

(To be totally honest, an extra division operation isn't going to bring your game to its knees. But, there are more "costly" operations we could ask Unity to perform, and learning to put things in variable buckets now is good practice to prepare us for the heavy lifting that we'll do later.)

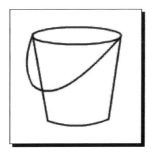

Time for action – Declaring a variable to store the screen midpoint

1. Modify your script so that it looks like this (you can get rid of the `Debug.Log()` function call):

```
function Update () {
    var halfW : float = Screen.width/2;
    transform.position.x = (Input.mousePosition.x -halfW)/halfW;
}
```

This code looks a lot cleaner. Not only is it easier to read, but we've knocked out some of those confusing brackets in the second line.

What just happened – we've gone too Var

We've used the special `var` keyword to declare our variable (bucket). I chose the name `halfW`, which is short for "half width"—half the width of the screen. You can choose any name you like for a variable as long as it isn't a reserved Unity keyword, and it doesn't break any of the naming rules that we discussed when we looked at naming functions. For example, `1myvar funfun` will **not** work, because it begins with a number and has a space in the middle. Also, it sounds ridiculous and doesn't make any sense. Try your best to keep your variable names logical.

F is for function

The biggest difference between naming a function and naming a variable in Unity is that a function name should start with a capital letter, while a variable name should not. This is not a hard and fast rule, but it's called a "best practice", which means that everyone else does it, so you should too. Jump off a bridge with us!

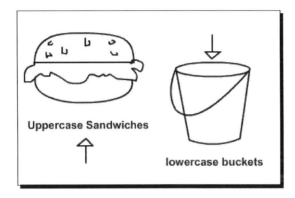

Uppercase Sandwiches

lowercase buckets

We stuck a colon and the word `float` on the end of our variable name. Why? By using a colon, we're telling Unity what type of variable we're using. This lets the program know how big of a bucket to create. Giving a variable a type speeds up our game because Unity doesn't have to keep guessing what type of bucket `halfW` is.

`float` is short for a single-precision floating point. To you and me, that's a number with a decimal point in it. Here are a few more data types that Unity uses:

- `String`: An alphanumeric bunch of characters like "Hello, my name is Herb" or "123 Fake St".

- `Boolean`: Like a light switch, a `Boolean` can be only one of two states—`true` or `false`.

- `int`: An integer like 28 or -7.

Our `halfW` variable is typed as a float because we need that decimal place. But, we're not splitting the atom or anything, so we don't need to make it a double, which is a more accurate numerical data type.

Save the script and test your game to make sure everything is working correctly.

Using all three dees

Now that we know how to track the mouse left and right with the paddle, it's not a huge leap of logic to make our paddle track the y position of the mouse, and translate it into z coordinates. Remember that we're working with two different planes here:

- The flat, two-dimensional plane of the computer screen
  - Horizontal X-axis
  - Vertical Y-axis
  - Origin point (0, 0) at the bottom-left of the screen

- The deep, three-dimensional intersecting planes of our game world
  - Horizontal X-axis
  - Vertical Y-axis
  - Deep Z-axis
  - Origin point (0, 0, 0) in the middle of the world where the three planes meet

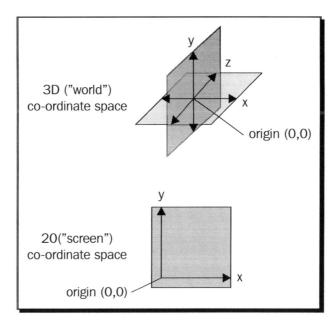

We're going to track the y movement of the mouse, and map it onto the z movement of the paddle to make it move toward and away from the player. If instead we map the mouse y position to the paddle's y position, the **Paddle** will move up and down from the ground to the sky, which is not quite what we're after.

Time for action – Following the Y position of the mouse

1. Modify your code to add a few familiar-looking lines:

```
function Update ()
{
    var halfW:float = Screen.width/2;
    transform.position.x = (Input.mousePosition.x - halfW)/halfW;
    var halfH:float = Screen.height/2;
    transform.position.z = (Input.mousePosition.y - halfH)/halfH;
}
```

The two new lines of code are almost identical to the first two lines. We've created a new variable and called it `halfH` (half height) instead of `halfW`. We're changing the `z` property of `Input.mousePosition` instead of `x`. When you save the script and test your game, you'll have a fully movable paddle to bounce your ball on.

Math effect

I actually put a little cheat into my code. I wanted the paddle to travel deeper and farther along the Z-axis with less mouse movement, so I changed my `halfH` variable declaration to this:

```
var halfH:float = Screen.height/3;
```

That's a third of the screen, not a half. Technically, I should change the name of my variable to something like "thirdH". But, do you want to get hung up on details all day or do you want to build a game? Fudge the number by changing that 2 to a 3, and let's move on. It'll be our little secret.

A keep-up game for robots

After all this effort for getting our paddle to move, the game still doesn't have much oomph to it. It's very easy to keep the ball bouncing because there's nothing to send it spinning off in any crazy directions. At least in Breakout or Arkanoid, you had interesting angles to work with. Our game doesn't have any walls to angle off, but we do have that paddle.

What if we angled the paddle as the player moved it around? An angled paddle would make the ball bounce in different directions and keep the player on his toes.

Once more into the breach

How do we make the paddle angle? Let's consult the language reference, armed with words that describe what we want to do: angle, rotation, rotate, spin, turn, bank, tilt, yaw, roll. Our second idea, rotation, holds the secret.

Time for action – Re-visiting the Unity Language Reference

1. Type **rotation** into your script. It lights up. It's one of the *magic* keywords!

2. Double-click to select the rotation keyword.

3. Press *Ctrl + ' or Command + '* to warp to the Unity Language Reference. You could also type **rotation** into the **Search** field of the reference if you already have it open.

A quick look at the resulting list turns up `Transform.rotation`. We've already been using `Transform.position` to move our paddle around—it's not such a stretch to figure out that this is what we need. Click on the link!

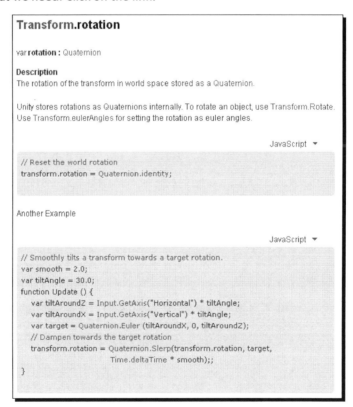

```
Transform.rotation

var rotation : Quaternion

Description
The rotation of the transform in world space stored as a Quaternion.

Unity stores rotations as Quaternions internally. To rotate an object, use Transform.Rotate.
Use Transform.eulerAngles for setting the rotation as euler angles.

                                                                    JavaScript  ▼

// Reset the world rotation
transform.rotation = Quaternion.identity;


Another Example

                                                                    JavaScript  ▼

// Smoothly tilts a transform towards a target rotation.
var smooth = 2.0;
var tiltAngle = 30.0;
function Update () {
    var tiltAroundZ = Input.GetAxis("Horizontal") * tiltAngle;
    var tiltAroundX = Input.GetAxis("Vertical") * tiltAngle;
    var target = Quaternion.Euler (tiltAroundX, 0, tiltAroundZ);
    // Dampen towards the target rotation
    transform.rotation = Quaternion.Slerp(transform.rotation, target,
                    Time.deltaTime * smooth);;
}
```

Our work here is done

Well, would you look at that—while we were sleeping, some kindly programmer elves cobbled together some shoes for us! The `Transform.rotation` page of the Language Reference has a chunk of code that "smoothly tilts a transform towards a target rotation". That sounds a lot like what we're trying to do.

Hey, I have an idea: I'll keep an eye on the door. You copy and paste this code into your game. If anyone asks, tell them "the book made me do it".

Time for action – Adding the sample code to your script

Add the new code to your existing game code. You'll need to shuffle a few lines around. Here it is with the new stuff highlighted:

```
var smooth = 2.0;
var tiltAngle = 30.0;
function Update ()
{
  var halfW:float = Screen.width/2;
  transform.position.x = (Input.mousePosition.x - halfW)/halfW;

  var halfH:float = Screen.height/3;
  transform.position.z = (Input.mousePosition.y - halfH)/halfH;

  // Smoothly tilts a transform towards a target rotation.
  var tiltAroundZ = Input.GetAxis("Horizontal") * tiltAngle;
  var tiltAroundX = Input.GetAxis("Vertical") * tiltAngle;
  var target = Quaternion.Euler (tiltAroundX, 0, tiltAroundZ);
  // Dampen towards the target rotation
  transform.rotation = Quaternion.Slerp(transform.rotation,
    target,Time.deltaTime * smooth);
}
```

Nobody's perfect

In my version of the Script Reference, there's a type-o. The last line ends with two semicolons instead of one. If your version has the same type-o, just delete the extra semicolon.

Note that two variables, `smooth` and `tiltAngle`, are outside the `Update` function at the top of the script. We'll discover why in a moment.

If you save the script and run the game now, the new rotation code won't work. We have to make a few adjustments. I've highlighted what you need to change in the following code:

```
var smooth = 5.0;
var tiltAngle = 30.0;

function Update ()
{
  var halfW:float = Screen.width/2;
  transform.position.x = (Input.mousePosition.x - halfW)/halfW;

  var halfH:float = Screen.height/3;
  transform.position.z = (Input.mousePosition.y - halfH)/halfH;

  // Smoothly tilts a transform towards a target rotation.
  var tiltAroundZ = Input.GetAxis("Mouse X") * tiltAngle * 2;
  var tiltAroundX = Input.GetAxis("Mouse Y") * tiltAngle * 2;
  var target = Quaternion.Euler (tiltAroundX, 0, tiltAroundZ);
  // Dampen towards the target rotation
  transform.rotation = Quaternion.Slerp(transform.rotation,
    target, Time.deltaTime * smooth);
}
```

Here's what's new:

- We bumped up the smooth variable from `2.0` to `5.0` to make the motion more... well, smooth.

- We asked Unity for `Mouse X` and `Mouse Y` instead of `Horizontal` and `Vertical`. `Horizontal` and `Vertical` are, by default, mapped to the arrow keys and the *WASD* keys on your keyboard. `Mouse X` and `Mouse Y` will report mouse movement.

- Finally, we doubled the tilt effect by multiplying the `tiltAroundZ` and `tiltAroundX` values by `2`.

Available for comment

Notice the line that says `Smoothly tilts a transform towards a target rotation`, and the one a bit farther down that says `Dampen towards the target rotation`. That sounds like plain English—not code at all. The double-slashes before these two lines make them comments. Comments are ignored by Unity when we run our game. Comments enable you to type whatever you want in your code as long as you've got those two slashes in front. Many programmers use comments to explain to other programmers (or to themselves, in the future) what a piece of code is supposed to do. While you learn Unity, you can use comments to take notes on the new code concepts that you're learning.

Save the script and test your game. The paddle should tilt as you move your mouse around. It sort of works, but the way it tilts around the Z-axis makes the paddle fire the ball into crazy town. Stop testing your game. We're close—very close.

One final tweak

One small adjustment stands between you and a fun keep-up game mechanic. We want the paddle to angle in the opposite direction to keep the ball bouncing inside the play area. Instead of multiplying by 2, we can multiply by -2 to flip the effect:

```
var tiltAroundX = Input.GetAxis("Mouse Y") * tiltAngle * -2;
```

Save and test. Hooray! The paddle tilts around the play area inclusively, keeping the ball more or less within our reach—unless we get twitchy, and then we drop the ball. But that's the fun of keep-up—moving the paddle just so to keep the ball in play.

What's a quaternion?

Well, that was lots of fun! We've got a working keep-up game mechanic. Now let's go and do something else.

Wait, what's a quaternion?

Oh, that? Don't worry about it. We have bigger fish to fry! In the next chapter, we'll...

WHAT THE HECK IS A QUATERNION??

Gosh, you're persistent. Can't you just leave it well enough alone?

I'm not going to sugarcoat it: 3D math is complex. A **quaternion** (like the one we used in our rotation code just now) is a beast of a mathematical concept. According to my mathematics dictionary (which I often pull out for light reads in the bathroom), "a quaternion forms a four-dimensional normed division algebra over the real numbers". There. Now do you understand?

Quaternions are clearly outside the scope of a beginner book. But, we can't just go swiping code from the Language Reference without even partially understanding it, so let's give it the old college try.

Educated guesses

These are the two lines from our code we'd like to better understand:

```
var target = Quaternion.Euler (tiltAroundX, 0, tiltAroundZ);
  // Dampen towards the target rotation
  transform.rotation = Quaternion.Slerp(transform.rotation,

    target,Time.deltaTime * smooth);
```

Let's actually start from the bottom up.

In the final line of code, we're setting `transform.rotation` to something, which will turn the paddle somehow. That much, we get. We can probably also guess that `Quaternion` is one of those built-in classes that we looked at, like `Input`—both `Quaternion` and `Input` start with a capital letter, and light up when we type them.

`Slerp` sounds weird, but it starts with a capital letter and has round brackets next to it. We've seen that same structure when we called functions earlier in our code, like `Input.GetAxis()` and `Debug.Log()`. And, just like those two functions, `Slerp()` needs some extra information to do what it does. These are called arguments, and we've used them a few times already. We stuck something inside the brackets of `Debug.Log()` to make it appear at the bottom of the Unity window. Giving data to a function to make it do what it does is called passing arguments.

So, what do we have? A class (or blueprint) called `Quaternion`, with a function called `Slerp()` that asks for three pieces of information—three arguments. For a better idea of which arguments `Slerp()` needs, type `Quaternion.Slerp()` into the script, and read the code hinting that pops up. `Slerp()` needs these three arguments to do what it does:

- **From**, which needs to be of type `UnityEngine.Quaternion`
- **to**, which needs to be of type `UnityEngine.Quaternion`
- **t**, which needs to be of type `float`

You can read "as" as "needs to be of type ..." if that makes things more clear. This just means that we can't pull any funny business by feeding the function a float type or a Boolean type when it's asking us for a Quaternion type.

We can already see that we're passing in the paddle's `transform.rotation` value as the **from** argument, which means that `transform.rotation` must be of type `Quaternion`.

For the **to** argument, we're passing `target`, which is a variable of type `Quaternion`. We defined it one line earlier.

Finally, for the **t** argument, we're passing `Time.deltaTime` and multiplying it by the value of our `smooth` variable, which we defined way up at the top of our script as `5.0`.

Time.deltaTime

You'll see `Time.deltaTime` very often in your Unity travels.
`deltaTime` is a property of the `Time` class; it represents the amount
of time that elapsed between this frame and the last. You usually use it
to make your game move according to time rather than according to the
frame rate. Frame rates can change depending on how powerful a player's
computer is, but time remains consistent.

More on Slerp

We've used our brains to try to figure out what this code is doing, so now it's time to fill in
our knowledge gaps a little more.

Slerp is a frankenword meaning **Spherical linear interpretation**. You might already have
guessed that it lets us move from one `Quaternion` rotation to another. The interpolation
(or spread-outedness of the motion) happens across *t*, or time.

If we were to pseudocode this statement:

```
transform.rotation = Quaternion.Slerp(transform.rotation,
    target,Time.deltaTime * smooth);
```

It might go something like this:

On every frame, rotate the paddle, starting at the paddle's current rotation. Rotate towards
our target rotation. Use the amount of time that's elapsed between frames to stretch out
(interpolate) the motion. Reduce the jerkiness of the motion by applying a smooth modifier.

Right on target

Last but not least, let's look at how we get that `target Quaternion`. We know why we
need it: because we have to feed a **to** Quaternion to the `Slerp()` function. To better
understand the penultimate line, let's break it down like we did before.

```
var target = Quaternion.Euler (tiltAroundX, 0, tiltAroundZ);
```

We're creating a variable called `target`, which is a bucket. Then, we're putting something
in that bucket that we know is going to be of type `Quaternion`. We're calling the `Euler`
function of the `Quaternion` class and passing it one argument.

Wait, did he just say "one" argument? I counted three. Yes, but try typing `Quaternion.Euler()` into your script, and reading the tooltip that pops up (sorry, Mac users, no tooltip for you. Try the Script Reference). The `Euler` function needs one argument of type `Vector3`. We've seen the `Vector3` class before (earlier in this chapter). A quick trip to the Language Reference reminds us that a `Vector3` is made up of three different parts: x, y, and z. That's why we're passing three arguments. If we already had a `Vector3` assembled, we could pass our single `Vector3` to the `Euler` function.

The rest is history. We're using our `TiltAroundX` and `TiltAroundZ` variables in the x and z slots, and because there's no change in the y rotation, we're passing zero. The `Euler` function gives us a return value, which is like putting money into a vending machine and getting change. We feed it values for x, y, and z (or a single `Vector3`), and it spits out a crazy-complex `Quaternion` for us that we probably couldn't have constructed on our own. With any luck, we'll get a candy bar too!

We take the resulting `Quaternion`, store it in a variable (bucket) called `target`, and use that as the **to** argument in the `Slerp()` function of the last line.

Have a go hero - Time to break stuff

But don't take my word for it. If you're still confused about what does what or you want to put this sample code through its paces, go for it. Here are a few things to try:

◆ Change the values for the smooth and/or `tiltAngle` variables, and test your game (make sure that whatever value you try still has a decimal point). What effect do the new numbers have on the movement of the paddle?

◆ Reverse any number in the code by putting a minus sign (-) in front of it.

◆ Divide instead of multiplying.

◆ Subtract instead of adding.

◆ Try creating separate variables called `tiltAngleX` and `tiltAngleZ` to control the x and z tilt amounts independently.

◆ Try creating a new variable of type `Vector3` using the `tiltAroundX`, 0, and `tiltAroundZ` values. Then, pass the resulting `Vector3` to the `Quaternion.Euler` function. Does your code still work?

Keep it up

That was some heavy-duty book-learnin'! Feel free to leave the room for a moment if you need to empty your brain. In this chapter, we:

- Wrote our first Unity JavaScript
- Applied the script to a **Game Object**
- Learned how to modify components through code
- Removed a script from a **Game Object**
- Moved a **Game Object** with code
- Hooked the position and rotation of a **Game Object** up to the mouse's position and movement
- Dove into the Unity Script Reference and Component Reference to understand and to "borrow" some code
- Took a crash course in programming to learn about:
  - functions and statement blocks
  - classes
  - data types
  - arguments
  - comments
  - logging

If you're still not grasping every little detail about programming, don't fret. Certain people are wired to just immediately get it, and some of us have to keep trying, failing, and trying again until that little light turns on. I tried and failed at programming my whole life, from the time I was about ten years old, until I gradually understood it. For me, it was less of a sudden light turning on, and more of a slow, steady burn, as the lightbulb filament steadily heated up as if on a dimmer switch. If you want to learn programming in Unity, you're not bound by your intelligence—only by your determination and drive.

Beyond the game mechanic

We've added code to our keep-up game to control the paddle, and the game mechanic is amusing, but it's not a game! There's *so* much more to game development than just the core mechanic. Our game needs a proper starting point; it needs an ending; it needs a cue telling the player that he's failed when the ball falls on the ground; it needs a ground. Currently, you have to shut down and restart the game every time you drop the ball—we need some kind of **Play Again** button. And, wouldn't it be nice to have a score counter on the screen telling the player how many bounces he got before dropping the ball? What about sound effects and music? And the box art! We *have* to have nice box art!

We may not get as far as shipping our game out to the shopping mall, but there's still a lot more we can do to make our game more gamey. We're going to come back to this game mechanic in a bit because there's definitely something promising here. But, first, we should learn how to put some of those crucial buttons and score counters on the screen. While we figure that out, we're going to use our new-found programming skillz to build a whole other game. Are you ready? Then journey with me to the laboratory of Professor Wrecker...

5
Game #2: Robot Repair

One of the secret aspects of game development is that getting a mechanic working is often less challenging than getting an entire GAME working.

Our keep-up game has a working mechanic, but it's clearly nothing like a finished game.

In this chapter, we'll take a break from our keep-up game to add an important tool to our Unity game development tool belt: Graphical User Interface programming. Graphical User Interfaces, or GUIs for short, include all of the buttons, sliders, drop-downs, arrows, and on-screen text that help players understand and move through your game. Unity has a whole separate GUI (pronounced "gooey") system that we'll start digging around in to flesh out our games a bit better. To get a good grasp on what the GUI system can do, we're going to program an entire working 2D flip n' match memory game in that system!

A language by any other name

There's nothing particularly Unity-centric about what we're going to learn in this chapter. The techniques you learn here can generally be applied to other scripting languages to build the same game. Programming a memory game in the Unity GUI is not much different from building one in VB6, Flash, XNA, or OBJ-C for the iPhone and iPad.

In this chapter, we'll:

◆ Build an entire working memory game called **Robot Repair** using only the Unity GUI controls

◆ Learn how to add buttons and images to the screen

◆ Connect multiple scenes with buttons

◆ Practice our programming, including one-dimensional and two-dimensional arrays

All set? Then let's get GUI!

You'll totally flip

Let's make sure we're on the same page when I say "flip n' match memory game". That's the kind of game where you take a deck of playing cards and lay them out in a grid on the table. Then, two or more players take turns flipping over a set of two cards. If the pair of cards matches (that is, two 10s, two queens, and so on), then that player clears the matching pair from the table and gets to flip again. Otherwise, the cards are turned back face down and the next player gets a turn. The game ends when the grid is cleared. The winning player is the one who collects the most matching cards.

To start, we're going to build the basic Solitaire flip n' match game in the Unity GUI, using robots on the cards. Here's how it will look when you're finished:

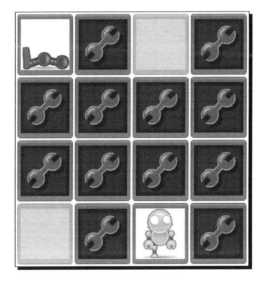

There are lots of things that make flip n' match memory an ideal learning game for new developers. It's extremely versatile! The pictures on the cards can be anything you like—you can skin the game in endless ways. You can build it for any number of players; a Solitaire version just needs a few extra goodies, like a timer, to make it more compelling. You can quite easily crank the difficulty up and down by tweaking the number of cards on the table, the timer length, and the types of allowable matches.

I can't wait to start! Let's go!

A blank slate

Start a new Unity project by clicking on **File | New Project...**. Create a new folder called `robotRepair` on your computer's operating system. Follow the same steps as before to choose a folder for the new project, call the project `robotRepair`, and click on **Create**. You don't need to import any extra unityPackage files if you don't want to—we won't be using anything from them in this project.

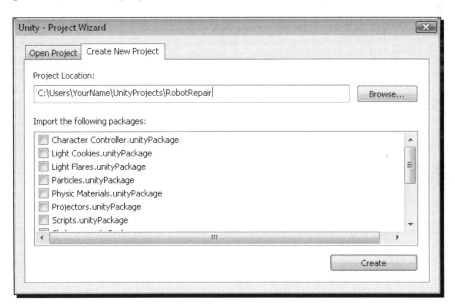

٦ity has finished building your project, you should see that big, wide-open, empty
      We're going to completely ignore the 3D world for this project and focus instead
..1e invisible 2D plane sitting in front of it. Imagine that your 3D world sits behind a sheet
of glass—that sheet of glass is where the Unity GUI controls exist. We'll tack up buttons and
images to that sheet of glass as if they're stickers that the player can interact with.

You're making a scene

Until now, we've only been working with one **Scene**. Unity lets you create multiple scenes,
and then daisy-chain them together. You can think of a scene as a level in your game. In our
case, we're going to create a scene for the title screen of our game and another scene for the
game itself.

Time for action – Setting up two scenes

The new project you just created automatically starts with a single scene. Let's rename it
to **title**.

1.   Click on **File | Save Scene As** and choose **title** for the name of the scene. You'll
     notice that the title bar in Unity now says **title.unity – robotRepair**. There's also a
     new scene in the **Project** panel called **title**. You can tell that it's a scene because it
     has a little black-and-white Unity logo next to it.

2. Create a second scene by clicking on **File | New Scene**.

3. Click on **File | Save Scene As...** and call this new scene **game**.

4. To keep things more organized, create a folder to hold your two scenes. Click on the **Create** button in the **Project** panel and choose **Folder**. A new folder called New Folder appears in the **Project** panel.

5. Rename the folder Scenes.

6. Click-and-drag your **game** and **title** scenes into the Scenes folder in the **Project** panel. All tidy!

7. Click on the little gray arrow to expand the Scenes folder. Double-click on the **title** scene to make it the active scene. You'll know that you've done it correctly if the Unity title bar says **Unity – title.unity – robotRepair**.

Now, we have a scene to hold our title screen, and a scene to hold all of our game logic. Let's get to work building that title screen!

No right answer

The more you explore Unity, the more you'll discover that there are many possible ways to do one thing. Often, there's no "right" way to do something—it all depends on what you're building and how you want it to look. There can, however, be better ways to do things: as we saw earlier, programmers call these preferred methods "best practices".

You can build a title screen for your game a number of different ways. If you have a 3D world, maybe you want the camera to fly around the world as a piece of 2D title work fades up over it? Maybe the title work should be in 3D, and you start the game by moving a controllable character through a doorway? For this introduction to Unity GUI controls, we'll take a flat 2D graphic of our game title work and add a **Play** button on top of it. This is how it will look when we're finished:

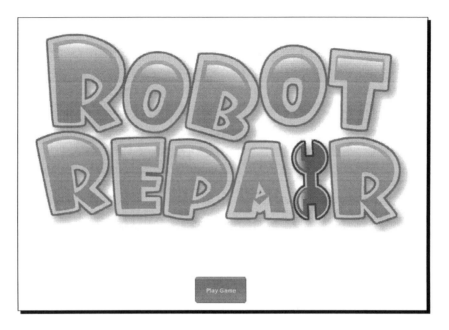

Time for action – Preparing the GUI

In Unity, GUIs are coded in scripts, which are attached to game objects. Let's create an empty **GameObject** and then attach a new script to it.

   1. Click on **GameObject | Create Empty**. A **GameObject** called "GameObject" appears in the **Hierarchy** panel.

2. Click on the **GameObject** in the **Hierarchy** panel and press *F2*. Rename it to **TitleScreen**.

3. In the **Inspector** panel, position the **TitleScreen Game Object** at x:0 y:1 z:0.

4. Right-click on a blank space in the **Project** panel and select **Create | JavaScript**.

5. Rename the new script **TitleGUI**.

6. Click-and-drag the **TitleGUI** script from the **Project** panel to the **TitleScreen Game Object** you just created in the **Hierarchy** panel. The **TitleScreen Game Object** should light up blue before you release the mouse button.

7. To make sure the **TitleGUI** script is linked to the **TitleScreen**, click on the **TitleScreen** in the **Hierarchy** panel. In the **Inspector** panel, you should see the **TitleGUI** script listed beneath the **Transform** as one of the components of the **TitleScreen**.

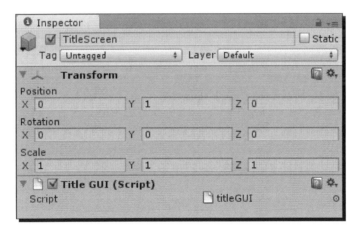

Our script won't get executed unless it's hooked up to a **Game Object**. We've created an empty **Game Object** called **TitleScreen** and connected our new **TitleGUI** script to it. We're almost ready to start scripting!

GUICam

Some developers prefer to hook their GUI scripts up to the main camera in the scene. If this makes more sense to you than hooking the script up to an empty **Game Object**, don't let me hold you back. Go for it!

The beat of your own drum

We're going to take a few extra steps to ensure that our GUI looks different from the standard built-in Unity GUI. If you visit the Unity game portals in *Chapter 1, That's One Fancy Hammer*, you may notice that the buttons and UI controls in many of the games look the same or similar: dark, semi-transparent buttons with gently-rounded corners. This is because those game developers haven't bothered to give their UI controls any unique flair.

Time for action – Creating and linking a custom GUI skin

Custom styling your UI controls is definitely more work than sticking to the Unity default, but the results are worth it! If you've ever worked with **Cascading Style Sheets** (**CSS**), you'll have a better idea of what's going on here. CSS enables you to define the way a website looks, how the images are displayed, the font and size of the text, and the spacing of elements. All of the website's pages use that stylesheet to display their elements the same way. So you've got the thing, and then you've got the way the thing looks. It's like putting a costume on a kid at a birthday party. You can make the kid look like a pirate, a princess, a superhero, or a giant walking cupcake. But, the foundation of the kid doesn't change. It's still little Billy under that foam cupcake suit. Two different websites can have the exact same content, but their stylesheets could make them appear radically different.

When you custom style your UI, you create a new "costume" for it. You can apply different costumes to the GUI, but the bones stay the same. You still have the same number of buttons at the same size and in the same position on the screen. Those buttons and controls all behave the same way as they did before—they're just wearing a different costume.

Let's take the first few steps towards setting up our game to use a custom UI—a different costume (or "skin") for our controls.

1. Double-click on the **TitleGUI** script in the **Project** panel to open the default script editor, **MonoDevelop**.

2. At the top of the script, create a variable to hold your custom GUI skin:

```
var customSkin:GUISkin;
function Update() {
}
```

3. Save and close the **TitleGUI** script.

4. Right-click or secondary click on any empty space in the **Project** panel, then click on **Create | GUI Skin**. You can also click on the **Create** button at the top of the **Project** panel.

5. Rename the newly created GUI Skin **MyGUI**.

6. Click on the **TitleScreen Game Object** in the **Hierarchy** panel.

7. Look for the **TitleGUI** script component in the **Inspector** panel. Notice that the customSkin variable that we just created is now listed in the **TitleGUI** script component!

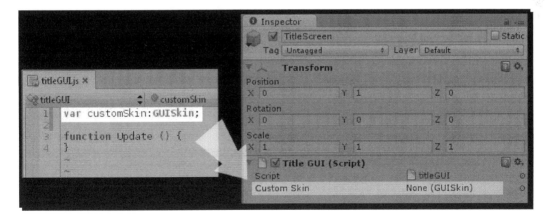

8. Click-and-drag the **MyGUI GUI Skin** that you just created and drop it into the `customSkin` variable in the **Inspector** panel. You can also choose **MyGUI** from the drop-down list in that same variable field.

What just happened?

We've created a skin for our GUI, which works like a costume on a kid at a birthday party. Now, we're all set up to fiddle with the fonts, colors, and other parameters of our custom **MyGUI** skin. We have the costume, now we just need to describe the kid underneath it. Let's build ourselves a button, and then we'll see the difference that a custom GUI skin can make.

Time for action – Creating a button UI control

We're going to add a button to the title screen through code, using Unity's built-in `OnGUI` function.

1. Double-click on the **TitleGUI** script, or switch over to the script editor if it's already open.

2. We won't need the `Update` function any longer. Instead, we'll be using the built-in `OnGUI` function. Change the word `Update` to `OnGUI`:

```
var customSkin:GUISkin;
function OnGUI() {

}
```

3. Add a button-creating a chunk of code inside the OnGUI function:

```
var customSkin:GUISkin;
function OnGUI() {
  if(GUI.Button(Rect(0,0,100,50),"Play Game"))  {
    print("You clicked me!");
  }
}
```

4. Save the script and click on the Unity **Play** button to test your game.

A button labeled **Play Game** appears at the top-left of the screen. When you click on it, the message **You clicked me!** appears in the status bar at the bottom of the Unity interface. It will also appear in the console window if you have it open.

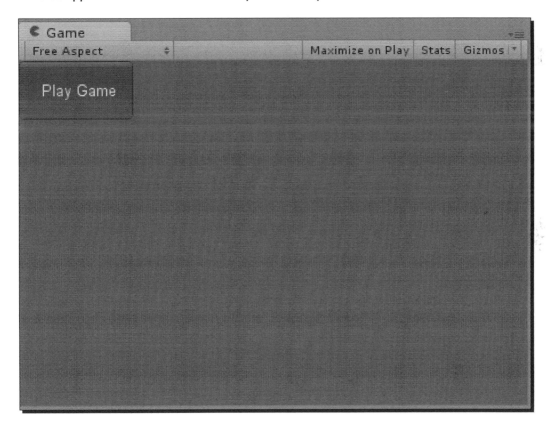

Great! With a very tiny bit of code, we have a working, labeled button up on the screen! It lights up when you roll over it. It goes back to normal when you roll off. Its appearance changes when you press and hold the mouse button on it. The text label is automatically centered inside the button. Somebody spent a bunch of time behind the scenes programming this GUI stuff to save us time. Thanks, Unity team!

Where it all begins

This **Play Game** button is a crucial element of our flip n' match memory game, and every game you'll ever build with Unity, or any other game-building tool for that matter! Its part of the understood language of the video game medium that games start in a paused state on a title screen and the player takes an action to start the game. In a coin-operated arcade setup, that action is inserting a quarter. In modern console gaming, that action is pressing a button on the controller. In a web game like ours, that action is clicking on a button that says **Start**, **Play**, or **Play Game**.

What just happened?

If you've never programmed user interfaces before, this should all seem peachy. But, if you *have* done some coding, you might be looking at the lines we just wrote with a completely confused look on your face. This isn't like any interface programming that you've ever seen before.

Unity uses what's called an **immediate mode GUI**. The term is borrowed from graphics programming, and it requires you to program a little differently than you may be used to. Let's break it down line by line.

```
if(GUI.Button(Rect(0,0,100,50),"Play Game"))
```

Like the `Update` function, the `OnGUI` function is called repeatedly as your game runs. This line is called twice a frame—once to create the button and once to see if the button has been clicked. On every frame, your entire interface is recreated from scratch based on the code in your `OnGUI` function.

So, if you picture this code as a split-second in time, your `if` statement asks whether the button that you're creating in this instant is being clicked on. It's kind of a strange thing to get used to, but it makes sense the more you use it. The `if` in this case is like saying "if the button was clicked".

The rest of the line is a bit easier to understand. The `GUI.Button` method needs two arguments—a rectangle defining the top-left corner and size of the button, and a label for the button.

```
if(GUI.Button(Rect(0,0,100,50),"Play Game"))
```

Rect takes four inputs: x position, y position, width, and height. The origin of the two-dimensional screen is at the top-left, so a value of 0,0 places the button at the top-left of the screen. (Note that this is in opposition to the bottom-left origin we just learned about when tracking mouse movement. This is the THIRD co-ordinate system we've encountered so far!) The width and height values of 100 and 50 make the button 100 pixels wide and 50 pixels tall.

```
print ("You clicked me!");
```

This line is straightforward. When the button is clicked, the message we typed is printed to the status bar and the console window's log. Remember that the status bar is the skinny 20-pixel-high gray bar at the bottom of the Unity interface. Let's check it out one more time with a big fat arrow to help us out:

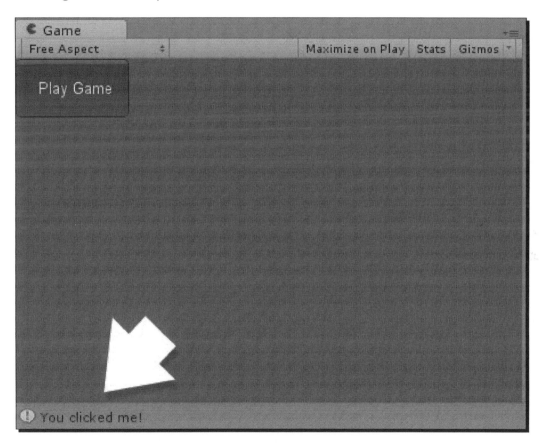

print is another way to throw messages to the **Console** window or the status bar. I prefer it to Debug.Log() because it's faster and easier to type, but be aware that it won't work in all situations. If you ever find yourself tearing your hair out because your print() statements aren't working, try switching to Debug.Log().

Have a go hero – No sense sitting around on your button

Why stop there? To fully appreciate what this code is doing, try this:

◆ Change the button label, the button position, and the button width and height.

◆ Change the message that gets printed when you click on the button.

◆ Try taking the button creation code out of the `if` statement. What happens?

Fiddling with this code is a sure-fire way to better understand it.

Want font?

As promised, we're going to try overriding the default look of the UI button control using our custom GUI skin (or "cupcake costume"). At the top of the `OnGUI` function, between the curly brackets, add this line:

```
GUI.skin = customSkin;
```

Save the script. Now, the custom GUI skin called **MyGUI** that we linked to this script will knock out the default skin like putting on a different costume. Let's make a quick change to **MyGUI** so that we can see the results.

Click on **MyGUI** in the **Project** panel. Now, check out the **Inspector** panel. There's a loooong list of goodies and controls that we can customize. This is why many of the Unity projects that you see use the default GUI—customizing all this stuff would take a long time!

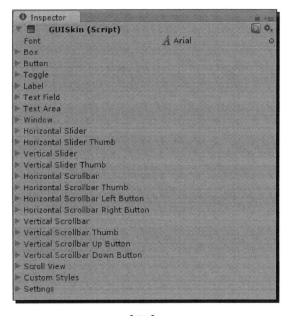

Click on the arrow next to **Button** to expand it, and then click on the arrow next to **Normal**. There's a color swatch here labeled **Text Color** (it has an eye dropper icon next to it). Click on the swatch and choose a new color—I chose light blue. Click on the **Play** button to test your game.

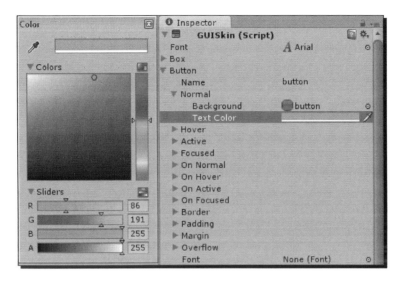

Voila! The text color on your button is blue! When you roll over the button, though, the text reverts to white. There are separate colors and graphics for the hover, normal, and pressed states of the button. Yikes! That's tedious.

To change the font on your buttons, navigate to a directory on your computer where you keep your fonts, and click-and-drag the font file into the **Project** panel. Now, you can choose that font from the drop-down list labeled **Font** in the **Inspector** panel of your **MyGUI** skin.

Where my fonts are?

If you're running Windows, your fonts are likely to be in the `C:\Windows\Fonts` directory. If you're a Mac user, you should look in the `/Library/Fonts/` folder.

You could spend hours messing around with your custom GUI skin. Don't let me hold you back! If you want to go nuts customizing **MyGUI**, be my guest. When you're ready to come back, we'll build out the rest of the title screen.

Cover your assets

Download the Assets package for this chapter (look for instructions in the Preface of this book). To import the package, click on **Assets | Import Package | Custom Package**. Navigate to wherever you saved the package and double-click to open it—an **Importing Package** dialog will open. All assets should be checked by default, so click on the **Import** button to pull them into your **Assets** folder.

Open the **Resources** folder in the **Project** panel. All of the graphics that we need to build the game are now in there, including the title screen graphic—it's the one called **title**. Click on it. You should see a preview of the **Robot Repair** title screen in the **Inspector** panel.

With the title screen graphic selected, click on **GameObject | Create Other | GUI Texture**. Unity analyzes the width and height of our graphic and sets it up as the background to our GUI. Click on the **Play** button to test your game—you should now see the **Play Game** GUI button superimposed over the **Robot Repair** title screen graphic (or floating off from the top-left corner of the image, depending on your screen resolution).

Don't forget to select the image

Unity does a few extra steps for us when we create a **GUI Texture** with an image selected. If you try to create a **GUI Texture** and the image is *not* selected, you'll have to manually hook up the image and set a few parameters for it. Why bother? Make sure that the **Robot Repair** image is selected first and you'll save a bit of time.

Beautify the background

Depending on your screen resolution, you may see the default blue background color around the edges of the title screen **GUI Texture**. To change this color, click on the **Main Camera** in the **Hierarchy** panel. Click on the color swatch labeled **Background** in the **Inspector** panel. Change the color to white—it looks the best.

Time for action – Nix the mip-mapping

There's an unwanted sparkly effect that can occur when a 3D camera gets closer and farther away from a 2D image. A technique called **mip-mapping** reduces this effect. Unity creates a series of images from your texture that are each half the size of the previous image, which allow the computer to figure out the best pixel colors to show to the player, reducing the sparkle effect.

Because our title screen is presented as is with no 3D camera movement, we're not really concerned about sparkle. And, as you can imagine, with all those extra images, mip-mapping adds a decent amount of processor "overhead" to our game—the amount of work the computer has to do to run it. As we don't need mip-mapping adding that extra strain, let's disable it.

1. With the title texture image selected, find the **Generate Mip Maps** checkbox in the **Inspector** panel.

2. Uncheck the box.

3. Click on **Apply** to save these changes.

4. The rest of the images that you imported should be un-mipmapped, but there's no harm in checking them for peace of mind.

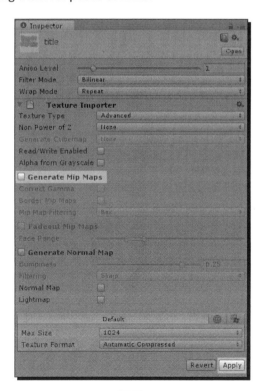

Front and center

Our title screen is almost complete, but a glaring problem is that the **Play Game** button is in a really goofy place, at the top-left of the screen. Let's change the code so that the button is centered on the screen and sits just beneath the title work.

Time for action – Centering the button

In order to center the button on the screen, you need to adjust the **TitleGUI** script.

1. Double-click on the **TitleGUI** script in the **Project** panel, or switch over to the script editor if it's already open.

2. Write a few new variables at the top of the `script`:

```
// button width:
var buttonW:int = 100;
// button height:
var buttonH:int = 50;

// half of the Screen width:
var halfScreenW:float = Screen.width/2;
// half of the button width:
var halfButtonW:float = buttonW/2;
```

3. Modify the button creation line in the `OnGUI` function to incorporate these new variables:

```
if(GUI.Button(Rect(halfScreenW-halfButtonW,560,buttonW,buttonH),
"Play Game");
```

What just happened – investigating the code

The code is just a touch hairier now, but those variable declarations help to clarify it. First, we're storing the width and height of the button that we're going to create:

```
// button width
var buttonW:int = 100;
  // button height
var buttonH:int = 50;
```

Next, we're storing the value of half the screen width, which we get by dividing the `Screen.width` property by 2. `Screen` refers to what Unity calls **Screen Space**, which is the resolution of the published player—the box or window through which the player experiences your game. By referring to **Screen Space**, we can center things on the screen regardless of the resolution our gamer's computer is running.

```
// half of the Screen width
var halfScreenW:float = Screen.width/2;
```

Below that, we're storing half of the button width by dividing our earlier stored value, `button`, **by** 2:

```
// half of the button width
var halfButtonW:float = utton/2;
```

We're storing all of these values so that we can clarify the button creation line, which looks like this:

```
if(GUI.Button(Rect(halfScreenW-halfButtonW,560,buttonW,buttonH),
"Play Game");
```

Note that if we didn't store these values ahead of time, the button creation line could have been written as:

```
if(GUI.Button(Rect((Screen.width/2)-(100/2),560,100,50),"Play Game"))
```

There are a few too many brackets and mysterious numbers in there for my liking! The line where we use variable names is a lot clearer to read.

Math will divide us

Computers are faster at multiplication than they are at division. If you are a stickler for speed, you can amp up this code by multiplying the values by 0.5 instead of dividing them by 2.

By declaring and defining these variables at the top of the script, any of our script's functions can refer to them. They'll also show up in the **Inspector** panel, where we can fiddle with their values without having to open a script editor.

So, what we're doing here is putting the button halfway across the screen. Because the button builds out from its top-left corner, we're bumping it back by half its own width to make sure it's perfectly centered. The only other thing we're doing here is placing the button at 560 pixels down the screen along the Y-axis. This puts the button just beneath the title work.

Here's what your complete code should look like:

```
var customSkin:GUISkin;
  var buttonW:int = 100;
  var buttonH:int = 50;
  var halfScreenW:float = Screen.width/2;
  var halfButtonW:float = buttonW/2;

function OnGUI () {
  GUI.skin = customSkin;
  if(GUI.Button(Rect(halfScreenW-halfButtonW,560,buttonW,buttonH),
      "Play"))
  {
    print("You clicked me!");
  }
}
```

Save your code and try out your game with **Maximize on Play** selected. It's starting to look pretty good!

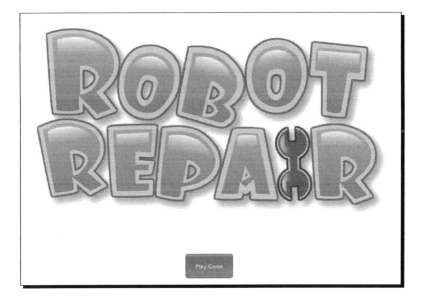

To the game!

The title screen is built and the button's in place. The only thing left to do is to link the **Play Game** button up to take us to the "game" scene.

Modify the line inside the button call where you're printing **You clicked me!**. Wipe out the whole line (or comment it out using double-slashes if you want to save it for later) and type this line:

```
Application.LoadLevel("game");
```

The `Application.LoadLevel` call moves us from this scene to whichever scene we pass as an argument. We're passing the name of our game scene, so that's where we'll end up when we click on the button.

Time for action – Adding both scenes to the Build List

There's just one last thing we need to do. Unity keeps a laundry list of scenes to bundle together when we run the game called the **Build List**. If we call a scene that is not on the **Build List**, Unity will throw an error and the game won't work. And we don't want that.

1. Click on **File | Build Settings...**; the **Build Settings** panel appears.

2. Click on the **Add Current** button to add the **title** scene to the **Build Settings** page.

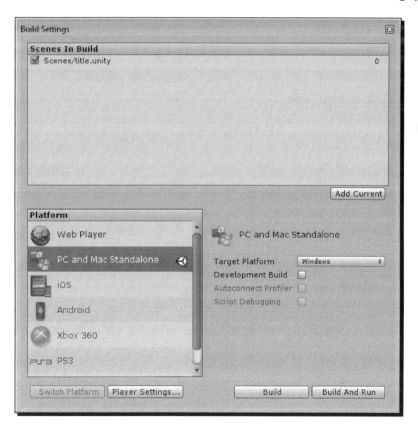

3. Close the **Build Settings** panel.

4. Click on **File | Save** to save the **title** scene.

5. In the **Project** panel, double-click on the **game** scene to switch to it.

6. Follow the same process to add the **game** scene to the **Build Settings**, and then close the **Build Settings** window. Alternately, you can click-and-drag the **game** scene from the **Project** panel into the **Build Settings** panel.

7. Click on the **Play** button to test the game.

Order! Order!

The order in which you add scenes to the **Build List** matters. Scenes appear from the top down. If you put your **title** scene at the bottom of the list, it won't appear first when you build or export your game. If you added the scenes in the wrong order, you can easily reorder them by clicking-and-dragging the scenes around in the **Build Settings list**.

Now that both of our scenes are on the **Build List**, the `Application.LoadLevel` call will take us to the **game** scene when you click on the **Play Game** button. When you click on the button, you should see a blank screen. That's because we haven't actually built anything in the **game** scene, but the button totally works! Huzzah!

Set the stage for robots

The excitement is palpable! We have a shiny-looking title screen promising something about robots. There's a glistening **Play Game** button that, when clicked, takes us to a new scene where our flip n' match memory game will live. It's time now to build that game.

Make sure your game's not still running—the **Play** button at the top of the screen should not be lit up. Double-click on the **game** scene in the **Project** panel. Unity may ask you to save the **title** scene if you haven't already—if that's the case, click on **Save**.

Just as we did with the **title** scene, we should change the camera color to white. Select the **Main Camera** from the **Hierarchy** panel, and change its view color by clicking on the color swatch in the **Inspector** panel.

Time for action – Preparing the game scene

We need to repeat a few steps that we followed in the **title** scene to set up our **game** scene.

1. Go to **GameObject | Create Empty** and rename the new **Game Object GameScreen**.

2. Create a new JavaScript file from the **Project** panel and name it **GameScript**.

3. If you'd like to stay tidy, create a folder in the **Project** panel and rename it as `Scripts`. Drag your **TitleGUI** and **GameScript** scripts into the new `Scripts` folder to keep them organized.

4. Drag-and-drop the **GameScript** script from the **Project** panel onto the **GameScreen Game Object** in the **Hierarchy** panel to link the script to a **Game Object**.

5. If you feel so inclined, you can set up a `customSkin` variable in the script, and link up your **MyGUI** custom GUI skin to the script. This step is not necessary to complete the rest of this chapter.

These steps are a repeat of what we've already done on our **title** scene. For more detailed instructions, just thumb back a few pages!

The game plan

One of the best ways to learn game development is to build a learning project. Choose a very basic game and recreate it on your own. Many programmers use Tetris as their learning project. For a very basic introduction to a language or tool, I like to use **Memory**.

"But, wait!" you say: "Memory games are stupid and boring, and they're for babies, and I'll positively die if I have to build one!" Of course, you're right. You're not going to be lauded by critics and raved about by gamers by building a simple memory game. But, it's a fun challenge to set for yourself: how can you take a game that everyone has played before a million times, and put a simple twist on it to make it more interesting? How can you work within those constraints to make it your own, and to showcase your creativity?

In **Robot Repair**, we'll lay out a 4x4 grid of 16 cards. There are four different robot types—a yellow robot, a red robot, a blue robot, and a green robot. To make things interesting, we're going to break these robots—rip off an arm here, tear off a leg there. The player has to match each broken robot with its missing body part!

Once the player wins, we'll give him the option to play again. The **Play Again** button will link him back to the title screen.

Starting your game development career by building simple starter games like Memory is like eating a big slice of humble pie. But, this is all in the spirit of crawling before you walk. While you're crawling, how can you make things interesting for yourself? And, if you can't flex a little creative muscle in the confines of a simple game, how will you survive building your dream project?

Have some class!

To start building **Robot Repair**, we need to write a custom class in our **GameScript** script. We've already seen some built-in Unity classes in the previous chapter—the `Renderer` class, the `Input` class, and so on. We're going to create our own class called `Card`. You guessed it—the `Card` class is going to represent the cards in the game.

1. Double-click to open the **GameScript** script.

2. Add the following code to the script, beneath (and outside) the `Update` function:

    ```
    class Card extends System.Object
    {
      var isFaceUp:boolean = false;
      var isMatched:boolean = false;
      var img:String;

      function Card()
      {
        img = "robot";
      }
    }
    ```

Just like the keyword `var` declares a variable, we use the keyword `class` to declare a class. Next comes the name of our class, `Card`. Finally, our `Card` class extends `System.Object`, which means that it inherits all of its stuff from the built-in `System.Object` class...much the same way I inherited my fabulous good looks and my withered left knee that smells like almond bark.

System.Object

What does it mean to inherit from `System.Object`? That class is like Adam/Alpha/the Big Bang—it's the class from which (generally speaking) everything in Unity is derived. It's about as nondescript as anything can get. You can think of `System.Object` as being synonymous with "thing" or "stuff". Every single other thing we build in Unity, including our Memory game's `Card` class, derives from this primordial ur-thing called `System.Object`.

In the next few lines, we declare some variables that all cards must have. `isFaceUp` determines whether or not the card has been flipped. `isMatched` is a true or false (aka "boolean") flag that we'll set to `true` when the card has been matched with its partner. The `img` variable stores the name of the picture associated with this card.

The function called `Card` inside the class called `Card` is a special piece of code called the constructor function. The constructor is the very first function that gets called, automatically, when we create a new card. Unity knows which function is the constructor function because it has the same name as the class. The only thing that we're doing in the constructor function is setting the `img` variable to `robot`.

Great! That's all we need in our `Card` class for now. Let's create some important game variables off the top of the script.

Time for action – Storing the essentials

There are a few crucial values we need to remember throughout our game. Let's declare some variables at the very top of the **GameScript** (remember that typing the comments is optional, but the comments may help you understand the code).

```
var cols:int = 4; // the number of columns in the card grid
var rows:int = 4; // the number of rows in the card grid
var totalCards:int = 16;
var matchesNeededToWin:int = totalCards * 0.5; // If there are 16
cards, the player needs to find 8 matches to clear the board
var matchesMade:int = 0; // At the outset, the player has not made any
matches
var cardW:int = 100; // Each card's width and height is 100 pixels
var cardH:int = 100;
var aCards:Array; // We'll store all the cards we create in this array
var aGrid:Array; // This array will keep track of the shuffled, dealt
cards
var aCardsFlipped:ArrayList; // This array will store the two cards
that the player flips over
var playerCanClick:boolean; // We'll use this flag to prevent the
player from clicking buttons when we don't want him to
var playerHasWon:boolean = false; // Store whether or not the player
has won. This should probably start out false :)
```

Speed kills

Remember that this line:

```
var matchesNeededToWin:int = totalCards * 0.5;
```

is exactly the same as this:

```
var matchesNeededToWin:int = totalCards / 2;
```

But, because the computer can multiply faster than it can divide, getting into the habit of multiplying could speed up your more complicated games in the future.

That's a big list of variables! Everything there should be straightforward, except what the heck is an array?

If a variable is a bucket that can hold one thing, an array is a bucket that can hold many things. We've defined some arrays to store a collection of cards, a list of cards on the table, and a list of the cards that the player has flipped over (Note that aCardsFlipped is actually an ArrayList—this is because an ArrayList has a few methods that the Array class doesn't have. Using an ArrayList will speed us up later on.)

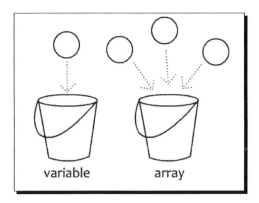

variable   array

"a" is for anal retentive

Programmers develop their own naming conventions for things. My own best practice when declaring arrays is to begin them with a lowercase letter "a". This is how I know, down the road, that I'm dealing with an array. It's just a code organization technique that helps me keep everything straight in my head.

Start me up

Remember that we're building this game with Unity GUI controls. Just as we created a clickable **Play Game** button on the title screen, we're going to build all of our clickable game cards using the same button control. Our grid of cards will be a grid of GUI buttons aligned on the screen.

Let's write a function called `Start` to get the ball rolling. `Start` is another one of those built-in Unity functions that gets called before `Update` or `OnGUI`, so it's a good place to initialize some stuff. Type this code near the top of your script, beneath the list of variables we just declared:

```
function Start()
{
  playerCanClick = true; // We should let the player play, don't you
think?


  // Initialize the arrays as empty lists:
  aCards = new Array();
  aGrid = new Array();
  aCardsFlipped = new ArrayList();

  for(i=0; i<rows; i++)
  {
    aGrid[i] = new Array(); // Create a new, empty array at index i

   for(j=0; j<cols; j++)
    {
     aGrid[i][j] =  new Card();
    }
  }
}
```

In these first few lines, we're flagging `playerCanClick` to `true` so that the player can start playing the game right away. Then, we're using the `new` keyword to create new instances of the `Array` (or `ArrayList`) class, and storing them to the `aCards`, `aGrid`, and `aCardsFlipped` buckets.

Going loopy

What follows is a touch trickier. We want to create 16 new cards and put them into the `aGrid` array. To do that, we're using a nested loop to create a two-dimensional array. A 2D array is one where everything you put in the array is, itself, an array. 2D arrays are very useful when you're creating grids, like we are now.

An iterative loop is a piece of code that repeats itself, with special instructions telling it when to start and when to end. If a loop never ends, our game crashes, and we're flooded with angry tech support calls.

This line begins an iterative loop:

```
for(i=0; i<rows; i++)
```

The variable `i` is called the **iterator**. That's what we use to figure out how many times to loop, and when to stop. You don't have to use the letter `i`, but you'll see it a lot in other people's code. And, as we'll see shortly, when you start putting loops inside other loops, you'll actually have to start using other letters, or else your code will break.

The anatomy of a loop

An iterative loop always starts with the `for` keyword. It has three important sections:

- Where to start.
- Where to end.
- What to do after every loop finishes.

1. In this case, we start by setting the iterator `i` to zero.

    ```
    i=0
    ```

2. Next, we say that we're going to loop as long as the value of `i` is less than (<) the value of `rows`. Because we've already set `rows` to 4, this code will loop four times.

    ```
    i<rows
    ```

3. In the third section, we increase the value of `i` by one. Here's how the interpreter chews through our loop:

    - Set a variable called `i` to `0`.
    - Run the code inside the loop.
    - When we're finished, increase `i` by one (`i++`).
    - Check to see if `i` is less than `rows` (4). 1 is less than 4, so let's keep going.
    - Run the code inside the loop.

❑ Repeat until we increase i to 4 on the fourth loop.

❑ Because i is no longer less than rows (4), stop repeating the loop.

To nest is best

The structure that we've set up is called a **nested loop** because we have one iterative loop running inside another. We're doing two things in our first loop—stuffing a new, empty array into aGrid[i] (which means we'll eventually have an array filled with four empty arrays) and running another loop.

Inside the second loop, we're using j as the iterator because i is already in use. We're using the new keyword to create a new card, and storing it as the **jth** element inside aGrid[i].

Talk it through and it's not too tricky to understand:

◆ The first time through the outside loop, we create a new array and add it to the aGrid array. Now, the aGrid bucket has one thing in it, at index 0: an empty array.

◆ Then, we loop four times and stuff a new card into the empty array that we just created. So, aGrid is a bucket with an array inside it and that array is a list of four cards.

◆ Next, we do the main loop again. We create an empty array and put it in the aGrid array. aGrid now contains an array of four cards at index 0 and an empty array at index 1.

◆ On to the inner loop, we cram four new cards into the empty array that we just created. Now, aGrid contains two arrays, each with four cards inside.

◆ We keep going until this whole thing plays out. At the end of the nested loop, aGrid contains four arrays, and each of those arrays has four cards in it, for a total of 16 cards.

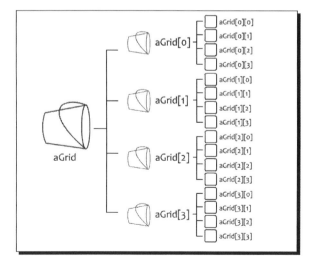

The reason why 2D arrays are so handy is that we can easily access stuff inside them using grid co-ordinates, just like in that old board game **Battleship**. If we want to talk about the card two slots over and one slot down, we call it using `aGrid[1][2]`. In fact, if we were building a digital version of Battleship, we might use nested loops to build 2D arrays to build that game as well.

Note that arrays are zero-based. The card at `aGrid[0][0]` is the card at the top-left of the grid. Next to that is the card in `aGrid[0][1]`. Next to that is the card in `aGrid[0][2]`. To get the card one row down, we increase the first index: `aGrid[1][2]`. Here's what you should try picturing in your head:

aGrid[0][0]	aGrid[0][1]	aGrid[0][2]	aGrid[0][3]
aGrid[1][0]	aGrid[1][1]	aGrid[1][2]	aGrid[1][3]
aGrid[2][0]	aGrid[2][1]	aGrid[2][2]	aGrid[2][3]
aGrid[3][0]	aGrid[3][1]	aGrid[3][2]	aGrid[3][3]

Hopefully, you're already seeing how a grid like this relates to a grid of cards laid out on the table for a Memory game.

Seeing is believing

So far, everything we've done has been theoretical. Our cards exist in some imaginary code space, but we've done nothing to actually draw the cards to the screen. Let's build our `OnGUI` function and put something on the screen to see where all this is leading.

On the title screen, we used a fixed layout to position our **Play Game** button. We decided exactly where on the screen to put the button, and how big it should be. We're going to build our grid of cards using an **Automatic Layout** to illustrate the difference.

With an automatic layout, you define an area and place your GUI controls inside it. You create your controls using the built-in `GUILayout` class, instead of the `GUI` class. The controls that you create with `GUILayout` stretch to fill the layout area.

Time for action – Creating an area to store the grid

Let's create one of these automatic layout areas in our **GameScript**.

1. We don't need the `Update` function in this script either. As we did earlier, change `Update` to `OnGUI` to create an `OnGUI` function:

```
function OnGUI () {
```

2. Begin and end the automatic layout area inside the `OnGUI` function:

```
function OnGUI ()
{
    GUILayout.BeginArea (Rect (0,0,Screen.width,Screen.height));
    GUILayout.EndArea();
}
```

The area will be the width and height of the screen, and it will start at the screen origin at the top-left of the screen.

These two statements are like bookends or HTML tags. Any UI controls we build between these bookends will be created within the area. Each new control will automatically stack vertically beneath the last. The controls will stretch to the width of the area, which in this case is the entire screen.

Have a go hero – Don't take my word for it!

If you'd like to stray off the beaten path and build a few buttons between the area statements to see what happens, I won't hold you back! Use the code we learned earlier in the chapter to create a button or two at different positions. You could also try adjusting the width, height, and start values of the area to see how that affects your UI buttons' placement.

Build that grid

Between the area statements, we want to build the grid of card buttons. But, to keep the code from getting hard to understand, we could make a function call out to a separate piece of code, just to keep things looking clean and easy to read. Modify your `OnGUI` code:

```
function OnGUI () {
    GUILayout.BeginArea (Rect (0,0,Screen.width,Screen.height));
    BuildGrid();
    GUILayout.EndArea();
    print("building grid!");
}
```

That `building grid!` line is just there so that you can be sure something's happening. I like to add statements like these so that I can see into the mind of my computer, and to make sure certain functions are getting executed. Remember that your `print` statements show up in the status bar at the bottom of the screen or in the console window if you have it open.

(Note that if we actually try to run the code now, we'll get an error. Unity has no idea what the `BuildGrid` function is, because we haven't written it yet!)

Let's write that `BuildGrid` function. Add this code to the bottom of the script, outside and apart from the other chunks:

```
function BuildGrid()
{
  GUILayout.BeginVertical();
    for(i=0; i<rows; i++)
    {
      GUILayout.BeginHorizontal();
      for(j=0; j<cols; j++)
      {
        var card:Object = aGrid[i][j];
        if(GUILayout.Button(Resources.Load(card.img),
            GUILayout.Width(cardW)))
        {
          Debug.Log(card.img);
        }
      }
      GUILayout.EndHorizontal();
    }
  GUILayout.EndVertical();
}
```

What just happened – grokking the code

We start by wrapping the whole thing in vertical layout tags. Controls are stacked vertically by default within a layout area, but we're explicitly calling `BeginVertical` and `EndVertical` because of some fancy layout gymnastics that we're going to perform a few steps later.

Next, we build a nested loop. Just as before, we're looping through the columns and rows. We wrap the inner loop in a horizontal layout area with the `BeginHorizontal` and `EndHorizontal` calls. By doing this, each new card button we lay down will be stacked horizontally instead of vertically.

Finally, inside the inner loop, we're using an unfamiliar statement to create a button:

```
if (GUILayout.Button(Resources.Load(card.img),

    GUILayout.Width(cardW)))
```

In that first parameter, we're passing `Resources.Load` to fill the button with a picture instead of a piece of text. We pass the name of the picture we want the `Resources.Load` called. Because every card's `img` variable is set to `robot`, Unity pulls the picture labeled `robot` from the `Resources` folder in the `Assets` library and sticks it on the button.

The second parameter is a sort of an override. We don't want our card buttons stretching to fill the width of the layout area, so we pass the `cardW` (which is set to 100 pixels at the top of the script) to the `GUILayout.Width` method.

The net result is that we loop four times, and on each loop we lay down a row of four buttons, each with a picture of a robot.

Save the script and test your game. You should see a 4x4 grid of buttons, each with a yellow robot picture on it.

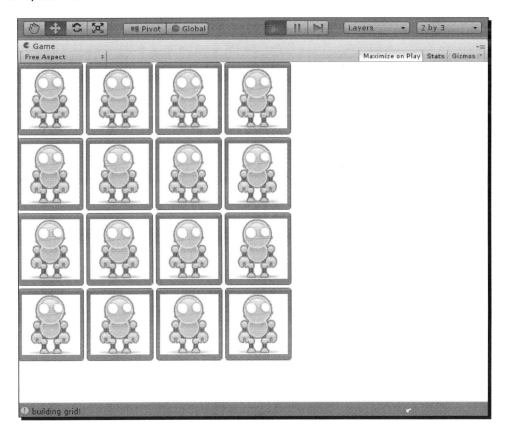

Now you're playing with power!

There's so much to learn about building Unity graphical user interfaces, and you've just taken the first important steps. So far, you know how to:

- Add button UI controls to the screen
- Tool up a custom GUI skin
- Create new scenes, add them to the **Build list**, and link them together using buttons
- Write a two-dimensional array using a nested loop
- Lay out UI controls with both automatic and fixed positioning

As we delve deeper into our **Robot Repair** game, we'll learn more about automatic positioning so that we can center the game grid. We'll also figure out how to flip over cards, and add the crucial game logic to make everything function properly. Join us, won't you?

6
Game #2: Robot Repair Part 2

As we've learned, building the game part of the game is only half the battle. A lot of your sweat goes into creating what's around the game—the buttons, menus, and prompts that lead the player in, around, and through your game. We're right in the middle of learning how to display buttons and other UI (user interface) controls on top of our Unity games. We'll take a break from the 3D environment, adding game logic to the UI controls to produce a fully functioning 2D game with the Unity GUI alone.

In this chapter, we'll:

- Discover some code to help us better position our UI controls on the screen
- Learn to control when the player can and can't interact with our game
- Unleash the terrifyingly awesome power of random numbers
- Hide and show UI controls
- Detect winning conditions
- Show a "Win" screen when the player finishes the game

From zero to game in one chapter

Let's make a quick list of the stuff we need to do to make this flip n' match memory game functional. Break all of the missing pieces into little bite-sized tasks. For smaller game projects, I like to put these steps in a list with checkboxes. Then, I can put a big 'X' in the box when I'm finished. There is nothing more satisfying to me, in any given working day, than to put Xs in boxes.

Here's what we need to do to get this game working:

☐ Center the grid on the screen.

☐ Put different images on the cards. (It would be great if the cards could be shuffled around every time you played!)

☐ Figure out how to break the robots and distribute their body parts on the cards properly.

☐ Make the cards flip over from back to front when you click on them.

☐ Prevent the player from flipping over more than two cards in a turn.

☐ Compare two flipped-over cards to see if they match (Note: if they match, we should remove the cards from the table. If they don't match, we should flip them back over.)

☐ If all of the cards have been removed from the table, show a victory message and a **Play Again** button. The **Play Again** button should restart the game when you click it.

Checkboxes are like ferocious dragons. Putting Xs in boxes is like slaying those dragons. With each dragon you slay, you've become stronger and wiser, and you're getting closer to your goal. And, sometimes, I like to pretend my desk chair is a pony.

Golly-GDD

The list we just created is a very simple example of a GDD, a **Game Design Document**. GDDs can be as simple as checklists, or as complicated as 1,000-page Word documents. I like to write my GDDs online in a wiki because it's easier to stay nimble and to change things. My whole team can commit new artwork, ideas, and comments to a living, breathing wiki GDD.

Putting a point on it

One interesting tip I've heard about writing GDDs is that you should end each task with a period. This gives the task more weight, as if you're saying, "It shall be so!" Periods, strangely, help to make GDD tasks seem more final, crucial, and concrete.

With this to-do list, and our description of gameplay from the previous chapter, we have our bare-bones GDD. Are you ready? Let's slay some dragons!

Finding your center

We've got our game grid set up, but it's crammed up to the top-left of the screen. That'll be the first thing we'll tackle. Advance warning: writing code isn't quite like writing a book. We're going to be bouncing around quite a bit from function to function. If it ever gets too hairy, don't worry: the complete script is listed at the end of this chapter, and you can always download my working file from the Packt website.

Time for action – Centering the game grid vertically

We'll use the `FlexibleSpace()` method of the `GUILayout` class to center the grid on the screen, first vertically and then horizontally.

1. Double-click on the **gameScript** script to open the code editor. Find the `BuildGrid()` function.

2. Insert two `GUILayout.FlexibleSpace()` calls inside the `GUILayout.BeginVertical()` and `GUILayout.EndVertical()` calls, like so:

    ```
    function BuildGrid()
    {
      GUILayout.BeginVertical();
      GUILayout.FlexibleSpace();
      for(i=0; i<rows; i++)
      {
        // the rest of the code is in here, but we've removed it for
          the sake of simplicity
      }
      GUILayout.FlexibleSpace();
      GUILayout.EndVertical();
    }
    ```

3. Save the script and test your game.

The game grid is now centered vertically on the screen. There's an equal amount of space above the grid as there is below it.

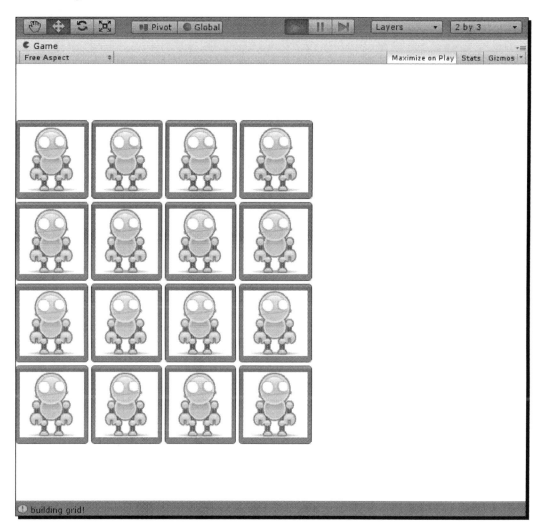

What just happened?

UI controls in an automatic layout like the one we're using want to fill all the space they're given, much like a goldfish will grow to fill the size of the tank it's in. The goldfish thing is actually a myth, but `FlexibleSpace()` is very, very real. Because we've given the grid the entire screen to fill by defining the size of our area rectangle with `Screen.width` and `Screen.height`, our UI controls want to spread out to fill all that space.

`FlexibleSpace` creates a kind of compactable spring that fills up any space that the UI controls aren't using. To get a better sense of what this invisible element does, try commenting the top `GUILayout.FlexibleSpace();` function call:

```
// GUILayout.FlexibleSpace();
```

Save the script and then test your game. There's no `FlexibleSpace` above the grid anymore, so the `FlexibleSpace` below the grid stretches out to fill as much of the area as possible. It automatically grabs any available space that's not filled by your UI controls.

Likewise, you can try commenting out only the bottom FlexibleSpace() function call and leave the top FlexibleSpace uncommented. Predictably, the top FlexibleSpace stretches its legs and pushes the grid to the bottom of the screen. Make sure both FlexibleSpace lines are uncommented, and let's forge ahead.

Time for action – Centering the game grid horizontally

By dropping two more FlexibleSpace function calls into your BuildGrid() function, you can horizontally center the grid on the screen.

1. Add a GUILayout.FlexibleSpace(); function call between the GUILayout. BeginHorizontal() and GUILayout.EndHorizontal() calls:

```
function BuildGrid()
{
  GUILayout.BeginVertical();
  GUILayout.FlexibleSpace();
  for(i=0; i<rows; i++)
  {
    GUILayout.BeginHorizontal();
    GUILayout.FlexibleSpace();
    for(j=0; j<cols; j++)
    {
      // Again, the code here has been removed for the sake of
        brevity
    }
     GUILayout.FlexibleSpace();
     GUILayout.EndHorizontal();
  }
  GUILayout.FlexibleSpace();
  GUILayout.EndVertical();
}
```

2. Save the script and test your game. Hooray! The game grid is now centered on the screen, both horizontally and vertically.

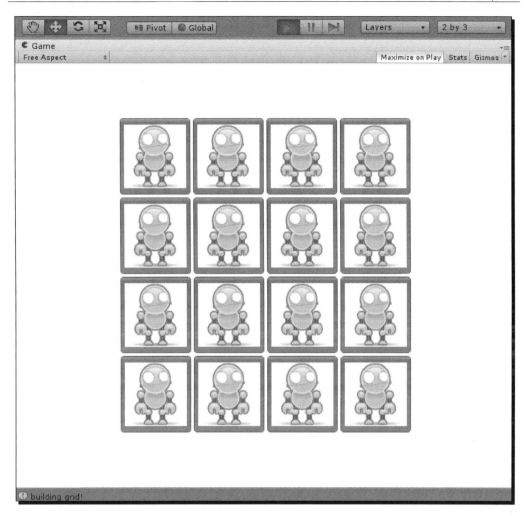

What just happened – coding like a ninja

What we've done here is stuck two springy, compactible `FlexibleSpace` elements at either end of each of our horizontal grid rows. At this point, we have ten `FlexibleSpace` elements: one on the top, one on the bottom, and two on either side of our four grid rows.

As with any programming task, there are many different ways you could have approached this problem. You could wrap your four grid rows in a single horizontal area, and stick two `FlexibleSpace` elements inside in order to have only four `FlexibleSpace` elements in total instead of ten. Or, you could do away with `FlexibleSpace` elements and automatic layouts altogether, and opt for a fixed layout. You could also put all of the buttons in an area (`GUILayout.BeginArea`) and center the area. Or, you could turn off your computer and go outside and play. It's up to you. This is just one solution available to you.

Any way you slice it, we've just knocked one item off our GDD task list:

☐ Center the grid on the screen

Take THAT, you fell beast! Giddy up, desk chair! Onward!

Down to the nitty griddy

Grids are a game development essential. As we saw in the previous chapter, a classic board game like *Battleship* is set up in a grid. So are about 50 other board games I can think of off the top of my head: *Connect Four, Guess Who, Stratego, chess, tic-tac-toe, Clue, checkers, chutes n' ladders, go, slider puzzles,* and so on—it's an absolutely huge list. Add to that the slew of digital games that use a grid layout: *MineSweeper, Tetris, Bejewelled, Puzzle League, Bomberman, Dr. Mario, Breakout.* And lest you think that only 2D games use grids, consider 3D turn-based strategy games—the action takes place on a grid! Grids are used in inventory screens, in image galleries, and on level select screens. A* (A-star), a popular method for moving characters around obstacles on the screen ("pathfinding"), can also use grids. In fact, your entire computer display is a grid of square pixels.

Mastering the grid is key to mastering game development. You'll use grids again and again, from the main mechanic to the interface to perhaps even the high score table at the end of the game. The 2D array method we learned in the last chapter is just one way of setting up a grid, but it's a great one to start with.

Do the random card shuffle

What fun is a flip n' match memory game if all the cards are face up, and they all have the same image on them? Answer: no fun. No fun at all. What we *want* is to deal out a bunch of different cards. And, as long as we're shooting for the moon here, why not deal out a *different* bunch of cards every time we play?

We're going to create an array to represent our entire deck of cards. Then, we'll randomly draw a card from that deck and put it on the table—just like we would in real life.

Time for action – Preparing to build the deck

Let's set up a deck-building function called `BuildDeck`.

1. Create a new function called `BuildDeck`. Write this function outside of and apart from your other functions—make sure it's not trapped inside the curly brackets of one of your other functions.

```
function BuildDeck()
{
}
```

2. Call the `BuildDeck` function in the `Start` function, just after you define the three card-related arrays:

```
function Start()
{
    playerCanClick = true; // We should let the player play,
        don't you think?

    // Initialize the arrays:
    aCards = new Array();
    aGrid = new Array();
    aCardsFlipped = new ArrayList();

    BuildDeck();

    // (the rest of this function has been omitted)
}
```

The very first function that gets called in our script is the `Start` function. After we set our `playerCanClick` flag and create a few empty arrays, `BuildDeck()` is the very first thing the script will do.

Let's break some robots

The way our game works, we have four different robots—a yellow one, a blue one, a red one, and a green one. Each robot will be missing a body part. The player has to match each robot to its missing body part. That accounts for eight cards—four robots and four missing body parts. Because there are sixteen cards in our 4x4 grid, we need to use each robot twice—two yellow robots with two missing yellow body parts, two blue robots with two blue missing body parts, and so on: **2*8=16**.

Each robot has three body parts that we can knock off: its head, its arm, or its leg. We have to be careful when we build our deck that we don't repeat a robot and body part combination of the same color. For example, our two green robots can't both be missing a head. Our player won't know which head goes with which robot! It's also possible that the player might flip over two green heads, and wonder why they aren't considered a match. Let's do whatever we can to avoid that.

Time for action – Building the deck

The strategy we'll use to build our deck is to create an array of possibilities, randomly choose one of those possibilities, and then remove that possibility as an option. Let's see how that works.

1. In the `BuildDeck` function, start off by declaring a few variables:

```
function BuildDeck()
{

    var totalRobots:int = 4;   // we've got four robots to
        work with
    var card:Object; // this stores a reference to a card
}
```

2. Next, build a loop to step through each of the four colored robot types:

```
    var card:Object; // this stores a reference to a card

    for(i=0; i<totalRobots; i++)
    {
    }
```

This loop will run four times because `totalRobots` is set to 4. Next, create an array called `RobotParts` that will house the names of the body parts we can knock off:

```
    for(i=0; i<totalRobots; i++)
    {
        var aRobotParts:Array = ["Head", "Arm", "Leg"];
    }
```

3. Now, we'll set up a nested loop to run twice. So, for all four robot types, we'll create two busted robots (in order to fill our 16-card quota):

```
    for(i=0; i<totalRobots; i++)
    {
        var aRobotParts:Array = ["Head", "Arm", "Leg"];
        for(j=0; j<2; j++)
```

```
        {
        }
}
```

The meat of the `BuildDeck` code goes inside that inner loop:

```
for(j=0; j<2; j++)
{
    var someNum:int = Random.Range(0, aRobotParts.length);
    var theMissingPart:String = aRobotParts[someNum];

    aRobotParts.RemoveAt(someNum);

    card = new Card("robot" + (i+1) + "Missing" + theMissingPart);
    aCards.Add(card);

    card= new Card("robot" + (i+1) + theMissingPart);
    aCards.Add(card);
}
```

Here's how the `BuildDeck` function looks when you're finished:

```
function BuildDeck()
{

    var totalRobots:int = 4;   // we've got four robots to work with
    var card:Object; // this stores a reference to a card

    for(i=0; i<totalRobots; i++)
    {
        var aRobotParts:Array = ["Head", "Arm", "Leg"];
        for(j=0; j<2; j++)
        {
            var someNum:int = Random.Range(0, aRobotParts.length);
            var theMissingPart:String = aRobotParts[someNum];

            aRobotParts.RemoveAt(someNum);

            card = new Card("robot" + (i+1) + "Missing" +
theMissingPart);
            aCards.Add(card);

            card= new Card("robot" + (i+1) + theMissingPart);
            aCards.Add(card);
        }
    }
}
```

What just happened – dissecting the bits

Let's step through that last chunk of code and figure out what it does.

```
var someNum:int = Random.Range(0, aRobotParts.length);
```

First, we're declaring a variable called someNum (short for "some crazy old random number"), which will be an integer. Then, we're using the Range() method of the Random class to pull a random number. We supply the minimum and maximum ends of the range to pull from—in this case, the low end is 0 (because arrays are 0-based), and the high end is the length of the aRobotParts array. The first time through the loop, aRobotParts.length has three parts ("Head", "Arm", and "Leg"). Our minimum and maximum values are 0 and 3. So, the first time through this loop, someNum will be a random number from 0-2.

Exclusive to the max

When using Random.Range with int data types, note that the minimum value is inclusive, while the maximum value is exclusive. That means that unless you supply the same number for your minimum and maximum values, Random.Range() will never pull your maximum value. That's why, in the previous example, you'll never get 3 from Random.Range(), even though we're supplying 3 as the maximum value.

Floats work a little differently than ints. When randomizing with floats, the maximum value is inclusive.

```
var theMissingPart:String = aRobotParts[someNum];
```

Here, we use our random number to pull a body part out of the aRobotParts array. If someNum is 0, we get "Head". If someNum is 1, we get "Arm". If someNum is 2, we get "Leg". We store this result in a String variable called theMissingPart.

```
aRobotParts.RemoveAt(someNum);
```

The RemoveAt() method of the Array class rips an element out of the array at the specified index. So, we specify the someNum index we just used to grab a body part. This removes that body part as an option to the next robot. This is how we avoid ever having two green robots, each with a missing head—by the time we choose a missing body part for the second robot, "Head" has been removed from our list of options. Note that the aRobotParts array is "reborn" with each new robot type, so the first of each pair of robots gets its pick of a new batch of body parts. The second robot of each type always has one less option to choose from.

```
card = new Card("robot" + (i+1) + "Missing" + theMissingPart);
aCards.Add(card);
card= new Card("robot" + (i+1) + theMissingPart);
aCards.Add(card);
```

With these final lines, we create two new instances of the Card class, and add references to those cards to the aCards array. The aCards array is the card deck we'll use to deal out the game.

Each time we create a new card instance, we're passing a new argument—the name of the image we want displayed on the card. The first time through the nested loop, for the first (yellow) robot type, let's say we randomly choose to break its head.

This String:

```
"robot" + (i+1) + "Missing" + theMissingPart
```

resolves to:

```
"robot1MissingHead"
```

and

```
"robot" + (i+1) + theMissingPart
```

resolves to:

```
"robot1Head"
```

Take a quick look at the images in the Resources folder of the **Project** panel. "robot1MissingHead" and "robot1Head" just so happen to be the names of two of our images!

Time for action – Modifying the img argument

Because we're passing a new argument to the Card class, we have to modify Card to accept it.

1. Change the Card class code from this:

```
class Card extends System.Object
{
  // (variables omitted for clarity)
  function Card()
  {
    img = "robot";
  }
}
```

to this:

```
class Card extends System.Object
{
    // (variables omitted for clarity)
```

```
function Card(img:String)
{
    this.img = img;
}

}
```

2. Now, find the nested loop in the `Start` function where we added all our new cards to the `aGrid` array. Change it from this:

```
for(j=0; j<cols; j++)
{
    aGrid[i][j] = new Card();
}
```

to this:

```
for(j=0; j<cols; j++)
{
    var someNum:int = Random.Range(0,aCards.length);
    aGrid[i][j] = aCards[someNum];
    aCards.RemoveAt(someNum);
}
```

What just happened?

This code should look familiar to you because we're pulling a very similar trick here. We have a deck of cards—the `aCards` array. We're grabbing a random number using `Random.Range()`, and we supply the length of the `aCards` array as the maximum value. This gives us a value that stays within the bounds of `aCards`.

Then, we use that random number to pull a card out of the deck and assign it to the `aGrid` 2D array (it gets dealt to the table later on, in the `BuildGrid()` function). Finally, we remove that card from the deck so that we don't accidentally deal it out multiple times.

Save the script and play your game! What you should see is an army of amputated androids. Awesome! Because the cards are dealt randomly and the deck itself is being built randomly, any pictures of the game that you see from here on may not match what you have on your screen.

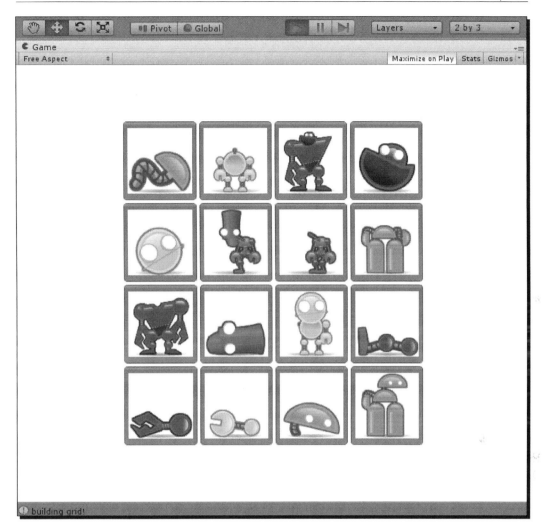

What exactly is "this"?

Did the `this.img = img;` line trip you up? Here's what's going on with that.

The `Card` class has an instance variable called `img`. We're also passing an argument to its constructor function with the exact same name, `img`. If we simply wrote `img = img;`, that means we'd be setting the value of the argument to the value of the argument. Hunh! That's not quite what we're after.

By specifying `this.img = img;`, we're saying that we want the `img` variable attached to this, the `Card` class, to have the same value as the argument called `img`.

It's a smidge confusing, I'll admit. So, why not just call the argument something different? You absolutely could! We did it this way because it's very common to see variables passed to the constructor function with the same name as the instance variables in the class. You may as well encounter it here with a full explanation, than come across it in the wild and let it gnaw your leg off.

Here's one more look at another, completely imaginary class that does the same kind of thing. Stare at it, absorb it, and be at peace with it.

```
class Dog extends System.Object
{
   var myName:String;
   var breed:String
   var age:int;

   function Dog(myName:String,breed:String,age:int)
   {
      this.myName = myName; // set the value of the instance variable
       "myName" to the value of the argument "myName"
      this.breed = breed; // set the value of the instance variable
       "breed" to the value of the argument "breed"
       this.age = age; // set the value of the instance variable "age"
          to the value of the argument "age"
   }
}
```

Have a go hero - Grokketh-thou Random.Range()?

As long as we're taking some time to let it all sink in, let's do another pass on this `Random.Range()` method. If `Random.Range()` is not clear to you yet, try building a test loop in the `Start()` function and logging the results:

```
for(i=0; i<1000; i++)
{
   Debug.Log(Random.Range(0,10));
}
```

Test and run. Make sure that the **Console** window is open (**Window | Console**), and make sure that **Collapse** is unchecked—otherwise, you'll see only the last few log lines. You should also ensure there are no other `print()` or `Debug.Log()` statements cluttering the console.

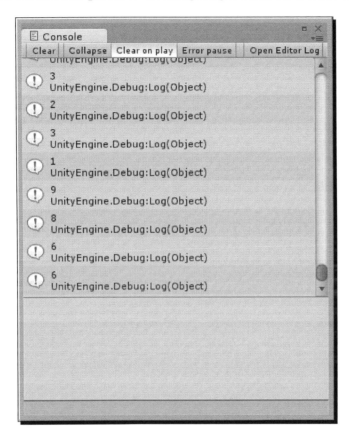

The number Unity spits out should never equal ten (provided you're using ints and not floats). Play around with the minimum and maximum values until you're completely confident, then delete your test loop and check out the rest of this code.

Random reigns supreme

Being able to pull and effectively use random numbers is another game development essential. With random numbers, you can make sure every card deal is different, like you've just done with your **Robot Repair** game. You can make enemies behave unpredictably, making it seem as though they're acting intelligently (without having to bother with complicated Artificial Intelligence programming!) You can make spaceships attack from surprising angles. You can build an avatar system with a **Shuffle** button that randomly dresses up your player's character.

The best game developers use random numbers to make their games meatier, more visually appealing, and more fun! The *worst* game developers use random numbers in all the wrong ways. Imagine a game where, whenever you shot a gun, the bullet traveled in a completely random direction! Random numbers can dramatically help or hinder your gameplay. Use them wisely, and they're an incredibly effective weapon in your game design arsenal.

Second dragon down

We've got some card faces displaying in the game, and we randomized. We just totally stabbed another one of our GDD dragons in the face (or cuddled another kitten, depending on the imagery you prefer). Well done!

☐ Put different images on the cards. (It would be great if the cards could be shuffled around every time you played!)

Time to totally flip

Let's move on to the next item in our list. **Robot Repair** lacks a certain amount of mystery at the moment. Let's add a bit of logic to make our cards two-sided, and to flip them over when the player clicks on them.

Time for action – Making the cards two-sided

We'll write some logic so that the cards show one image or another depending on whether or not they've been flipped over.

1. Find this line in your `BuildGrid` function:

```
if(GUILayout.Button(Resources.Load(card.img),

    GUILayout.Width(cardW)))
```

2. Change `card.img` to `img` so that the line reads like this:

```
if(GUILayout.Button(Resources.Load(img), GUILayout.Width(cardW)))
```

3. Just above that line, find the `card` variable definition:

```
var card:Object = aGrid[i][j];
```

4. Insert this line just after it:

```
var img:String;
```

5. Finally, after that line, write this conditional statement:

```
if(card.isFaceUp)
{
    img = card.img;
}
else
{
    img = "wrench";
}
```

The whole function should look like this when you're finished:

```
function BuildGrid()
{
  GUILayout.BeginVertical();
  GUILayout.FlexibleSpace();
  for(i=0; i<rows; i++)
  {
    GUILayout.BeginHorizontal();
    GUILayout.FlexibleSpace();
    for(j=0; j<cols; j++)
    {
      var card:Object = aGrid[i][j];
      var img:String;

      if(card.isFaceUp)
      {
        img = card.img;
      }
      else
      {
        img = "wrench";
      }

      if(GUILayout.Button(Resources.Load(img),
          GUILayout.Width(cardW)))
      {
        Debug.Log(card.img);
      }
    }
    GUILayout.FlexibleSpace();
    GUILayout.EndHorizontal();
  }
  GUILayout.FlexibleSpace();
  GUILayout.EndVertical();
}
```

So, instead of showing the card's image (`card.img`) when we draw each card button, we're showing the name of a card that we're storing in a new variable called `img`. Note that `img` and `card.img` are two different variables—`card.img` belongs to an instance of our `Card` class, while `img` is just a temporary variable that we're defining inside our loop, with the line `var img:String;`.

Next, we have a conditional statement. If the `isFaceUp` Boolean flag on the card is `true`, we set the value of our temporary `img` variable to match the `card.img` name. But, if the card is not face up, we'll show a generic "wrench" picture. The wrench picture will be the standard reverse image for all of our cards. You can find it in the `Resources` folder of the **Project** panel, if you're the kind of person who likes to peek at presents before your birthday.

Time for action – Building the card-flipping function

This card-flipping code looks pretty good, but there's no way to test it without adding some way of flagging that `isFaceUp` variable to `true`. Let's build a new function to do just that, and call it whenever a card button is clicked.

1. Create a new function called `FlipCardFaceUp`. As you did with the `BuildDeck` function earlier, write this function outside of and apart from your other functions— make sure it's not trapped inside the curly brackets of one of your other functions.

```
function FlipCardFaceUp()
{

}
```

2. Call the `FlipCardFaceUp` function from inside the card creation code:

```
if(GUILayout.Button(Resources.Load(img), GUILayout.Width(cardW)))
{
    FlipCardFaceUp();
    Debug.Log(card.img);
}
```

3. We need to tell the `FlipCardFaceUp` function *which* card has been flipped. Modify the line to pass a reference to the clicked-on card as an argument:

```
FlipCardFaceUp(card);
```

4. Now, we need to accept that card as an argument in our function definition. Modify your `FlipCardFaceUp` definition:

```
function FlipCardFaceUp(card:Card){

}
```

5. Now that we're passing a reference to the clicked-on card to our `FlipCardFaceUp` function, and the function is receiving that reference as an argument, we can do as we please with the card:

```
function FlipCardFaceUp(card:Card)
{
    card.isFaceUp = true;
}
```

Mismatched arguments

The name of the variable that you pass as an argument to a function does not need to match the name of the argument you receive in that function. For example, we could pass a variable called monkeyNubs (`FlipCardFaceUp(monkeyNubs)`), and we could name the argument butterFig function (`FlipCardFaceUp(butterFig :Card)`). As long as the type of the thing getting passed and received is the same (in this case, an object of type `Card`), it'll work. We can't pass a `String` and receive an `int`, no matter what the variable is called on either end.

Reference versus value

Another picky thing about many programming languages, including UnityScript, is that some data types are passed to functions by reference, while some are passed by value. Large structures like classes and arrays are passed by reference, which means that when we accept them as arguments in our functions and start fiddling around with them, we're making changes to the actual structure that was passed in. But, when we pass something like an `int`, it gets passed by value. It's like we're getting a copy of it, not the original. Any changes we make to something passed by value does not affect the original variable.

Save the script and test your game. Because all of the cards default to isFaceUp = false, the grid is dealt "wrench side up". When you click on each of the cards, the isFaceUp Boolean for each clicked-on card is flagged to true. The next time the interface is redrawn OnGUI (which is fractions of seconds later), Unity sees that isFaceUp=true for the clicked-on cards, and loads card.img instead of "wrench".

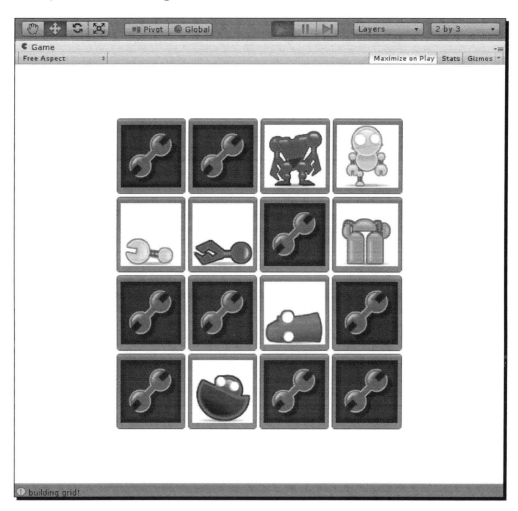

What's that I smell? Why, it's the stench of a dying dragon (or a cuddled kitten). We figured out how to flip over the cards, so let's knock another item off our list:

☐   Make the cards flip over from back to front when you click them.

You'll notice, of course, that there's no way to flip the cards back over. Let's take care of that now.

Time for action – Building the card-flipping function

The game will let the player flip over two cards. Then, it will pause for a brief moment and flip the cards back over. We'll worry about detecting matches for our grand finale in just a moment.

1. Add the following code to your `FlipCardFaceUp` function:

```
function FlipCardFaceUp(card:Card)
{
  card.isFaceUp = true;
  aCardsFlipped.Add(card);

  if(aCardsFlipped.Count == 2)
  {
    playerCanClick = false;

    yield WaitForSeconds(1);

    aCardsFlipped[0].isFaceUp = false;
    aCardsFlipped[1].isFaceUp = false;

    aCardsFlipped = new ArrayList();

    playerCanClick = true;
  }
}
```

2. Then, make a small change to one line in the `BuildGrid` function:

```
if(GUILayout.Button(Resources.Load(img),
    GUILayout.Width(cardW)))
{
  if(playerCanClick)
  {
    FlipCardFaceUp(card);
  }
  Debug.Log(card.img);
}
```

3. Save and test. You should be able to flip over two cards before your incessant clicking falls on deaf ears. After a one-second pause, the cards flip back over.

What just happened – dissecting the flip

Let's take a look at what we've just done:

```
aCardsFlipped.Add(card);
```

In this line, we're adding the card to our `aCardsFlipped ArrayList`.

```
if (aCardsFlipped.Count == 2)
```

Next, our conditional checks to see if the player has flipped over two cards—in that case, the `Count` property should be 2. Remember that `aCardsFlipped` is from the `ArrayList` class, not the `Array` class, so it's a bit of a different beast. To check the length of an `Array`, we use `Length`. To check the length of an `ArrayList`, we use `Count`. The count of our array goes up when we use the `ArrayList.Add()` method, which throws additional items into the list.

```
playerCanClick = false;
```

Our `playerCanClick` flag comes in handy here—by setting it to `false`, we prevent the fiendish player from flipping over more cards than he ought to.

```
yield WaitForSeconds(1);
```

This straightforward piece of code waits for one second before allowing the next line of code to execute.

```
aCardsFlipped[0].isFaceUp = false;
aCardsFlipped[1].isFaceUp = false;
```

These lines flag the two flipped-over cards back to their unflipped states. The next time the `OnGUI` function runs, which will be very soon, the cards will be drawn wrench side up.

```
aCardsFlipped = new ArrayList();
```

By reinitializing the `aCardsFlipped ArrayList`, we're emptying it out to hold two brand new flipped-over cards.

```
playerCanClick = true;
```

Now that it's safe to start flipping cards again, we'll flag the `playerCanClick` variable back to `true`.

```
if (playerCanClick)
{
    FlipCardFaceUp(card);
}
```

By adding this simple condition at the beginning of the `FlipCardFaceUp()` function call, we can control whether or not the player is allowed to flip over the card.

Pumpkin eater

If you hail from Cheaty-Pants land, you may have figured out that you can flip over the same card twice. This isn't technically cheating, but when you break the game, you're only cheating yourself. We also have to be careful because a click-happy player might accidentally double-click the first card, and then think that the game is broken when he can't flip over a second card. Let's wrap the `FlipCardFaceUp` in a conditional statement to prevent this from happening:

```
function FlipCardFaceUp(card:Card)
{
   card.isFaceUp = true;
   if(aCardsFlipped.IndexOf(card) < 0)
   {
      aCardsFlipped.Add(card);

      // (the rest of the code is omitted)
   }
}
```

What just happened?

This is where we finally get some mileage out of our `ArrayList` class. `ArrayList` has a method called `IndexOf` that searches itself for an element, and returns the index point of that element.

Take a look at this example (the log's "answers" are commented at the end of each line):

```
var aShoppingList:ArrayList = ["apples", "milk", "cheese",
                              "chainsaw"];
Debug.Log(aShoppingList.IndexOf("apples")); // 0
Debug.Log(aShoppingList.IndexOf("cheese")); // 2
Debug.Log(aShoppingList.IndexOf("bicarbonate of soda")); // -1
```

Note that `ArrayList` returns `-1` when the element can't be found.

So, for our purposes, we do a quick check of the `aCardsFlipped ArrayList` to make sure it doesn't already contain a reference to the card. If the card is already in `aCardsFlipped`, that means that the player clicked on the same card twice. If we do detect a double-flip, we simply don't execute the remainder of the card-flipping code.

The `Array` class doesn't have this handy `IndexOf()` method—we would have had to write our own. Thumbs up for less work!

Stabby McDragonpoker rides again

There's one more item off our checklist. Make an X, pat yourself on the back, and steel your will against the next challenge!

☐ Prevent the player from flipping over more than two cards in a turn.

Game and match

The last piece of crucial functionality in our flip n' match game is to detect, and react to, a match. We currently have no way of knowing, through code, if two cards match, so we'll fix that first. Then, we'll detect the match, and remove the cards from the table. After that, we just need to check for the endgame scenario (all matches found) before zipping it up and calling it a game.

Time for action – ID the cards

Let's revisit our card-creation code and give each card an ID number. We'll use that number to detect matches.

1. In the `BuildDeck` function, add this line:

    ```
    function BuildDeck()
    {
        var totalRobots:int = 4; // we've got four robots to work with
        var card:Object; // this stores a reference to a card
        var id:int = 0;
    ```

2. Look a little further down the code. Pass the `id` value to the `Card` class with each robot and missing body part card, and then increment the ID number:

    ```
    card = new Card("robot" + (i+1) + "Missing" + theMissingPart,
                    id);
    aCards.Add(card);

    card= new Card("robot" + (i+1) + theMissingPart, id);
    aCards.Add(card);
    id++;
    ```

3. Add `id` as a property of the `Card` class. Accept `id` as an argument in the `Card` class constructor function, and set the card's `id` instance variable to that value:

    ```
    class Card extends System.Object
    {
      var isFaceUp:boolean = false;
      var img:String;
      var id:int;
    ```

```
  var isMatched:boolean = false;

  function Card(img:String, id:int)
  {
    this.img = img;
    this.id = id;


  }
}
```

What just happened?

What you've done is given each matching set of cards its own ID number. A yellow robot with a missing head, and its missing head, will each have an ID of 0. The next two cards added to the deck might be a yellow robot with a missing arm, and its missing arm, which each get an ID of 1. With this logic in place, it should be much easier to tell if two cards match—we'll just compare their IDs!

Time for action – Comparing the IDs

To compare the IDs, we need to make some changes to the `FlipCardFaceUp` function.

1. Note that we're folding two existing lines of code inside a new conditional statement:

```
function FlipCardFaceUp(card:Object)
{
  card.isFaceUp = true;

  if(aCardsFlipped.IndexOf(card) < 0)
  {
    aCardsFlipped.Add(card);

    if(aCardsFlipped.Count == 2)
    {
      playerCanClick = false;

      yield WaitForSeconds(1);

      if(aCardsFlipped[0].id == aCardsFlipped[1].id)
      {
       // Match!
       aCardsFlipped[0].isMatched = true;
       aCardsFlipped[1].isMatched = true;

      }
       else
       {
```

```
                    aCardsFlipped[0].isFaceUp = false;
                    aCardsFlipped[1].isFaceUp = false;
                }

            aCardsFlipped = new ArrayList();

            playerCanClick = true;
        }
    }
}
```

Here, we check to see if the two flipped-over cards have the same ID value. If they do, we set each card's isMatched flag to true. If they don't match, we just flip the cards back over as before.

2. We should add a little bit of logic to our BuildGrid function to make sure the player can't flip over a card that's been matched:

```
function BuildGrid()
{
// (some stuff was omitted here for clarity)
var card:Object = aGrid[i][j];
var img:String
if(card.isMatched)
  {
    img = "blank";
  }
  else
  {
    if(card.isFaceUp)
    {
      img = card.img;
    }
    else
    {
      img = "wrench";
    }
  }

GUI.enabled = !card.isMatched;
if(GUILayout.Button(Resources.Load(img), GUILayout.Width(cardW)))
{
if(playerCanClick)
{
  FlipCardFaceUp(card);
}
Debug.Log(card.img);
}
GUI.enabled = true;
```

What just happened?

So, we wrap our first piece of logic in a conditional that says if the card is matched, set its image to some blank white picture.

The next new lines are pretty interesting. We're setting GUI.enabled, which is a Boolean value, to whatever card.isMatched is NOT. The exclamation mark operator means "is not". So, if card.isMatched is true, then GUI.enabled is false. If card.isMatched is false, then GUI.enabled is true. GUI.enabled, as you probably guessed, enables or disables GUI control functionality.

When we're finished drawing our card button and setting its click behavior (which is ignored if GUI.enabled is false), we need to remember to re-enable the GUI—otherwise, none of our other cards will be clickable!

Save the script and repair some robots. Just like the second **Death Star**, your game is fully operational, baby!

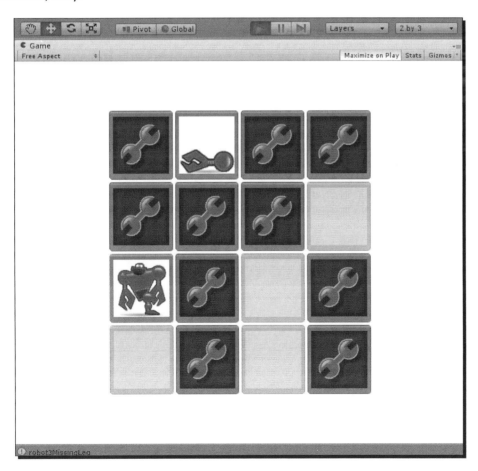

On to the final boss

With that last step, we've slain or cuddled the penultimate dragon or kitten:

☐ Compare two flipped-over cards to see if they match (Note: if they match, we should remove the cards from the table. If they don't match, we should flip them back over.)

The last checkbox awaits: detecting victory and showing the endgame message with a **Play Again** button. Onward, to victory!

Endgame

With the amount of emotional and temporal engagement you're expecting from your players with this game, it would be criminal to skimp on the endgame. Let's close the loop by showing the player a congratulatory message with an option to play again when we detect that all of the matches have been found.

Time for action – Checking for victory

Our `matchesMade`, `matchesNeededToWin`, and `playerHasWon` variables have been standing at the ready this whole time. Let's finally make use of them.

1. Add these few lines to the `FlipCardFaceUp` function, where you're detecting a match:

```
if(aCardsFlipped[0].id == aCardsFlipped[1].id)
{
  // Match!
  aCardsFlipped[0].isMatched = true;
  aCardsFlipped[1].isMatched = true;

  matchesMade ++;

  if(matchesMade >= matchesNeededToWin)
  {
    playerHasWon = true;
  }
}
```

2. Add a new function call to the `OnGUI` function:

```
function OnGUI () {
  GUILayout.BeginArea (Rect (0,0,Screen.width,Screen.height));
  GUILayout.BeginHorizontal();
  BuildGrid();
```

```
        if(playerHasWon) BuildWinPrompt();
        GUILayout.EndHorizontal();
        GUILayout.EndArea();
    }
```

3. And, now, we'll use some `GUILayout` commands that we learned in the last chapter to display a "win" prompt to the player. Write this new function apart from the other functions, and make sure it's not wedged inside any other function's curlies:

```
function BuildWinPrompt()
{
    var winPromptW:int = 100;
    var winPromptH:int = 90;

    var halfScreenW:float = Screen.width/2;
    var halfScreenH:float = Screen.height/2;

    var halfPromptW:int = winPromptW/2;
    var halfPromptH:int = winPromptH/2;

    GUI.BeginGroup(Rect(halfScreenW-halfPromptW,
        halfScreenH-halfPromptH, winPromptW, winPromptH));
     GUI.Box (Rect (0,0,winPromptW,winPromptH),
        "A Winner is You!!");
     if(GUI.Button(Rect(10,40,80,20),"Play Again"))
     {
        Application.LoadLevel("Title");
     }
     GUI.EndGroup();
}
```

What just happened?

This method uses 90% recycled knowledge. We store a few variables to help us remember where the middle of the screen is, store the half width and height of the prompt we're about to draw, and then draw and position it using a fixed layout (instead of an automatic layout, like our grid of cards).

The remaining unknown 10% uses a wrapper called a **Group**, which helps us collect UI controls together.

```
    GUI.Box (Rect (0,0,winPromptW,winPromptH), "A Winner is You!!");
```

This draws a box at the origin point of the **Group** (which is centered on the screen). Feel free to change the box label, "A Winner is You!!", to something equally sarcastic.

10 pixels in and 40 pixels down inside that box, we draw a **Button** control with the label **Play Again**. When clicked, we link the player to the **Title Scene** where the game starts all over again and much fun is repeatedly had, until the player dies of old age and the Earth crashes into the sun.

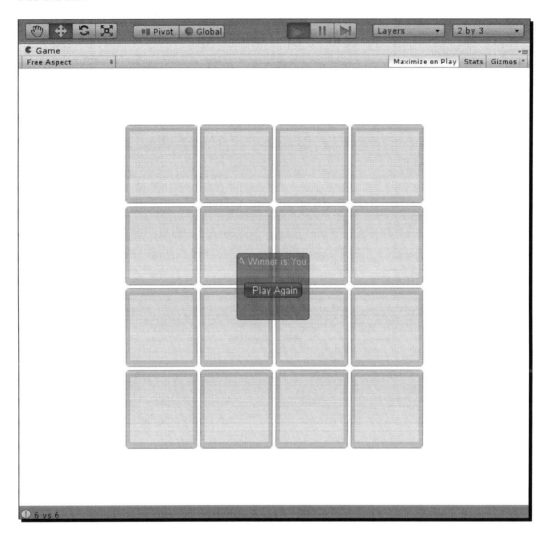

Have a go hero – Extra credit

As you now know how to create label, and position buttons; create scenes, and link scenes to each other with buttons; and draw text and graphics to the screen, here are a few challenges for you that will give your already complete game even more bells and whistles:

- Create a **Credits** screen, and link to it from either the **Title Scene** or the **Play Again** prompt. Be sure to credit yourself for absolutely everything, with perhaps a token nod to grandma. You've earned it!

- Create an **Instructions** screen. This is really an excuse to throw some color into the game, and church up what is really just a simple flip n' match memory game. Here's some copy for you to use and adapt:

  "Professor Wrecker had a wild night and smashed up the robotics lab again! Can you put the ruined robots back together while the Professor sleeps it off?"

  Hilarious *and* kid-friendly.

- Create some new elements near the edge of your grid—eight cards with silhouettes of the robots on them. As the player finds matches and the clickable cards are blanked out, swap the silhouettes for the repaired robots. This may give the player a stronger sense of a goal.

- Create a new set of graphics with four additional robots. Add them to your `Resources` folder, name them properly, and see if you can adjust the code so that all eight robots get dealt into the deck.

- Explore the other UI controls Unity has to offer. Try expanding those game instructions to a 30-page-long epic (NOT a good idea in real life, but we're just practicing here). Hook those monstrous instructions up to a scroll bar. Add a checkbox for the player stating, "I have read and agreed to these instructions." Do not let your player play the game until he has scrolled to the bottom of the instructions. This is probably a terrible design decision, but we'll make some concessions for the sake of your education. Just be sure to hide your home address from the player so that you don't get any bricks through your window or flaming bags of poo on your doorstep.

Endgame

You've created a fully working flip n' match memory game that'll be a sure-fire hit with grandma, especially if she sees her shout-out in the credits. In this chapter, you:

- Used `FlexibleSpace` to center your automatic `GUILayout`

- Learned how to pull random numbers and bend them to your nefarious will

- Figured out how to disable the GUI, flip Boolean flags, pause code execution, and prevent the player from clicking on stuff he's not supposed to

◆ Built an entire functioning game using only the Unity GUI system

◆ Learned how to break a game's design into smaller functional steps that you can add to a to-do list

Remember that any 3D game will likely require a decent amount of 2D programming. User interfaces like shops, inventory screens, level select screens, and character creation tools usually display items in grid layouts with selectable buttons, changing pictures, control-limiting logic, and a lot of the same stuff we've covered in this chapter. Consider these past two chapters training for all the amazing user interfaces you'll build for your games.

Astronauts don't train in space—they train in simulators. And, just like an astronaut in a NASA-constructed spinning thrill ride, this chapter may have left your head reeling! We covered a *lot* of ground here, but the good news is that the pages in this book aren't going anywhere. Meditate on them. Read them again and again. Take your time to let it all sink in before charging on to the next chapter.

Bring. It. On.

Are you ready to continue? Then, it's time to slather that wonderful brain of yours with awesome sauce. With Unity UI mastery under your belt, it's time to learn how to build a one-off GUI component that you could end up using in every game you'll ever build. How's that for a cliffhanger ending? Turn that page!

Here is the completed **GameScript** for Robot Repair:

```
var cols:int = 4; // the number of columns in the card grid
var rows:int = 4; // the number of rows in the card grid
var totalCards:int = 16;
var matchesNeededToWin:int = totalCards * 0.5; // If there are 16
cards, the player needs to find 8 matches to clear the board
var matchesMade:int = 0; // At the outset, the player has not made any
matches
var cardW:int = 100; // Each card's width and height is 100 pixels
var cardH:int = 100;
var aCards:Array; // We'll store all the cards we create in this array
var aGrid:Array; // This array will keep track of the shuffled, dealt
cards
var aCardsFlipped:ArrayList; // This array will store the two cards
that the player flips over
var playerCanClick:boolean; // We'll use this flag to prevent the
player from clicking buttons when we don't want him or her to
var playerHasWon:boolean = false; // Store whether or not the player
has won. This should probably start out false :)

function Start()
{
```

```
    playerCanClick = true; // We should let the player play, don't you
think?

    // Initialize the arrays as empty lists:
    aCards = new Array();
    aGrid = new Array();
    aCardsFlipped = new ArrayList();

    BuildDeck();

    for(i=0; i<rows; i++)
    {
      aGrid[i] = new Array(); // Create a new, empty array at index i

     for(j=0; j<cols; j++)
      {
        var someNum:int = Random.Range(0,aCards.length);
        aGrid[i][j] = aCards[someNum];
        aCards.RemoveAt(someNum);
      }
    }
}

function BuildDeck()
{
    var totalRobots:int = 4;  // we've got four robots to work with
    var card:Object; // this stores a reference to a card
    var id:int = 0;

    for(i=0; i<totalRobots; i++)
    {
        var aRobotParts:Array = ["Head", "Arm", "Leg"];
        for(j=0; j<2; j++)
        {
            var someNum:int = Random.Range(0, aRobotParts.length);
            var theMissingPart:String = aRobotParts[someNum];

            aRobotParts.RemoveAt(someNum);

            card = new Card("robot" + (i+1) + "Missing" + theMissingPart,
id);
            aCards.Add(card);
            card= new Card("robot" + (i+1) + theMissingPart, id);
            aCards.Add(card);
            id++;
        }
    }
}
```

```
function BuildWinPrompt()
{
    var winPromptW:int = 100;
    var winPromptH:int = 90;

    var halfScreenW:float = Screen.width/2;
    var halfScreenH:float = Screen.height/2;

    var halfPromptW:int = winPromptW/2;
    var halfPromptH:int = winPromptH/2;

    GUI.BeginGroup(Rect(halfScreenW-halfPromptW,
    halfScreenH-halfPromptH, winPromptW, winPromptH));
    GUI.Box (Rect (0,0,winPromptW,winPromptH), "A Winner is You!!");

    if(GUI.Button(Rect(10,40,80,20),"Play Again"))
    {
        Application.LoadLevel("Title");
    }
    GUI.EndGroup();
}




function OnGUI () {
    GUILayout.BeginArea (Rect (0,0,Screen.width,Screen.height));
    BuildGrid();
    if(playerHasWon) BuildWinPrompt();
    GUILayout.EndArea();
    //print("building grid!");
}

function BuildGrid()
{
    GUILayout.BeginVertical();
    GUILayout.FlexibleSpace();
    for(i=0; i<rows; i++)
    {
        GUILayout.BeginHorizontal();
        GUILayout.FlexibleSpace();
        for(j=0; j<cols; j++)
        {
            var card:Object = aGrid[i][j];
            var img:String;

            if(card.isMatched)
            {
            img = "blank";
            }
            else
```

```
        {
            if(card.isFaceUp)
            {
                img = card.img;
            }
            else
            {
                img = "wrench";
            }
        }

        GUI.enabled = !card.isMatched;

        if(GUILayout.Button(Resources.Load(img),
        GUILayout.Width(cardW)))
        {
            if(playerCanClick)
            {
                FlipCardFaceUp(card);
            }
            Debug.Log(card.img);
        }
        GUI.enabled = true;
    }
    GUILayout.FlexibleSpace();
    GUILayout.EndHorizontal();
    }
    GUILayout.FlexibleSpace();
    GUILayout.EndVertical();
}
function FlipCardFaceUp(card:Card)
{
    card.isFaceUp = true;
    if(aCardsFlipped.IndexOf(card) < 0)
    {
        aCardsFlipped.Add(card);

        if(aCardsFlipped.Count == 2)
        {
            playerCanClick = false;

            yield WaitForSeconds(1);

            if(aCardsFlipped[0].id == aCardsFlipped[1].id)
            {
                // Match!
                aCardsFlipped[0].isMatched = true;
                aCardsFlipped[1].isMatched = true;

                matchesMade ++;
```

```
            if(matchesMade >= matchesNeededToWin)
            {
                playerHasWon = true;
            }

        }
        else
        {
            aCardsFlipped[0].isFaceUp = false;
            aCardsFlipped[1].isFaceUp = false;
        }

        aCardsFlipped = new ArrayList();

        playerCanClick = true;
      }
    }
}


class Card extends System.Object
{
  var isFaceUp:boolean = false;
  var isMatched:boolean = false;
  var img:String;
  var id:int;

  function Card(img:String, id:int)
  {
    this.img = img;
   this.id = id;
  }
}
```

7

Don't Be a Clock Blocker

We've taken a baby game like Memory and made it slightly cooler by changing the straight-up match mechanism and adding a twist: matching disembodied robot parts to their bodies. Robot Repair is a tiny bit more interesting and more challenging thanks to this simple modification.

There are lots of ways we could make the game even more difficult: we could quadruple the number of robots, crank the game up to a 20x20 card grid, or rig Unity up to some peripheral device that issues a low-grade electrical shock to the player's fiddly bits every time he doesn't find a match. NOW who's making a baby game?

These ideas could take a lot of time though, and the Return-On-Investment (ROI) we see from these features may not be worth the effort. One cheap, effective way of amping up the game experience is to add a clock. Games have used clocks to make us nervous for time immemorial, and it's hard to find a video game in existence that doesn't include some sort of time pressure—from the increasing speed of falling Tetris pieces, to the countdown clock in every Super Mario Bros. level, to the egg timers packaged with many popular board games like Boggle, Taboo, and Scattergories.

Apply pressure

What if the player only has x seconds to find all the matches in the Robot Repair game? Or, what if in our keep-up game, the player has to bounce the ball without dropping it until the timer runs out in order to advance to the next level? In this chapter, let's:

◆ Program a text-based countdown clock to add a little pressure to our games

◆ Modify the clock to make it graphical, with an ever-shrinking horizontal bar

◆ Layer in some new code and graphics to create a pie chart-style clock

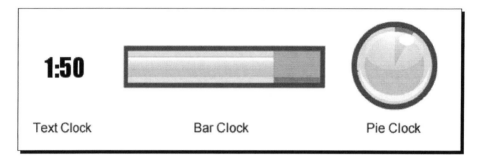

| Text Clock | Bar Clock | Pie Clock |

That's three different countdown clocks, all running from the same initial code, all ready to be put to work in whatever Unity games you dream up. Roll up your sleeves—it's time to start coding!

Time for action – Preparing the clock script

Open your Robot Repair game project and make sure you're in the **game Scene**. As we've done in earlier chapters, we'll create an empty **GameObject** and glue some code to it.

1. Go to **GameObject | Create Empty**.

2. Rename the empty **Game Object** as **Clock**.

3. Create a new JavaScript and name it **clockScript**.

4. Drag-and-drop the **clockScript** onto the **Clock Game Object**.

No problem! We know the drill by now—we've got a **Game Object** ready to go with an empty script where we'll put all of our clock code.

Time for more action – Preparing the clock text

In order to display the numbers, we need to add a **GUIText** component to the **Clock GameObject**, but there's one problem: **GUIText** defaults to white, which isn't so hot for a game with a white background. Let's make a quick adjustment to the game background color so that we can see what's going on. We can change it back later.

1. Select the **Main Camera** in the **Hierarchy** panel.

2. Find the **Camera** component in the **Inspector** panel.

3. Click on the color swatch labeled **Back Ground Color**, and change it to something darker so that our piece of white **GUIText** will show up against it. I chose a "delightful" puce (R157 G99 B120).

4. Select the **Clock Game Object** from the **Hierarchy** panel. It's not a bad idea to look in the **Inspector** panel and confirm that the **clockScript** script was added as a component in the preceding instruction.

5. With the **Clock Game Object** selected, go to **Component | Rendering | GUIText**. This is the **GUIText** component that we'll use to display the clock numbers on the screen.

6. In the **Inspector** panel, find the **GUIText** component and type **whatever** in the blank **Text** property.

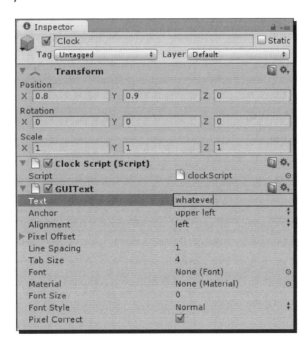

In the **Inspector** panel, change the clock's **X** position to **0.8**, its **Y** position to **0.9** and its **Z** position to **0** to bring it into view. You should see the word **whatever** in white, floating near the top-right corner of the screen in the **Game** view.

Right, then! We have a **Game Object** with an empty script attached. That **Game Object** has a **GUIText** component to display the clock numbers. Our game background is certifiably hideous. Let's code us some clock.

Still time for action – Changing the clock text color

Double-click on the **clockScript**. Your empty script, with one lone `Update()` function, should appear in the code editor. The very first thing we should consider is doing away with our puce background by changing the **GUIText** color to black instead of white. Let's get at it.

1. Write the built-in `Awake` function and change the **GUIText** color:

```
function Awake()
{
    guiText.material.color = Color.black;
}
function Update() {
}
```

2. Save the script and test your game to see your new black text.

`Awake` is a built-in function just like `Start`, but it happens even earlier. `Awake` is the first function that gets called when our script runs. This is Unity's default behavior, but there are knobs you can twist to change the order in which those built-in functions are called.

If you feel comfy, you can change the game background color back to white by clicking on the **Main Camera Game Object** and finding the color swatch in the **Inspector** panel. The white **whatever GUIText** will disappear against the white background in the **Game** view because the color-changing code that we just wrote runs only when we test the game (try testing the game to confirm this). If you ever lose track of your text or it's not displaying properly, or you just really wanna *see* it on the screen, you can change the camera's background color to confirm that it's still there.

If you're happy with this low-maintenance, disappearing-text arrangement, you can move on to the *Prepare the clock code* section. But, if you want to put in a little extra elbow grease to actually *see* the text, in a font of your choosing, follow these next steps.

Time for action rides again – Creating a font texture and material

Ha! I knew you couldn't resist. In order to change the font of this **GUIText**, and to see it in a different color without waiting for the code to run, we need to import a font, hook it up to a **Material**, and apply that **Material** to the **GUIText**.

1. Find a font that you want to use for your game clock. I like the LOLCats standby *Impact*. If you're running Windows, your fonts are likely to be in the `C:\Windows\Fonts` directory. If you're a Mac user, you should look in the `/Library/Fonts/` folder. Stick with a `.ttf` (TrueType font) if you want to have the most success.

2. Drag the font into the **Project** panel in Unity. The font will be added to your list of **Assets**. (Remember to create a `Fonts` folder to store it, if you want to keep your **Project** panel tidy.)

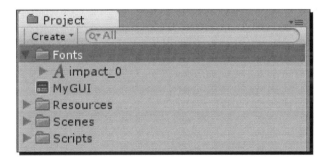

3. Right-click (or secondary-click) on an empty area of the **Project** panel and choose **Create | Material**. You can also click on the **Create** button at the top of the panel.

4. Rename the new **Material** to something useful. Because I'm using the Impact font, and it's going to be black, I named mine "BlackImpact" (incidentally, "Black Impact" is also the name of my favorite exploitation film from the 70s). Again, you can place the new material in a folder that you create called `Materials`.

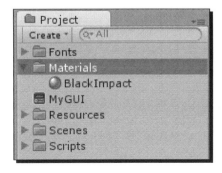

5. Click on the **Material** you just created in the **Project** panel.

6. In the **Inspector** panel, click on the color swatch labeled **Main Color** and choose black (R0 G0 B0), then click on the little red **X** to close the color picker.

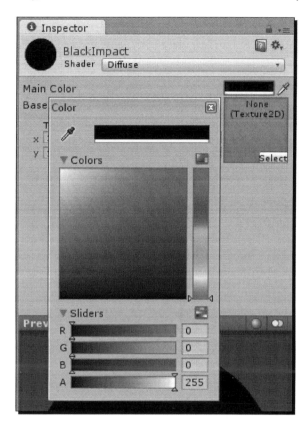

7. In the empty square area labeled **None (Texture 2D)**, click on the **Select** button, and choose your font from the list of textures (mine was labeled **impact - font texture**). If your font texture doesn't appear in the list, open the font in the **Project** panel, and drag/drop the font texture into the **None (Texture 2D)** area.

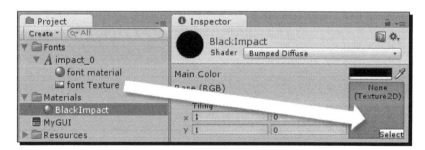

8. At the top of the **Inspector** panel, there's a drop-down labeled **Shader**. Select **Transparent | Diffuse** from the list.

9. Click on the **Clock Game Object** in the **Hierarchy** panel.

10. Find the **GUIText** component in the **Inspector** panel.

11. Click-and-drag your font—the one with the letter **A** icon—from the **Project** panel into the parameter labeled **Font** in the **GUIText** component. You can also click on the circular button next to the parameter labeled **None (Font)** and choose your font from the pop-up list.

12. Similarly, click-and-drag your **Material**—the one with the gray sphere icon—from the **Project** panel into the parameter labeled **Material** in the **GUIText** component. You can also click on the circle button (the parameter should say **None (Material)** initially) and choose your **Material** from the list.

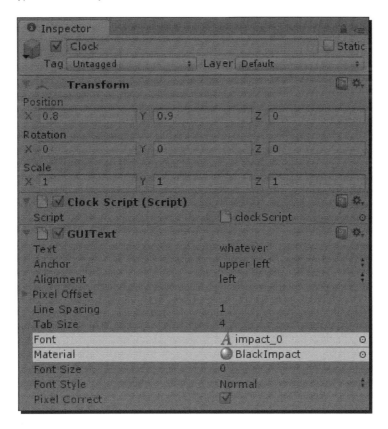

Just as you always dreamed about since childhood, the **GUIText** changes to a solid black version of the fancy font you chose! Now, you can definitely get rid of that horrid puce background and switch back to white for the remainder of the project. If you made it this far and you're using a **Material** instead of the naked font option, it's also safe to delete the guiText.material.color = Color.black; line from the **clockScript**.

Time for action – What's with the tiny font?

The Impact font, or any other font you choose, won't be very... impactful at its default size. Let's change the import settings to biggify it.

1. Click on your imported font—the one with the letter **A** icon—in the **Project** panel.

2. In the **Inspector** panel, you'll see the **True Type Font Importer**. Change the **Font Size** to something respectable, like 32, and press the *Enter* key on your keyboard.

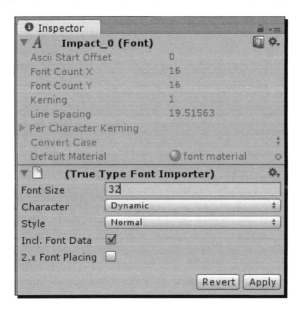

3. Click on the **Apply** button. Magically, your **GUIText** cranks up to 32 points (you'll only see this happen if you still have a piece of text like "whatever" entered into the **Text** parameter of the **GUIText** of the **Clock Game Object** component).

What just happened - was that seriously magic?

Of course, there's nothing magical about it. Here's what happened when you clicked on that **Apply** button:

When you import a font into Unity, an entire set of raster images is created for you by the **True Type Font Importer**. **Raster images** are the ones that look all pixelly and square when you zoom in on them. Fonts are inherently vector instead of raster, which means that they use math to describe their curves and angles. Vector images can be scaled up any size without going all Rubik's Cube on you.

But, Unity doesn't support vector fonts. For every font size that you want to support, you need to import a new version of the font and change its import settings to a different size. This means that you may have four copies of, say, the Impact font, at the four different sizes you require.

When you click on the **Apply** button, Unity creates its set of raster images based on the font that you're importing.

Time for action – Preparing the clock code

Let's rough in a few empty functions and three variables that we'll need to make the clock work.

1. Open up the **clockScript** by double-clicking it. Update the code:

```
var clockIsPaused : boolean = false;
var startTime : float; //(in seconds)
var timeRemaining : float; //(in seconds)
function Awake()
{
}

function Update() {
  if (!clockIsPaused)
  {
     // make sure the timer is not paused
     DoCountdown();
  }
}

function DoCountdown() {
}

function PauseClock()
```

```
{
    clockIsPaused = true;
}

function UnpauseClock()
{
    clockIsPaused = false;
}

function ShowTime()
{
}

function TimeIsUp()
{
}
```

What just happened – that's a whole lotta nothing

Here, we've created a list of functions that we'll probably need to get our clock working. The functions are empty, but that's okay—roughing them in like this is a really valid and useful way to program. We have a `DoCountdown()` function that we call on every update, as long as our `clockIsPaused` flag is `false`. We have `PauseClock()` and `UnpauseClock()` functions—each of them needs only one simple line of code to change the `clockIsPaused` flag, so we've included that. In the `ShowTime()` function, we'll display the time in the **GUIText** component. Finally, we'll call the `TimeIsUp()` function when the clock reaches zero.

At the top of the script are three hopefully self-explanatory variables: a Boolean to hold the clock's paused state, a floating point number to hold the start time, and another to hold the remaining time.

Now that we have the skeleton of our clock code and we see the scope of work ahead of us, we can dive in and flesh it out.

Time for action – Creating the countdown logic

Let's set the `startTime` variable, and build the logic to handle the counting-down functionality of our clock.

1. Set the `startTime` variable:

```
function Awake() {
    startTime = 5.0;
}
```

Note: Five seconds to beat the game is a bit ridiculous.
We're just keeping the time tight for testing. You can crank
this variable up later.

2. Decrease the amount of time on the clock:

```
function DoCountdown()
{
    timeRemaining = startTime - Time.time;
}
```

3. If the clock hits zero, pause the clock and call the `TimeIsUp()` function:

```
timeRemaining = startTime - Time.time;
if (timeRemaining < 0)
{
    timeRemaining = 0;
    clockIsPaused = true;
    TimeIsUp();
}
```

4. Add some `Debug` statements so that you can see something happening:

```
function DoCountdown()
{
    // (other lines omitted for clarity)
    Debug.Log("time remaining = " + timeRemaining);
}

function TimeIsUp()
{
    Debug.Log("Time is up!");
}
```

5. Save the script and test your game.

You should see the `Debug` statements in the information bar at the bottom of the screen.
When the clock finishes ticking down through five seconds, you'll see the **Time is up!**
message... (if you're a mutant with super-speed vision). The **Time is up!** message gets wiped
out by the next "time remaining" message. If you want to see it with normal-people vision,
open the console window (**Window | Console** in the menu) and watch for it in the list of
printed statements.

Note: If the "building grid!" print statement from the previous chapters is cluttering up your console window, it's safe to comment that line out with a double slash //.

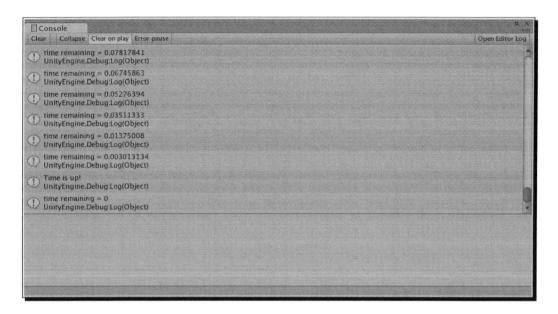

Time for action – Displaying the time onscreen

We know from the Debug statements that the clock is working, so all we need to do is stick the timeRemaining value into our **GUIText** to see it on the screen. But, it won't look very clock-like unless we perform a tiny bit of math on that value to split it into minutes and seconds so that five seconds displays as 0:05, or 119 seconds displays as 1:59.

1. Call the ShowTime() function from within the DoCountdown() function (you can delete or comment the Debug.Log() statement):

```
function DoCountdown()
{
  timeRemaining = startTime - Time.time;
  // (other lines omitted for clarity)
  ShowTime();
  Debug.Log("time remaining = " + timeRemaining);
}
```

2. Create some variables to store the minutes and seconds values in the `ShowTime()` function, along with a variable to store the string (text) version of the time:

```
function ShowTime() {
    var minutes : int;
    var seconds : int;
    var timeStr : String;
}
```

3. Just below that, divide the `timeRemaining` by `60` to get the number of minutes that have elapsed:

```
    var timeStr : String;
    minutes = timeRemaining/60;
```

4. Store the remainder as the number of elapsed seconds:

```
    minutes = timeRemaining/60;
    seconds = timeRemaining % 60;
```

5. Set the text version of the time to the number of elapsed minutes, followed by a colon:

```
    seconds = timeRemaining % 60;
    timeStr = minutes.ToString() + ":";
```

6. Append (add) the text version of the elapsed seconds:

```
    timeStr = minutes.ToString() + ":";
    timeStr += seconds.ToString("D2");
```

7. Finally, push the `timeStr` value to the **GUIText** component:

```
    timeStr += seconds.ToString("D2");
    guiText.text = timeStr; //display the time to the GUI
```

8. To gaze at your clock longingly as it counts down every delectable second, crank up the `startTime` amount in the `Awake` function:

```
    startTime = 120.0;
```

9. Save and test.

Your beautiful new game clock whiles away the hours in your own chosen font at your own chosen size, formatted with a colon like any self-respecting game clock should be.

What just happened – what about that terrifying code?

There are a few kooky things going on in the code we just wrote. Let's hone in on the new and weird stuff.

```
minutes = timeRemaining/60;
```

We set the value of the `minutes` variable by dividing `timeRemaining` by `60`. If there were 120 seconds left, dividing by 60 means there are two minutes on the clock. If there were only 11 seconds left on the clock, dividing by 60 gives us 0.183 repeating.

The reason why we don't see 0.1833333 in the "minutes" portion of our clock is a sneaky data type trick: `timeRemaining` is a `float` (floating point number), so it can remember decimal places. Our `minutes` variable is an `int` (integer), which *can't* remember decimal places. So, when we feed 0.183333 into an `int` variable, it just snips off everything after the decimal. It can't remember that stuff, so why bother? The result is that `minutes` is set to 0, which is what we see on the clock.

I know that earlier, we said it's slightly less processor intensive to multiply than to divide. So why are we dividing by 60 to get our minutes count? We are doing this because the alternative is to multiply by 0.0166666666666666666666666666667, which frightens me.

```
seconds = timeRemaining % 60;
```

This unnerving little percent-symbol beastie performs a modulo operation, which is like those exercises you did in grade three math class when you were just about to learn long division. A *modulo* operation is like a division, except it results in the remainder of your operation. Here are a few examples:

◆ 4 % 2 = 0 because 2 goes into 4 twice with no remainder

◆ 11 % 10 = 1 because 10 goes into 11 once with 1 as the remainder (10+1 = 11)

◆ 28 % 5 = 3 because 5 goes into 28 five times (5*5=25), with a remainder of 3 (25+3 = 28)

```
timeStr = minutes.ToString() + ":";
```

The `int.ToString()` method works exactly as advertised, converting an integer to a String. Many data types have `ToString()` methods. At the end of this line, we're tacking on a colon (`:`) to separate the minutes from the seconds.

```
timeStr += seconds.ToString("D2");
```

The += operator, you'll remember, takes what we've already got and adds something new to it—in this case, it's seconds.ToString();. We're passing the special argument D2 to the ToString() method to round to the nearest two decimal places so that the clock looks like this:

4:02

instead of this:

4:2

Nifty!

Whatever is the problem?

If you still have **whatever** as your placeholder text, now's a good time to consider ditching it. It shows up onscreen for a split-second before the numbers appear. Yuck! Click on the **Clock GameObject** in the **Hierarchy** panel, and clear out the value marked **Text** in the **GUIText** component in the **Inspector** panel.

Picture it

Number clocks look alright, but graphical clocks really get me revved up and ready for some pressurized pants-wetting. Nothing denotes white-knuckled urgency like a bar that's slowly draining. We don't need to do much extra work to convert our number clock into a picture clock, so let's go for it!

Time for action – Grabbing the picture clock graphics

As per our agreement, all the pretty pictures are pre-drawn for you. Download the Unity assets package for this chapter. When you're ready to import it, click on **Assets | Import Package | Custom Package...** and find the .unitypackage file. Open it up, and there it is! If only obtaining game graphics in a real production environment was this easy.

Let's get right to work by creating some code to make use of two of the graphics in the package—a blue clock background bar, and a shiny yellow foreground bar that will slowly shrink as time marches on.

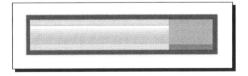

1. Let's go back to the top of the `clockScript` and create a variable to store the elapsed time as a percentage:

    ```
    var clockIsPaused : boolean = false;
    var startTime : float; //(in seconds)
    var timeRemaining : float; //(in seconds)
    var percent:float;
    ```

2. Create some variables to store the textures, as well as the initial width of the yellow foreground bar:

    ```
    var percent:float;
    var clockBG:Texture2D;
    var clockFG:Texture2D;
    var clockFGMaxWidth:float; // the starting width of the foreground
    bar
    ```

3. Save the script and go back to Unity.

4. Click on the **Clock Game Object** in the **Hierarchy** panel.

5. Find the **clockScript** component in the **Inspector** panel.

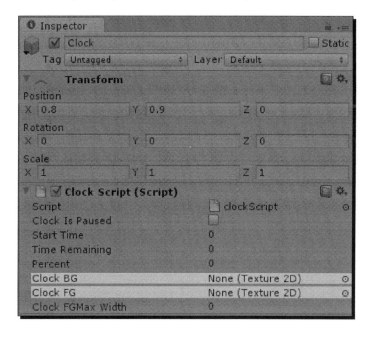

6. The new `clockBG` and `clockFG` variables we just created are now listed there. Click-and-drag the `clockBG` texture from the **Project** panel to the `clockBG` slot, and then click-and-drag the `clockFG` texture into its slot.

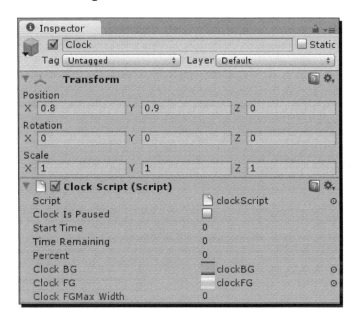

What just happened – you can do that?

This is yet another example of Unity's drag-and-drop usefulness. We created the two `Texture2D` variables, and the variables appeared on the **Script** component in the **Inspector** panel. We dragged-and-dropped two textures into those slots, and now whenever we refer to `clockBG` and `clockFG` in code, we'll be talking about those two texture images.

Handy, yes?

Time for action – Flexing those GUI muscles

Let's take a trip down memory lane to the previous chapter, where we became `OnGUI` ninjas. We'll use the GUI techniques we already know to display the two bars, and shrink the foreground bar as time runs out.

1. In the `DoCountdown` function of the `clockScript`, calculate the percentage of time elapsed by comparing the `startTime` and the `timeRemaining` values:

```
function DoCountdown()
{
    timeRemaining = startTime - Time.time;
```

```
   percent = timeRemaining/startTime * 100;
   if (timeRemaining < 0)
   {
     timeRemaining = 0;
     clockIsPaused = true;
     TimeIsUp();
   }
   ShowTime();
}
```

2. Store the initial width of the `clockFG` graphic in a variable called `clockFGMaxWidth` in the `Awake` function:

```
function Awake()
{
   startTime = 120.0;
   clockFGMaxWidth = clockFG.width;
}
```

3. Create the built-in `OnGUI` function somewhere apart from the other functions in your script (make sure you don't create it inside the curly brackets of some other function!)

```
function OnGUI()
{
   var newBarWidth:float = (percent/100) * clockFGMaxWidth; // this
is the width that the foreground bar should be
   var gap:int = 20; // a spacing variable to help us position the
clock
}
```

4. Create a new group to contain the `clockBG` texture. We'll position the group so that the `clockBG` graphic appears 20 pixels down, and 20 away from the right edge of the screen:

```
function OnGUI()
{
   var newBarWidth:float = (percent/100) * clockFGMaxWidth; // this
is the width that the foreground bar should be
   var gap:int = 20; // a spacing variable to help us position the
clock
   GUI.BeginGroup (new Rect(Screen.width - clockBG.width - gap,
     gap, clockBG.width, clockBG.height));
   GUI.EndGroup ();
}
```

5. Use the `DrawTexture` method to draw the `clockBG` texture inside the group:

```
GUI.BeginGroup (new Rect (Screen.width - clockBG.width - gap,
  gap, clockBG.width, clockBG.height));
GUI.DrawTexture (Rect (0,0, clockBG.width, clockBG.height),
  clockBG);
GUI.EndGroup ();
```

6. Nest another group inside the first group to hold the `clockFG` texture. Notice that we're offsetting it by a few pixels (5,6) so that it appears inside the `clockBG` graphic:

```
GUI.BeginGroup (new Rect (Screen.width - clockBG.width - gap,
  gap, clockBG.width, clockBG.height));
GUI.DrawTexture (Rect (0,0, clockBG.width, clockBG.height),
  clockBG);
    GUI.BeginGroup (new Rect (5, 6, newBarWidth,
    clockFG.height));
    GUI.EndGroup ();
GUI.EndGroup ();
```

Here, I've indented the second group to make the code easier to read.

7. Now, draw the `clockFG` texture inside that nested group:

```
GUI.BeginGroup (new Rect (5, 6, newBarWidth, clockFG.height));
GUI.DrawTexture (Rect (0,0, clockFG.width, clockFG.height),
  clockFG);
GUI.EndGroup ();
```

Did you punch that in correctly? Here's what the entire function looks like all at once:

```
function OnGUI ()
{
  var newBarWidth:float = (percent/100) * clockFGMaxWidth; // this
    is the width that the foreground bar should be
  var gap:int = 20; // a spacing variable to help us position the
    clock
  GUI.BeginGroup (new Rect (Screen.width - clockBG.width - gap,
    gap, clockBG.width, clockBG.height));
  GUI.DrawTexture (Rect (0,0, clockBG.width, clockBG.height),
    clockBG);
      GUI.BeginGroup (new Rect (5, 6, newBarWidth,
      clockFG.height));
```

```
        GUI.DrawTexture (Rect (0,0, clockFG.width,
          clockFG.height),
      clockFG);
        GUI.EndGroup ();
    GUI.EndGroup ();
  }
```

Save the script and jump back into Unity. Let's turn off the old and busted number clock so that we can marvel at the new hotness—our graphical clock. Select the **Clock GameObject** in the **Hierarchy** panel. Locate the **GUIText** component in the **Inspector** panel, and uncheck its check box to turn off its rendering.

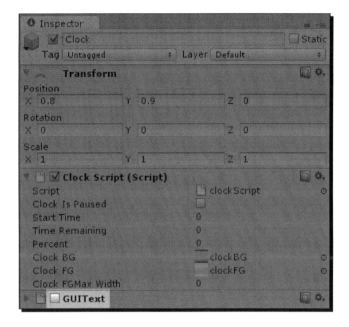

Now, test your game.

Fantastic! Your new graphical clock drains ominously as time runs out. That'll really put the heat on, without compromising your player's doubtless lust for eye candy.

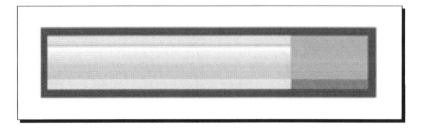

What just happened – how does it work?

The math behind this magic is simple ratio stuff that I, for one, conveniently forgot the moment I escaped the sixth grade and ran away to become a kid who enjoys watching the circus. We converted the time elapsed into a percentage of the total time on the clock. Then, we used that percentage to figure out how wide the `clockFG` graphic should be. Percentage of time elapsed is to 100, as the width of the `clockFG` graphic is to its original width. It's simple algebra from there.

The only math you need to know

I often say that this dead-simple ratio stuff is the only math you need to know as a game developer. I'm half-kidding, of course. Developers with a firm grasp of trigonometry can create billiard and pinball games, while developers who know differential calculus can create a tank game where the enemy AI knows which way to aim its turret, taking trajectory, wind, and gravity into account (hey, kids! Stay in school).

But, when people ask sheepishly about programming and how difficult it is to learn, it's usually because they think you can only create games by using complex mathematical equations. We've hopefully debunked this myth by creating two simple games so far with equally simple math. These ratio calculations are used ALL THE TIME in gaming, from figuring out health bars, to player positions on a mini-map, to level progress meters. If you're arithmophobic like I am, and you relearn only *one* piece of math from your long-forgotten elementary school days, make it this one.

The incredible shrinking clock

We've seen in earlier chapters that the `GUI.BeginGroup()` and `GUI.EndGroup()` functions can wrap our fixed-position UI controls together so that we can move them around as a unit. In the preceding code, we made one group to hold the background bar, and another inside it to hold the foreground bar, offset slightly. The outer group is positioned near the right edge of the screen, using the gap value of 20 pixels to set it back from the screen edges.

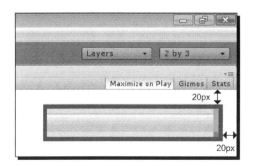

When we draw the foreground clock bar, we draw it at its normal size, but the group that wraps it is drawn at the shrinking size, so it cuts the texture off. If you put a 500x500 pixel texture inside a 20x20 pixel group, you'll only see a 20x20 pixel portion of the larger image. We use this to our advantage to display an ever-decreasing section of our clock bar.

Keep your fork—there's pie!

The third type of clock we'll build is a pie chart-style clock. Here's what it will look like when it's counting down:

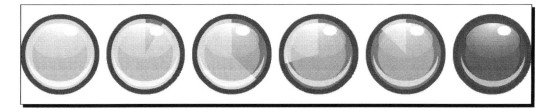

Pop quiz – How do we build it?

Before reading any further, stare at the picture of the pie clock and try to figure out how you would build it if you didn't have this book in front of you. As a new game developer, you'll spend a significant amount of time trying to mimic or emulate different effects you see in the games you enjoy. It's almost like watching a magic show and trying to figure out how they did it. So, how'd they do it?

(If you need a hint, take a look at the unused textures in the **Project** panel that you imported earlier in the chapter.)

How they did it

The pie clock involves a little sleight of hand. Here are the pieces that make up the clock:

It's a bit like a sandwich. We start by drawing the blue background. Then, we layer on the two yellow half-moon pieces. To make the clock look pretty, we apply the lovely, shiny gloss picture in front of all these pieces.

We rotate the right half-moon piece halfway around the circle to make the slice of yellow time appear to grow smaller and smaller.

At the halfway point, we slap a half-moon section of the blue background on top of everything, on the right side of the clock. We're all done with the right half-circle, so we don't draw it.

Now, we rotate the left half-moon piece, and it disappears behind the blocker graphic, creating the illusion that the rest of the clock is depleting.

When time is up, we slap the red clock graphic in front of everything.

A little flourish of the wrist, a puff of smoke, and the audience doesn't suspect a thing!

Time for action – Rigging up the textures

We know most of what we need to get started. There's just a little trick with rotating the textures that we have to learn. But, first, let's set up our clock with the variables we'll need to draw the textures to the screen.

1. Add variables for the new pie clock textures at the top of the **clockScript**:

```
var clockFGMaxWidth:float; // the starting width of the foreground
bar

var rightSide:Texture2D;
var leftSide:Texture2D;
var back:Texture2D;
var blocker:Texture2D;
var shiny:Texture2D;
var finished:Texture2D;
```

2. In the **Hierarchy** panel, select the **Clock Game Object**.

3. Just as we did with the bar clock, drag-and-drop the pie clock textures from the **Project** panel into their respective slots in the **clockScript** component in the **Inspector** panel. When you're finished, it should look like this:

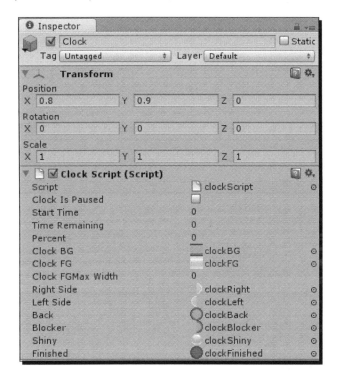

Time for action – Writing the pie chart script

With these `Texture2D` variables defined, and the images stored in those variables, we can control the images with our script. Let's lay down some code, and pick through the aftermath when we're finished:

1. Because of the switcheroo we have to pull off with the two yellow half-moon pieces, knowing when the clock has passed the halfway point is pretty important with this clock. Let's create an `isPastHalfway` variable inside our `OnGUI` function:

```
function OnGUI ()
{
    var isPastHalfway:boolean = percent < 50;
```

(Confused? Remember that our `percent` variable means "percent remaining", not "percent elapsed". When percent is less than 50, we've passed the halfway mark.)

2. Define a rectangle in which to draw the textures:

```
var isPastHalfway:boolean = percent < 50;
var clockRect:Rect = Rect(0, 0, 128, 128);
```

3. On the next line, draw the background blue texture and the foreground shiny texture:

```
var clockRect:Rect = Rect(0, 0, 128, 128);
GUI.DrawTexture(clockRect, back, ScaleMode.StretchToFill, true,
    0);
GUI.DrawTexture(clockRect, shiny, ScaleMode.StretchToFill, true,

    0);
```

4. Save the script and play the game. You should see your shiny blue clock glimmering at you in the top-left corner of the screen:

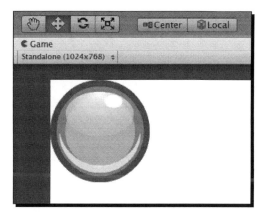

5. Next, we'll add a condition check and draw the red "finished" graphic over the top of everything when percent goes below zero (which means that time is up). Add that bit just above the "shiny" texture draw so that the shiny picture still layers on top of the red "finished" graphic:

```
GUI.DrawTexture(clockRect, back, ScaleMode.StretchToFill, true,
0);
if(percent < 0)
{
    GUI.DrawTexture(clockRect, finished, ScaleMode.StretchToFill,
      true, 0);
}
GUI.DrawTexture(clockRect, shiny, ScaleMode.StretchToFill, true,

    0);
```

6. Save the script and play the game again to confirm that it's working. When time runs out, your blue clock should turn red:

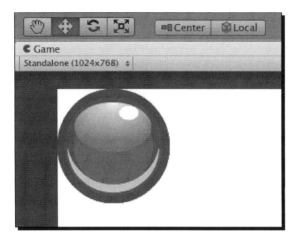

7. Let's set up a `rotation` variable at the top of the OnGUI function. We'll use the percent value to figure out how far along the 360 degree spectrum we should be rotating those yellow half-circle pieces. Note that once again, we're using the same ratio math that we used earlier with our bar clock:

```
var clockRect:Rect = Rect(0, 0,128,128);
var rot:float = (percent/100) * 360;
```

If you want to see it working, try adding a `Debug.Log()` or `print()` statement underneath to track the value of `rot`. The value should hit 360 when the clock times out.

8. We have to set two more variables before the fun begins—a `centerPoint` and a `startMatrix`. I'll explain them both in a moment:

```
var rot:float = (percent/100) * 360;
var centerPoint:Vector2 = Vector2(64, 64);
var startMatrix:Matrix4x4  = GUI.matrix;
```

What just happened?

One important thing to know is that, unlike 3D Game Objects like the **Paddle** and **Ball** from our keep-up game, GUI textures can't be rotated. Even if you apply them to a **Game Object** and rotate the **Game Object**, the textures won't rotate (or will skew in a very strange way). We know we need to rotate those two half-circle pieces to make the pie clock count down, but because of this limitation, we'll have to find a creative workaround.

Here's the game plan: we're going to use a method of the GUIUtility class called RotateAroundPivot. The centerPoint value we created defines the point around which we'll rotate. RotateAroundPivot rotates the entire GUI. It's as if the GUI controls were stickers on a sheet of glass, and instead of rotating the stickers, we're rotating the sheet of glass.

So, we're going to follow these steps to rotate those half-circles:

1. Draw the blue clock background.

2. Rotate the GUI using the rot (rotation) value we set.

3. Draw the yellow half-circle pieces in their rotated positions. This is like stamping pictures on a piece of paper with a stamp pad. The background has already been stamped. Then, we rotate the paper and stamp the half-circles on top of it.

4. Rotate the GUI back to its original position.

5. Draw or stamp the "finished" graphic (if the timer is finished) and the shiny image.

So, the background, the red "finished" image, and the shiny image all get drawn when the GUI is in its normal orientation, while the half-circle pieces get drawn when the GUI is rotated. Kinda neat, huh? That's what the startMatrix variable is all about. We're storing the matrix transformation of the GUI so that we can rotate it back to its "start" position later.

Time for action – Commencing operation pie clock

Let's lay down some code to make those half-circle pieces rotate.

1. Set up a conditional statement so that we can draw different things before and after the halfway point:

    ```
    GUI.DrawTexture(clockRect, back, ScaleMode.StretchToFill, true,
      0);
    if(isPastHalfway)
    {
    } else {
    }
    ```

2. If we're not past halfway, rotate the GUI around the centerPoint. Draw the right side half-circle piece on top of the rotated GUI. Then, rotate the GUI back to its start position.

    ```
    if(isPastHalfway)
    {
    }
    else
    {
    ```

```
    GUIUtility.RotateAroundPivot(-rot, centerPoint);
    GUI.DrawTexture(clockRect, rightSide, ScaleMode.StretchToFill,
       true, 0);
    GUI.matrix = startMatrix;
}
```

3. Save the script and test your game. You should see the right side half-circle piece rotating around the clock. But, we know it's not really rotating—the entire GUI is rotating, and we're stamping the image on the screen before resetting the rotation.

4. Draw the left half-circle once the GUI is back into position.

```
GUI.matrix = startMatrix;
GUI.DrawTexture(clockRect, leftSide, ScaleMode.StretchToFill,
    true, 0);
```

5. You can save and test at this point, too. The right half-circle disappears behind the left half-circle as it rotates; creating the illusion we're after.

6. It all comes crashing down after the halfway point, though. Let's fix that:

```
if(isPastHalfway)
{
    GUIUtility.RotateAroundPivot(-rot-180, centerPoint);
    GUI.DrawTexture(clockRect, leftSide, ScaleMode.StretchToFill,
      true, 0);
    GUI.matrix = startMatrix;
```

7. Save and test. Once we're past the halfway point, the left half-circle does its thing, but the illusion is ruined because we see it rotating into the right side of the clock.

8. We just need to draw that blocker graphic to complete the illusion:

```
GUI.matrix = startMatrix;
GUI.DrawTexture(clockRect, blocker, ScaleMode.StretchToFill,
    true, 0);
```

9. Save and test one last time. You should see your pie clock elapse exactly as described in the sales brochure.

What just happened – explaining away the loose ends

Hopefully, the code is straightforward. Notice that in this line:

```
GUIUtility.RotateAroundPivot(-rot, centerPoint);
```

We're sticking a minus sign on the `rot` value—that's like multiplying a number by negative-one. If we don't do this, the half-circle will rotate in the opposite direction (try it yourself! Nix the minus sign and try out your game.)

Similarly, in this line:

```
GUIUtility.RotateAroundPivot(-rot-180, centerPoint);
```

We're using the negative `rot` value, and we're subtracting 180 degrees. That's because the left half-circle is on the other side of the clock. Again, try getting rid of the `-180` and see what effect that has on your clock.

Another thing that you may want to try is changing the `centerPoint` value. Our pie clock graphics are 128x128 pixels, so the center point is at 64, 64. Mess around with that value and check out the funky stuff the clock starts doing.

```
GUI.matrix = startMatrix;
```

It's worth mentioning that this line locks the GUI back into position, based on the `startMatrix` value we stored.

```
GUI.DrawTexture(clockRect, leftSide, ScaleMode.StretchToFill, true,

    0);
```

Did I catch you wondering what `ScaleMode.StretchToFill` was all about? There are three different settings you can apply here, all of which fill the supplied rectangle with the texture in a different way. Try to look them up in the Script Reference to read about what each one does.

Time for action – Positioning and scaling the clock

The pie clock is pretty neat, but it's sadly stuck to the top-left corner of the screen. It would be great if we could make it any size we wanted, and if we could move it anywhere on the screen.

We're not far off from that goal. Follow these steps to get a dynamically positioned and scaled pie clock:

1. Create these variables at the top of the `OnGUI` function:

```
var pieClockX:int = 100;
var pieClockY:int = 50;

var pieClockW:int = 64; // clock width
var pieClockH:int = 64; // clock height

var pieClockHalfW:int = pieClockW * 0.5; // half the clock width
var pieClockHalfH:int = pieClockH * 0.5; // half the clock

  height
```

   In this example, `100` and `50` are the X and Y values where I'd like the pie clock to appear on the screen. The clock builds out from its top-left corner. 64 and 64 are the width and height values I'd like to make the clock—that's exactly half the size of the original clock.

Note: Scaling the clock will result in some ugly image artifacting, so I don't really recommend it. In fact, plugging in non-uniform scale values like 57x64 will destroy the illusion completely! But, learning to make the clock's size dynamic is still a worthwhile coding exercise, so let's keep going.

2. Modify the `clockRect` declaration to make use of the new x, y, width, and height variables:

```
var clockRect:Rect = Rect(pieClockX, pieClockY, pieClockW,

    pieClockH);
```

3. Modify the `centerPoint` variable to make sure we're still hitting the dead-center of the clock:

```
var centerPoint:Vector2 = Vector2(pieClockX + pieClockHalfW,

    pieClockY + pieClockHalfH);
```

4. Save the script and test your game. You should see a pint-sized clock (with a few ugly pixels here and there) at x100 y50 on your screen.

Have a go hero – Rock out with your clock out

There's lots more you could add to your clock to juice it up. Here are a few ideas:

◆ Add some logic to the `TimeIsUp()` method. You could pop up a new GUI window that says **Time is up!** with a **Try Again** button, or you could link to another **Scene** showing your player's character perishing in a blazing inferno... whatever you like!

◆ Create a pause/unpause button that starts and stops the timer. The `clockScript` is already set up to do this—just toggle the `clockIsPaused` variable, keep track of how many seconds elapse while the game is paused, and subtract that number from `timeRemaining`.

◆ In a few chapters, we'll talk about how to add sound to your games. Bring that knowledge back with you to this chapter to add some ticking and buzzer sound effects to your clock.

◆ Create a button that says **More Time!**. When you click on it, it should add more time to the clock. When you get this working, you can use this logic to add power-ups to your game that increase clock time.

◆ Use the skills that you've already acquired to tie this clock into any game that you create in Unity, including the keep-up and robot games you've built with this book.

Unfinished business

With this chapter, you've mastered an important step in your journey as a game developer. Understanding how to build a game clock will serve you well in nearly all of the games you venture off to build. Games without some kind of clock or timer are uncommon, so adding this notch to your game developer tool belt is a real victory. Here are some skills you learned in this chapter:

◆ Creating a font material

◆ Displaying values onscreen with **GUIText**

◆ Converting numbers to strings

◆ Formatting string data to two decimal places

◆ Ratios: the only math you'll ever need (according to someone who doesn't know math)!

◆ Storing texture images in variables

◆ Scaling or snipping graphics based on script data

◆ Rotating, and then unrotating, the GUI

◆ Converting hardcoded script values to dynamic script values

With three chapters behind you on linking scenes with buttons, displaying title screens, adding clocks and onscreen counters, the keep-up game that we started so long ago is starting to seem a little weak. Let's return home like the mighty conquerors we are, and jazz it up with some of the new things we've learned. Then, we'll go even further, and start incorporating 3D models built in an actual 3D art package into our game **Scenes**.

8
Ticker Taker

Now that your veins are coursing with Unity GUI superpowers, the keep-up game that you built a few chapters ago is looking pretty feeble. Get used to it: as you grow your skills, you'll look at your earlier games and think, "Gee, I could have done that a different way and wound up with a much better product," or more likely, "MAN, that game is weak".

It's high time we revisit that keep-up game and add the stuff we said we would add to make it play properly. Open up your keep-up game Unity project by going to **File | Open Project...** *. If you don't have the file any more, you can download it from the Packt website (*www.packtpub.com*). When the project finishes loading, double-click on the* **Game Scene** *to see the ball and the paddle, just as we left them.*

In this chapter, we'll:

- ◆ Replace our boring primitives with real 3D models
- ◆ "Skin" the keep-up game to make it more awesome
- ◆ Add a keep-up counter to the screen to keep track of our score
- ◆ Detect when the player drops the ball, and then add a score recap and a **Play Again** button

Welcome to Snoozeville

Let's face it: the keep-up game is dull. You've got a ball and a paddle. We're going to add a score counter, but that's just not going to cut it. We need a fun theme to hold the player's interest, and to set our Unity game apart from the rest.

How's this? Let's call the game **Ticker Taker**. We'll replace the ball with a human heart and the paddle with a pair of hands holding a teevee dinner tray. We'll string these bizarre elements together with a compelling story:

Mr. Feldman needs a heart transplant—stat—and there's no time to lose! Help Nurse Slipperfoot rush a still-beating human heart through the hospital hallways to the ER, while bouncing it on a dinner tray! Drop the heart, and it's lights-out for Feldman!

With a simple story re-skin, we now have a time-limited life and death drama. Doesn't that sound more exciting than "bounce the ball on the paddle"? Which game would you rather play?

To pull this off, we need to import the assets package for this chapter. When the **Importing package** dialog game: Importing package dialog" pops up, leave everything selected and click on the **Import** button.

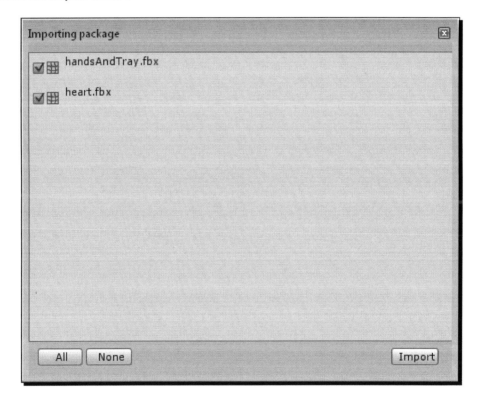

Model behavior

Let's take a look at what we just added to the Project folder: two items with mysterious blue icons called **handsAndTray** and **heart**. These models were created in a free 3D software package called Blender and exported to the .fbx file format.

When things don't mesh

Remember that Unity doesn't actually ship with any 3D modeling tools. If you want your game to contain more than just primitives—spheres, boxes, cylinders, and so on—you'll need to get your hands on some 3D models. You can buy them, create them yourself, or cozy up with a 3D artist and bat your eyelashes at him.

Just as the 2D images for the *Robot Repair* game were created in a drawing package and then imported, these 3D models were built in Blender and brought into the project. All imported assets wind up in the **Assets** folder behind the scenes which, you'll recall, is not to be fiddled with outside of Unity. There is complex metadata keeping track of everything in that folder, and monkeying around with it could break your project. Check the indices of this book for different resources you can use to create or buy assets for your own games.

Time for action – Exploring the models

Click on the little gray arrow next to the **handsAndTray** model. This model contains two separate meshes—a pair of hands, and a hospital dinner tray. There seem to be two instances of each, with two different icons next to them—a blue cube icon with a little white page and a black meshy/spiderwebby-looking icon.

Here's what's happening. The top-level **handsAndTray** parent is the `.fbx` file that Unity imported. Before you can use this file inside the program, Unity runs it through an import process to make sure that the models are the right size and orientation, along with a slew of other settings. The routine that preps the models for use in Unity is the **FBXImporter**. You can see it by clicking on the parent **handsAndTray** model in the **Project** panel.

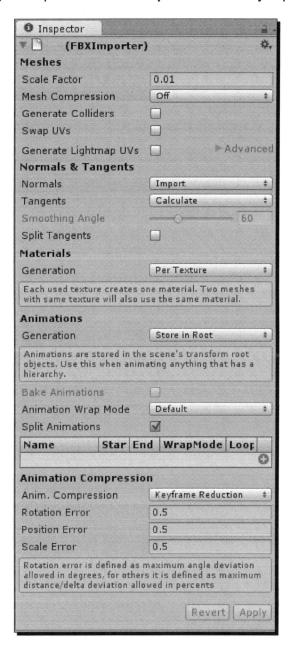

There's a lot of fancy stuff going on with the **FBXImporter**. Thankfully, we don't have to touch much of it. Our biggest concern is that the models are facing the right way, and are the right size. Different models from different 3D software packages can import in funny ways, so this is like our check-in counter to make sure everything's okay before we admit the model into our Hotel de Game. At the very bottom of the **FBXImporter**, you can see what the model looks like.

Rank and file

Unity has superpowers. It's true. Even better, it's like one of those superheroes that can absorb other superheroes' powers. Unity doesn't have modeling or art tools itself, but as we've seen, it can import meshes and images from the outside world. And if you have a supported 3D software package (like 3D Studio Max, Maya, or Blender) or 2D software package (like Photoshop) installed on your computer, Unity can import the native file format. That means your .max, .ma, .blend, and .psd files will be sitting right there in the Assets folder. If you double-click on one of these assets, Unity is smart enough to launch the corresponding program for you. And if you make a change to the file and save it, the results are automatically updated right inside your project's Assets folder. No need to re-import the file!

You can also tell Unity which program you'd like to launch when you double-click on a file with a format that can be read by many different programs, like .fbx or .jpg. Here's a list of native 3D file formats and software packages that Unity supported at the time of writing:

- Maya .mb and .ma
- 3D Studio Max .max
- Cheetah 3D .jas
- Cinema 4D .c4f
- Blender .blend
- Carrara
- Lightwave
- XSI 5.x
- SketchUp Pro
- Wings 3D
- 3D Studio .3ds
- Wavefront .obj
- Drawing Interchange Files .dxf
- Autodesk FBX .fbx

The ability to handle native file formats for a number of major software applications is one of the coolest things about Unity. If you work a lot with Photoshop, you'll appreciate that you don't have to flatten your image and save it as another format—just hide or show your various layers, and save the file. Unity automatically flattens the PSD for you and updates the image.

Time for action – Hands up!

Let's get the hands and tray into our **Scene!**

1. Click on **GameObject | Create Empty**. This is the **GameObject** that will contain the hands and tray models.

2. Rename the new **Game Object** as **HandsAndTray**.

3. Click-and-drag the **handsAndTray** model, which contains the **Tray_mesh** and **Hands_mesh** models, from the **Project** panel to the new **HandsAndTray Game Object** that you just created in the **Hierarchy** panel. You'll see the models appear indented beneath the **GameObject**, which will gain a gray arrow to indicate that it's now a parent.

4. Click on the **HandsAndTray** Game Object in the **Hierarchy** panel, and change its position/rotation/scale settings in the **Inspector** panel:

   Position   X: -0.18   Y: -0.4   Z: -0.2

   Rotation   X: 8   Y: 180   Z: 0

   Scale   X: 1   Y: 1   Z: 1

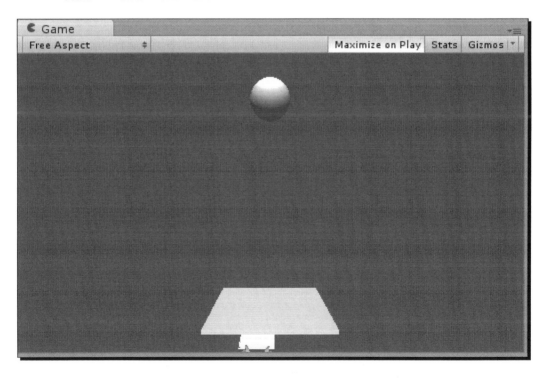

What just happened – size matters

When you change the position and rotation values, the **HandsAndTray** Game Object swings into view near our old **Paddle Game Object**, but the meshes are disappointingly tiny. Clearly, something went wrong during the FBX import process. We could scale the models' transforms up inside Unity, but strange things have been known to happen when you mess with a model's scale after it's been imported. Animations break, colliders stop colliding properly, the sun turns blood-red... it's a bad scene.

Time for action – Changing the FBX import scale settings

Let's revisit the **FBXImporter** and crank up the scale to make our models the proper size with no breakage.

1. Click on the blue **HandsAndTray** model in the **Project** panel. The **FBXImporter** will appear in the **Inspector** panel.

2. Change the **Scale** factor near the top of the **FBXImporter** from **0.01** to **0.03**.

3. Click on the **Generate Colliders** checkbox. (We'll find out what this does very shortly.)

4. Click on the **Apply** button near the bottom of the **FBXImporter**. You may have to scroll down, depending on your screen size.

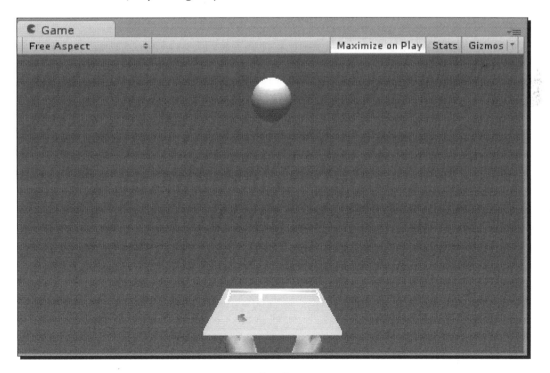

You should see the **handsAndTray** models scale up within the **Game** view to a reasonable size. That's better!

Auto-generating colliders

The checkbox that we ticked in the **FBXImporter** tells Unity to put a collider cage around our model once it's imported. You may remember that the spherical **Ball Game Object** and the cubic **Paddle Game Object** both got their own collider components when we created them—a **Sphere Collider** for the **Ball**, and a **Cube Collider** for the **Paddle**.

Unity uses an additional copy of the mesh as the collision "cage" around the object. This is great if you have a strangely-shaped mesh, and you want things to collide with it naturally. The trouble is that your game will take a performance hit with a more complex collider. If you can get away with adding your own primitive (**Cube/Sphere/Capsule**) collider to your model to make things less complicated for the physics engine, you should. Our *Ticker Taker* game has very little complexity, so I think we can indulge ourselves with a fancier collider on our tray model. Maybe later, we'll take a long soak in the tub and paint our toenails?

Time for action – Making the mesh colliders convex

Provided our mesh is made from fewer than 255 triangles, one thing that we can do to make our **Mesh Colliders** behave better is to mark them as "convex". Game Objects that are in motion (like our **HandsAndTray** soon will be) tend to react better with other moving colliders if we make this small change.

1. In the **Hierarchy** panel, hold down the *Alt* key on your keyboard and click on the grey arrow. Instead of just expanding the top-level item, this expands the entire tree beneath the parent GameObject.

2. Select **Hands_Mesh**.

3. In the **Inspector** panel, under the **Mesh Collider Component**, check the box labeled **Convex**.

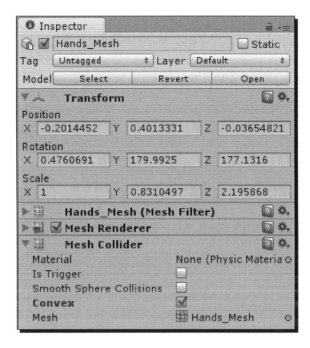

4. Do the same for **Tray_Mesh**.

Now we're all set up to put some motion in the ocean. Let's turn our eyes towards making this imported mesh move around the same way our boring primitive paddle does.

Time for action – Making the hands and tray follow the mouse

Any script that we create in Unity is reusable, and we can attach scripts to multiple Game Objects. Let's attach our **MouseFollow** script to the **HandsAndTray** Game Object.

1. Find the **MouseFollow** script in the **Project** panel (I put mine inside a `Scripts` folder), and drag it onto the **HandsAndTray** Game Object in the **Hierarchy** panel. (Make sure to drop it on the parent **HandsAndTray** Game Object, not the child **handsAndTray** model.)

2. Test your game by clicking on the **Play** button.

The hands and tray should follow your mouse the very same way the paddle does. Because we generated a collider on the tray in the **FBXImporter** settings, the **Ball** should bounce on the tray just as it does with the **Paddle**.

The only trouble is that the hands and tray may be flipped backwards. That's because in the **MouseFollow** script, we're telling the paddle to constantly tilt towards $y=0$. Our **HandsAndTray** Game Object is rotated 180 degrees in the Y axis. No worries—it's an easy fix.

Open the **MouseFollow** script and find this line of code:

```
var target = Quaternion.Euler (tiltAroundX, 0, tiltAroundZ);
```

Change the y rotation target to 180, like so:

```
var target = Quaternion.Euler (tiltAroundX, 180, tiltAroundZ);
```

Et voila—the hands and tray point in the correct direction.

What just happened – monkey see, monkey do

Because both the **Paddle** Game Object and the **HandsAndTray** Game Object have the same script attached, they both do exactly the same thing. Imagine a game where you have a number of enemies onscreen, all following the same **Script**:

1. Hunt the player.
2. Eat his face.

Reusable scripts make rampant face-eating possible, with just a single script.

Time for action – Get your heart on

Just as we did with the hands and tray models, we're going to create a new **Heart** Game Object and parent it to our imported heart model, with a few adjustments in the **FBXImporter**.

1. In the **Project** panel, click on the **heart** model.

2. Change the **Scale** factor of the **heart** model in the **Inspector** panel to 0.07.

3. Leave **Generate Colliders** unchecked.

4. Click on the **Apply** button.

5. Drag the heart model from the **Project** panel into the **Scene**.

6. In the **Inspector** panel, change the heart's position values to **X:0, Y:0, Z:0**.

7. In the **Hierarchy** panel, click on the gray arrow on the **heart** Game Object to reveal the **Heart_Mesh** inside.

8. Click to select the **Heart_Mesh**, and in the **Inspector** panel, change its **Transform** position to **X:0, Y:0, Z:0**.

By setting everything to position 0, we ensure that the collider we're about to add will appear at roughly the same spot where the heart model is. Now instead of using a special **Mesh Collider**, let's add a more primitive **Capsule** collider, and set up the heart so that it bounces.

9. Select the parent **heart** Game Object in the **Hierarchy** panel, and navigate to **Component | Physics | Rigidbody** to add a **Rigidbody** component to it. This includes the heart in the physics simulation. A message will appear, warning us that we'll be **Losing prefab**, whatever that means. Click on **Add** to ignore this message. Notice that the **heart** Game Object label in the **Hierarchy** panel is no longer blue, indicating that we've broken its prefab connection. (We'll learn more about prefabs shortly.) The heart's **Rigidbody** component appears in the **Inspector** panel.

10. Click on **Component | Physics | Capsule Collider** to add a pill-shaped collider to the heart. A green cage-like **Collider** mesh appears around the heart in the **Scene** view.

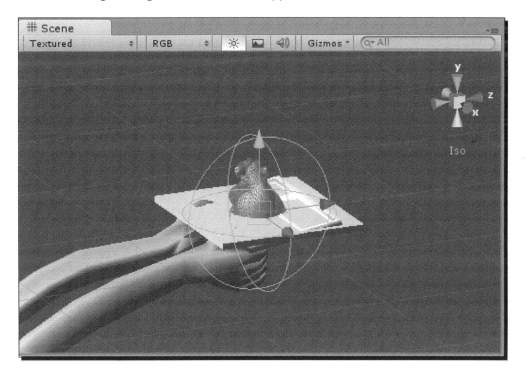

11. Change the settings on the **Capsule Collider** in the **Inspector** panel to:

Center

   X: -0.05   **Y: 0.05**   **Z: 0**

Radius: 0.2

Height: 0.6

That should make the **Capsule Collider** fit snugly around the heart model.

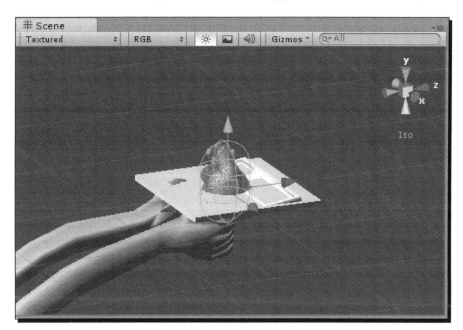

12. Still in the **Capsule Collider Component**, click on the little circle button in the field labeled **Material**, and choose the custom **BouncyBall PhysicMaterial** (which we created in an earlier chapter). This is what will give the **heart** its bounce.

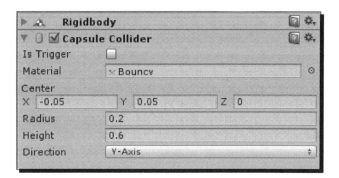

13. Finally, adjust the **heart** Game Object's **Transform** position in the **Inspector** panel to **X: 0.5, Y: 2.0, Z: -0.05**. This will place the **heart** right next to the **Ball**.

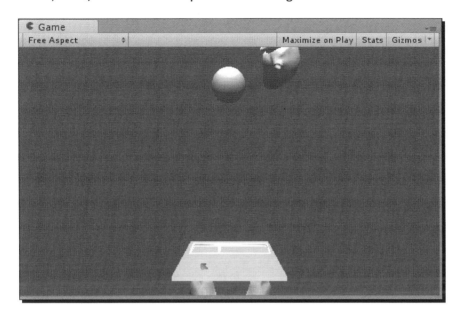

14. Save the **Scene** and test the game by clicking on the **Play** button. Paddles, trays, hearts, and balls should all be bouncing around. In fact, it's a smidge confusing. Let's take the old **Paddle** and **Ball** out of the equation and focus on the new stuff.

Time for action – Ditch the ball and paddle

Click on the **Paddle** in the **Hierarchy** panel, and uncheck the checkbox next to its name in the **Inspector** panel to make it disappear. Do the same for the **Ball**. Retest the game. The **Ball** and **Paddle** are turned off; you should see only the **heart** bouncing on the tray.

What just happened – bypass the aorta

The reason we're using a **Capsule Collider** on the heart instead of a **Mesh Collider** is that the **heart** model is pretty weird and irregular. It could catch its aorta on the corner of the tray and go spinning unpredictably out of control. The **Capsule Collider** gives the **heart** a little more predictability, and it won't be glaringly obvious that the **heart** isn't colliding perfectly. (Of course, a capsule shape is a little wonkier than the **Sphere Collider** we were using earlier. This capsule is kind of a compromise.)

Time for action – Material witness

Currently, the models we're using are about as exciting as clipping your toenails over the sink. All three models are a dull, default gray. Let's change that by creating some custom **Materials**, and applying them to the models.

Out with the old

If you had eaten your Wheaties this morning, you may have noticed that when we imported the models, their Materials were imported as well. The **Project** panel has a folder called `Materials` in it, which includes the three drab, boring Materials that we currently see on our models. Unity will import the materials that we create for our models depending on the 3D software package we used. Since these three models were not given Materials in Blender, they came in with default gray Materials. Now's a good time to select the `Materials` folder in the **Project** panel and press the *Delete* key (*Command + Delete* if you're on a Mac) to get rid of it. After confirming this action, the models turn pinky-purple. Don't worry—we'll fix that.

1. Right-click/secondary-click any empty area in the **Project** panel (or click on the **Create** button at the top of the panel) and choose **Create | Material**. A **New Material** appears in the **Project** panel.

2. Rename the **New Material** as **Skin Material**.

3. Select the **Skin Material** and click on the color swatch (next to the eyedropper) in the **Inspector** panel.

4. Choose a skin color for **Nurse Slipperfoot**. I chose **R 251 G 230 B 178** for a Caucasian nurse, but feel free to make her whatever color you like.

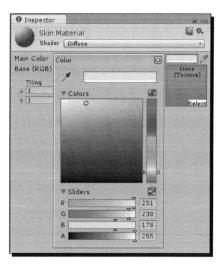

5. Close the color window by clicking on the X icon in the top-right corner (top-left corner on a Mac).

6. Click-and-drag the **Skin Material** from the **Project** panel to the **Hands_Mesh** in the **Hierarchy** panel. You may have to click on the gray arrows to expand the parent/child tree beneath the **HandsAndTray** Game Object in order to see the **Hands_Mesh**.

In a twinkling, Nurse Slipperfoot's hands go from a hot fuschia to a rosy peach.

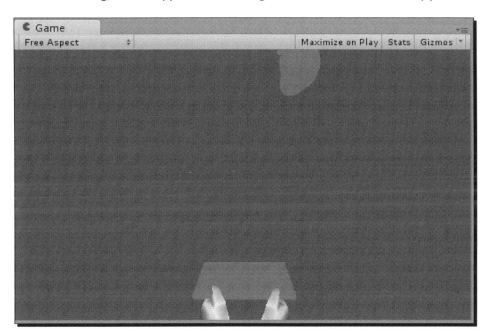

What just happened – understanding Materials

We've used Materials in a few other situations so far for fonts and other goofy things, but applying Materials to models is the classic example. If meshes are like chicken wire, Materials are like the **papier-mâché** coating we lay over them to give them "skin". A **Material** is a collection of shaders and textures that affect how light bounces off our models.

This diffuse, flat color is about as simple as a Material can get. If we wanted to go all-out, we could draw a more realistic image of Nurse Slipperfoot's skin, complete with freckles, beauty marks, and fingernails, in a program like Photoshop. Then we'd import the texture into Unity as an image file, and drag-and-drop it into that Texture2D slot that you see beneath the Material's color swatch. Suddenly, Nurse Slipperfoot's arms would look far more realistic. (It should be obvious, though, that realism isn't exactly what we're going for with this game.)

UV mapping

Any textures that we apply to our models this way may wind up disappointingly maligned. There's a process in 3D texturing called UV mapping, which is where you adjust the position and orientation of your textures in relation to your models. Most textures that get wrapped around anything more complex than a primitive shape require some monkeying around with the models' UV settings, which happens in your 3D art package outside Unity.

You can use textures in combination with Shaders to pull off even more impressive effects. One popular Shader called a **Bump Map** (**Bumped Specular** or **Bumped Diffuse** in Unity) lets you paint the "high" and "low" areas that the light will hit. By creatively painting a flat 2D texture with light and dark tones, you can indicate which parts of the image you want to appear to be raised, and which ones should appear to recede. A bump map could give Nurse Slipperfoot's thumbs the illusion that there are modeled fingernails on their ends. The advantage is that you get this illusion without the cost of actually modeling these extra details—the Shader is doing all the work, and is tricking the light into seeing more complex geometry than we actually have. Remember that more polygons (mesh geometry) require more computer power to draw and move around the screen, so faking this complexity is a great plan.

If you're so inclined, you can even program your own Shaders to pull off custom lighting and texturing effects on your models. That topic is way outside the scope of a beginner book, but if writing custom Shaders interests you, don't let me hold you back. Go forth and code! You can find some good resources for learning about more complex stuff like custom Shaders in the back of this book.

Have a go hero – Adding Materials to the other models

Now that you know how to create your own Materials, create two more Materials for your other models—one for the tray and one for the heart. I chose a bright red color for the heart (**R:255 G:0 B:0**), and made it revoltingly wet-looking and shiny by choosing **Specular** from the **Shader** drop-down. Then I cranked the "Shininess" slider up. If you had the inclination, you could draw a veiny texture in your favorite 2D program and import it into Unity, and then drag it onto the **Heart Material**. Gross!

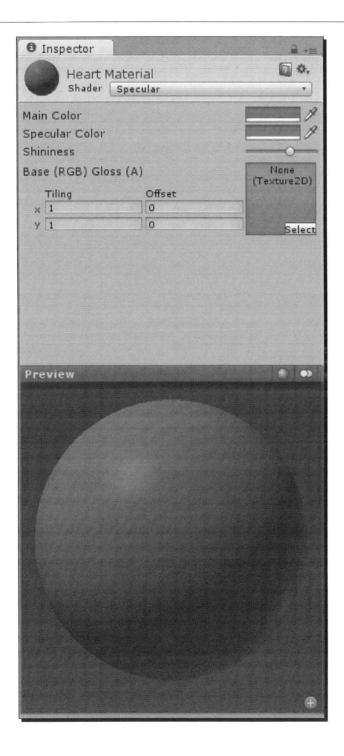

When you're finished creating and adding new Materials to the tray and the heart, and dropping them into a new folder called "Materials", let's continue.

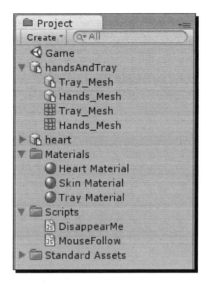

This just in: this game blows

Despite all the work we've done to add a fun theme, there's still a fundamental problem with our keep-up game. 2D is one thing, but because we're expecting the player to bounce the heart in three dimensions, the game is nigh impossible. I can only get a few bounces in before the heart goes flying off into Siberia. But thanks to the miracle of cheating, we can actually fix this problem, and the player will feel much better about playing our game.

Time for action – Multiple erections

We're going to erect four invisible walls around the play area to keep the heart reined in.

1. Click on **GameObject | Create Other | Cube**.

2. Rename the new **Cube GameObject** as **Wall Back**.

3. Give the **Cube** these transform settings in the **Inspector** panel:

   Position X:-0.15 Y: 1.4 Z: 1.6

   Rotation: X: 0 Y: 90 Z: 0

   Scale: X: 0.15 Y: 12 Z: 6

4. Uncheck the **Mesh Renderer** checkbox in the **Inspector** panel to make the back wall invisible to the player.

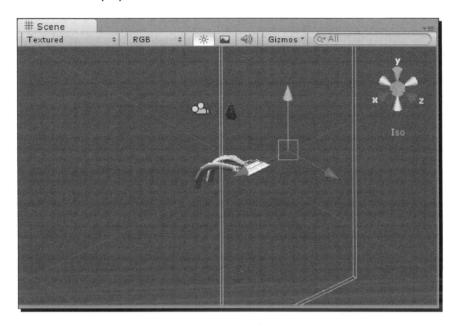

5. Repeat these steps to create three more cubes called **Wall Front**, **Wall Left**, and **Wall Right**. The best way to do this is to duplicate the **Front Wall** three times. Just right-click/alternate click on the **Wall Front** Game Object and choose **Duplicate** from the context menu. These are the settings I used to place the other walls, but feel free to tweak them to suit your taste:

Wall Front

Position   X: -0.7   Y: 1.4   Z: -2.4

Rotation   X: 0   Y: 90   Z: 0

Scale   X: 0.15   Y: 12   Z: 6

Wall Left

Position   X:- 2   Y: 1.4   Z: 0.56

Rotation   X: 0   Y: 17.6   Z: 0

Scale   X: 0.15   Y: 12   Z: 6

Wall Right

Position   X: 1.6   Y: 1.4   Z: -0.06

Rotation   X: 0   Y: 348   Z: 0

Scale   X: 0.15   Y: 12   Z: 6

6. Remember to turn off the **Mesh Renderer** settings for each wall. You can turn them back on in case you need to fine-tune the positioning of each wall.

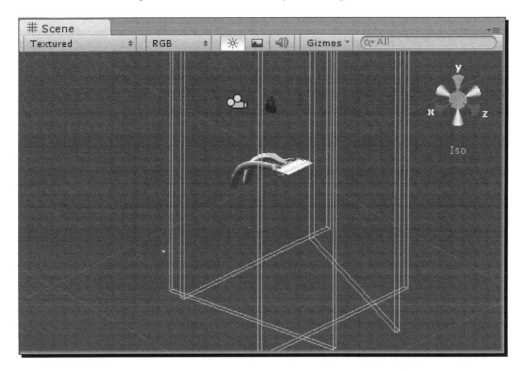

7. I made a slight tweak to the **handsAndTray** transform, nudging the **X** rotation value to **16**.

It's like TRON up in here! Save the **Scene** and test the game. To the player, it seems as if the **heart** is bouncing off Nurse Slipperfoot's forehead, or the edges of the screen, but we know better. We've actually cheated in favor of the player, to help him have more fun and success with our game.

In defense of the cube

If you've poked around Unity a little on your own, you may have wondered why we placed four cubes instead of four planes. For starters, planes are one-sided and they disappear when you look behind them, making it a little more difficult to position them into place. And because they're one-sided, we risk having the heart pass right through them if they're oriented the wrong way.

For the home stretch, we'll repeat a few of the steps we've already learned to display the number of hits the player achieves while playing, and to add a **Play Again** button when we detect that the heart has plummeted past the tray and into the abyss.

Time for action – Creating a font texture

First, let's create a custom font texture to display some **GUIText** showing the player how many times he's bounced the heart.

1. Create a new **GUIText** object and call it **Bounce Count**. Follow the instructions in *Chapter 7* (in the *Creating a font texture and material section*) for creating a **GUIText** object and mapping a font material to it. This time, I chose a font called "Cajun Boogie" because it's ridiculous.

2. Change the font size in the **Font Exporter**. I chose 45 pts for the font—your mileage may vary.

3. In the **Inspector** panel, set the **Bounce Count** transform position to **X:0.9 Y:0.9 Z:0** to place it in the upper-right corner of the screen.

4. Choose **Anchor: Upper Right** and **Alignment: Right** from the **GUIText** component settings in the **Inspector** panel.

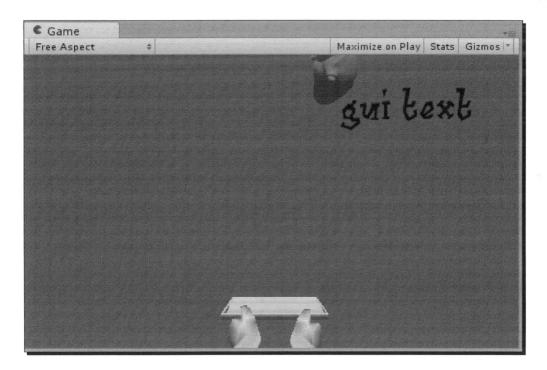

Now we have a fun onscreen **GUIText GameObject** to display the player's bounce score.

Time for action – Creating the HeartBounce script

We need to attach a new script to the **heart**. The script will respond to two important situations: when the **heart** hits the tray, and when the **heart** misses the tray completely and dive-bombs into the great beyond. Let's create the script and add some simple code to it.

1. Right-click/secondary-click on the **Project** panel (or use the **Create** button) and choose **Create | JavaScript**.

2. Rename the new script as **HeartBounce**.

3. Double-click to open the script in the script editor.

4. Add the following code to the top of the script above the Update function:

```
function OnCollisionEnter(col : Collision) {
  if(col.gameObject.tag == "tray") {
     Debug.Log("yes! hit tray!");
  }
}
```

What just happened – charting a collision course

There's some new code happening here. OnCollisionEnter is a built-in function that gets called when the Game Object's collider touches (or collides with) another Game Object's collider, as long as one of those colliders is attached to a Game Object with a non-kinematic **Rigidbody Component** (like our **heart**). We use the variable col (short for collision) to store the argument that gets passed in. That argument contains a reference to whatever it was we hit.

One of the ways we can find out exactly what we hit is to ask for its tag. Here we're asking whether the collision's **Game Object** is a tagged **tray**. In order for this to work, we need to learn how to tag things.

Time for action – Tagging the tray

Save and close the **HeartBounce** script—we'll come back to it in a jiffy. First, let's tag the **tray** Game Object so that we can determine if the **heart** has collided with it.

1. Click on the **HandsAndTray** Game Object in the **Hierarchy** panel.

2. In the **Inspector** panel, just beneath the Game Object's name, is a drop-down labeled **Tag**. Choose **Add Tag** from the bottom of this drop-down list. (By default, all Game Objects are marked "Untagged")

3. We're taken to the **Tag Manager**. Click on the gray arrow beside the word **Tags** at the top of the list.

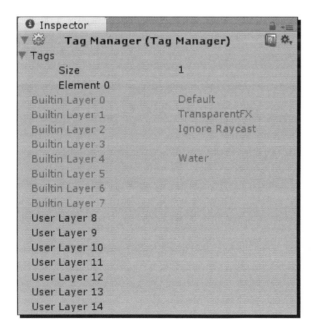

4. There's an invisible text field next to the line labeled **Element 0**. This takes a leap of faith the first time you do it. Click on the blank area beneath the **1** on the **Size** line. Then type the word **tray**. Press the *Enter* key to make it stick. Notice that Unity adds a new blank tag for us, labeled **Element 1**.

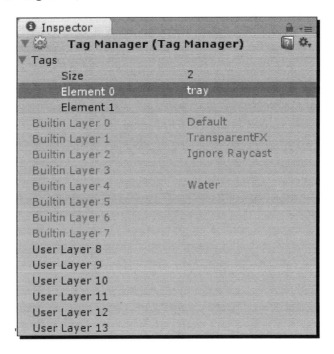

5. Click to select the **Tray_Mesh** in the **Hierarchy** panel (you may need to click on the gray arrows to expand the hierarchy beneath the **HandsAndTray** Game Object). When we chose "Add Tag," you may have thought that we were adding a tag called "tray" to the **HandsAndTray GameObject**. In fact, "Add Tag" actually means "add a tag to the list of tags we can choose from". The new tag isn't automatically added to any GameObject.

Now that we've *added* the **tray** tag, we can select it from the drop-down list.

6. With the **Tray Mesh** selected, choose **tray** from the **Tags** drop-down in the **Inspector** panel to tag the **Tray Mesh**.

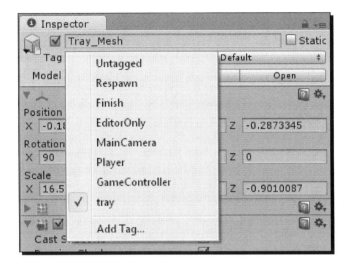

7. Tag the **Hands_Mesh** with the **tray** tag as well.

8. Click-and-drag the **HeartBounce** script to the **heart** Game Object to attach it.

Save the **Scene** and test your game. Keep an eye on the message bar at the bottom of the screen. When the heart hits the tray or hands models, you should see a message saying **yes! Hit tray!**

Time for action –Tweak the bounce

Now that we can detect when the heart is hitting the tray, there's no end to the fun we can have! While we're in the code, let's make a quick change to make the gameplay slightly better.

1. Double-click to open the **HeartBounce** script.

2. Type the following at the top of the script:

```
var velocityWasStored = false;
var storedVelocity : Vector3;
function OnCollisionEnter(col : Collision) {
  if(col.gameObject.tag == "tray") {
    Debug.Log("yes! hit tray!");
    if (!velocityWasStored) {
      storedVelocity = rigidbody.velocity;
      velocityWasStored = true;
```

```
        }
        rigidbody.velocity.y = storedVelocity.y;
    }
}
```

Save the script and test the game. You may not notice a difference at first, but we've made a clear improvement to our mechanic.

What just happened – storing velocity

The trouble with Unity's physics simulation is that it's almost too good. Left to its own devices, our heart will bounce less and less until it eventually runs out of steam and comes to rest on the dinner tray. Realistically, this might actually be what a still-beating human heart would do, given the circumstances. I'm too squeamish to find out for sure.

But this isn't realism—this is video games, baby! This is the land of gigantic guns and anthropomorphic mushrooms! We want that heart to bounce forever, with no degradation over time when the heart bounces against the tray and the walls.

That's what our little script does. The first time the heart bounces, we store its velocity (distance over time) in a variable. Then we inject a little high-velocity serum into the heart every time it hits the tray, overriding the slowly degrading velocity that the heart suffers from hitting our invisible walls. We use the `velocityWasStored` flag to determine whether the heart has bounced yet.

Time for action – Keeping track of the bounces

Let's introduce a few more variables to record how many times the player has bounced the heart.

1. Change the code to add these three variables at the top:

    ```
    var hitCount:GUIText;
    var numHits:int = 0;
    var hasLost:boolean = false;
    var velocityWasStored = false;
    var storedVelocity : Vector3;
    ```

2. Save the script and return to Unity.

3. Select the **Heart** in the **Hierarchy** panel.

4. We've created a variable (bucket) to hold a **GUIText** object. Drag the **Bounce Count GUIText** Game Object from the **Hierarchy** panel into the **GUIText** slot of the heart in the **Inspector** panel (or choose it from the pop-up menu). Now, whenever we refer to `hitCount` in our script, we'll be talking about our **GUIText** Game Object.

5. Add the following code to the Update function:

```
function Update() {
  var str:String = "";

  if(!hasLost){
    str = numHits.ToString();
  }
  else {
    str = "Hits:" + numHits.ToString() + "\nYour best:" +
     bestScore;

    if(bestScore > lastBest) str += "\nNEW RECORD!";
  }

  hitCount.text = str;
}
```

What this script will do is check the hasLost flag on every Update, and change the hitCount **GUIText** to show either just the bounce count, or a big score recap at the end of the game that will look like this:

Hits: 32
Your Best: 12
NEW RECORD!

Note that we don't have any logic yet to flip the hasLost flag, nor do we have any code to increment the numHits variable. Let's add those two things next.

\n

This code creates a line break. Whenever you see it, you can think of it as if someone has hit the *Enter* key to space out some text. Be aware that it only works inside Strings.

Time for action – Adding the lose condition

The easiest way to figure out if the player has lost is to check the `transform.position.y` value of the heart. If the heart has fallen through the floor, the player obviously isn't bouncing it on the tray any longer.

1. Add the logic for incrementing the player's score (number of hits/bounces before losing):

```
function OnCollisionEnter(col : Collision) {
  if(col.gameObject.tag == "tray") {
    //Debug.Log("yes! hit tray!");
    if (!velocityWasStored) {
      storedVelocity = rigidbody.velocity;
      velocityWasStored = true;
    }
    if(rigidbody.velocity.y > 1) {
      numHits ++;
    }
    rigidbody.velocity.y = storedVelocity.y;
}
```

2. Add the "lose the game" check to the `Update` function:

```
function Update() {
  var str:String = "";

  if(!hasLost){
      str = numHits.ToString();
  } else {
    str = "Hits:" +  numHits.ToString() + "\nYour best:" +
      bestScore;

    if(bestScore > lastBest) str += "\nNEW RECORD!";
  }
  hitCount.text = str;
  if(transform.position.y < -3){
    if(!hasLost) {
      hasLost = true;
      lastBest = bestScore;
      if(numHits > bestScore) {
        bestScore = numHits;
      }
    }
  }
}
```

3. Add these variables to the top of the script:

```
var hitCount:GUIText;
var numHits:int = 0;
var hasLost:boolean = false;
var bestScore:int = 0;
var lastBest:int = 0;
var velocityWasStored = false;
var storedVelocity : Vector3;
```

What just happened – understanding the code

We start by incrementing numHits whenever the heart hits the tray:

```
if(rigidbody.velocity.y > 1) {
  numHits ++;
}
```

Why is velocity a positive number, when the heart is actually falling down (through the negative range of the Y axis)? Because velocity doesn't describe distance—it describes distance over (divided by) time. What we're actually checking here is whether the heart is moving significantly in any direction. We put this conditional check on the heart's velocity so that the player doesn't score any points if he catches the heart on the tray and it just starts rolling around.

```
if(transform.position.y < -3){
    if(!hasLost) {
      hasLost = true;
```

This is like saying "if the heart is through the floor (transform.position.y is less than negative 3), and the player hasn't lost yet, make the player lose".

Next, we record what the last high score was.

```
lastBest = bestScore;
```

If the number of hits the player pulled off in this round beats the player's best score, reset the best score to the player's number of hits.

```
if(numHits > bestScore) {
    bestScore = numHits;
}
```

Save the script and test the game. The onscreen score counter updates with every hit you get, and when you drop the heart, you get a recap of your last and best scores.

Time for action – Adding the Play Again button

The very last thing we need to do is to add a button to the end of the game so that the player can play again. Let's revisit our good friend GUI from the last few chapters.

1. Add the OnGUI function to the **HeartBounce** script:

```
function OnGUI(){
  if(hasLost){
    var buttonW:int = 100; // button width
    var buttonH:int = 50; // button height

    var halfScreenW:float = Screen.width/2; // half of the Screen
      width
    var halfButtonW:float = buttonW/2; // Half of the button width

    if(GUI.Button(Rect(halfScreenW-halfButtonW, Screen.height*.8,
      buttonW, buttonH), "Play Again"))
      {
        numHits = 0;
        hasLost = false;
        velocityWasStored = false;
        transform.position = Vector3(0.5,2,-0.05);
        rigidbody.velocity = Vector3(0,0,0);
      }
  }
}
```

What just happened?

For GUI pros like us, this script is a piece of cake.

The whole function is wrapped in a "has the player lost the game?" conditional statement.

We start by storing some values for half of the screen's width and height, and the width or height of the button.

```
var buttonW:int = 100; // button width
var buttonH:int = 50; // button height

var halfScreenW:float = Screen.width/2; // half of the Screen width
var halfButtonW:float = buttonW/2; // Half of the button width
```

Next, we draw the button to the screen, and reset some game variables if the button is clicked:

```
if(GUI.Button(Rect(halfScreenW-halfButtonW, Screen.height*.8,
    buttonW, buttonH),"Play Again")){
    numHits = 0;
    hasLost = false;
    velocityWasStored = false;
    transform.position = Vector3(0,2,0);
    rigidbody.velocity = Vector3(0,0,0);
}
```

It's important that we reset the heart's starting position and the velocity of its **Rigidbody** component. Try commenting out either of these lines or both of these lines and see what happens!

Save the script and try it out. *Ticker Taker* now uses 3D models and an onscreen score counter to elevate a standard, dull keep-up game to a madcap emergency ward adventure.

Ticker taken

Let's recap the mad skillz we picked up in this chapter. We:

- Added 3D models to our game
- Created some simple Materials
- Learned how to tag Game Objects
- Detected collisions between Game Objects
- Overrode the physics simulation with our own code
- Programmed an onscreen score counter and recap

We could still do a much better job of conveying the story and setting to the player in *Ticker Taker*, so let's put another pin in this game and return to it in a later chapter. In the next action-packed installment, we'll get a little more practice with **GameObject** collisions, and we'll learn what all the fuss was about when Unity popped up that mysterious prefab warning. Prefabs will change the way you use Unity! I can't wait.

9

Game #3: The Break-Up

We've been learning pieces of game development like Lego bricks. We've chugged along merrily on two tracks simultaneously, learning about what we need to build to have a complete game, and how we can use Unity to build those pieces.

The Break-Up will be a simple catch game. "Catch" is in a genre of what we now call "mini-games"—often, they are games within games. Catch, like keep-up, has a very simple mechanic. The player controls a thing, (like a paddle, a character, a bucket, or a trampoline), usually at the bottom of the screen, and other things fall or move towards the player-controlled thing from the top of the screen. In a catch game, the player has to connect his controllable thing with the falling things (people jumping out of buildings, cherries falling from a tree, and so on) to catch or collide with them. A common feature upgrade is to add bad things that the player must avoid.

That's how the unskinned mechanic works. Of course, you can skin it in a million different ways. One of the earliest catch games I ever played was called Kaboom! on the Atari 2600. The player controlled a group of buckets, and had to catch bombs dropped by the Mad Bomber villain at the top of the screen.

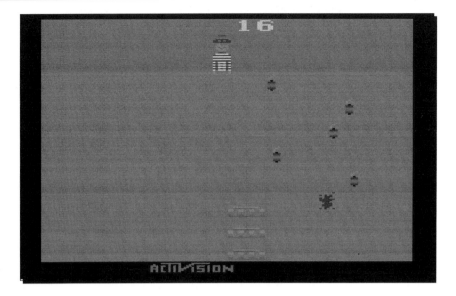

The skin I've cooked up for The Break-Up puts you in the role of a guy who's been kicked out of his apartment by his girlfriend. Your most prized possessions are your beer steins of the world collection and your cartoon bomb collection, and your ex-girlfriend is throwing both of them out the window! The bombs, naturally, are lit. You have to catch the fragile beer steins and avoid the bombs.

That skin is clearly just a little West of nuts, but it shows how far you can go with the fictional wallpaper on a simple mechanic.

So what are we going to need? We should have some kind of backdrop to set the scene, some beer steins and bomb models, and a character. Ideally, that character should be animated. Oh and we should probably learn how to blow stuff up too, because blowing stuff up is awesome. In this chapter, let's learn:

- How to set up animations from external models
- How to create particle effects like explosions and sparks
- How to use **Prefabs** to handle multiple copies of the same Game Object
- How to write one script to control multiple objects
- How to make things appear onscreen out of thin air

As before, the first thing you should do is start a new Unity project for this chapter, and call it **The BreakUp**. Be sure to include the `Particles.unityPackage` file from the list. Once your project starts up, save the default **Scene** and call it **Game**. Next, download and import the assets package for this chapter and all of the goodies you need to build the game will show up in the **Project** panel, in their own **Materials** and **Models** folders.

Conversion perversion

As with the heart, hands and tray models from our Ticker Taker project, these particular goodies were created in Blender—a free 3D modeling package. Then they were exported to the .fbx format, a common format among different 3D software packages. The drawback in converting your work to a common format is that certain things can be lost in translation—faces can be flipped inside out, textures can show up in the wrong place or not at all, and the model might not look the way you want it to. Remember that Unity can handle a number of native 3D file formats. There are advantages and disadvantages to working with native file formats instead of common formats like .fbx, which you'll discover as you gain more experience with Unity.

Time for action – Bombs away!

Let's cut right to the chase here: big round cartoon bombs are great. Real-life bombs aren't quite as much fun, so let's keep it cartoony. We'll set up our cartoon bomb model and add a special effect called a **Particle System** to make it look as though the fuse is lit.

1. In the **Project** panel, open the **Models** folder by clicking on the gray arrow to expand it.

2. Drag the bomb model into the **Scene** view.

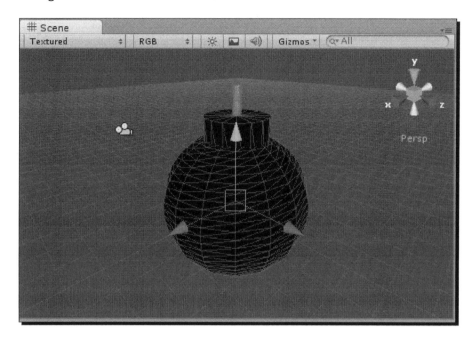

3. In the **Inspector** panel, change the bomb's **Transform Position** values to **0, 0, 0** on the **X**, **Y**, and **Z** axes to place the bomb at the origin of your 3D world. You can also click on the gray gear icon and choose **Reset Position** from the dropdown.

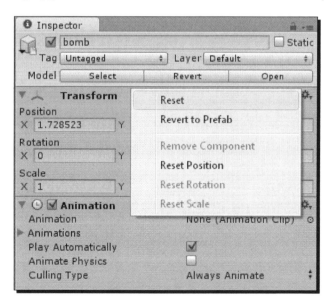

4. Hover your mouse over the **Scene** view and press the *F* key. This places focus on the bomb, which zooms into view.

5. Click on **GameObject | Create Other | Particle System**.

6. In the **Inspector** panel, change the **X, Y, Z Position** values of the **Particle System** to **0, 3, 0**. This places the **Particle System** at the tip of the fuse.

7. In the **Hierarchy** panel, rename the **Particle Effect** as **Sparks**.

Particle systems give games their zest. They can be used to depict smoke, fire, water, sparks, magic, jetstreams, plasma, and a pile of other natural and unnatural phenomena. Essentially, they're a ton of tiny little images that turn to face the camera, in a common 3D technique called **billboarding**. Each little picture can be textured, just like the Material on a 3D model. The little pictures support transparency, so they don't have to look like squares. **Particle Systems** have an emitter, which is where the particles come from. The built-in **Particle System** that ships with Unity lets you control a dizzying array of additional parameters, such as the number, color, frequency, direction, and randomness of the particles.

In pursuit of shiny objects

Many game developers use particle effects as a cheap trick to reward their players. For many casual gamers, the best piece of feedback in a puzzle game is a satisfying sound effect paired with an explosion of particles. Games like *Bejeweled* and *Peggle* put particle systems to work with great results.

Right now, our **Particle Effect** looks like spooky forest fairy magic floating around our bomb. We want something closer to the classic Warner Bros. Wile E. Coyote bomb, with sparks shooting out of the fuse. Let's explore the wide range of settings that Unity's **Particle Systems** offer.

Click on the **Sparks Particle System** in the **Hierarchy** panel if it's not already selected.

Check out the **Inspector** panel. There are a metric ton of settings and dials for tweaking particle systems! We won't discuss them exhaustively because that's what software manuals are for. Suffice it to say, the best way to get what you want out of particle systems is to poke things until it looks right. Let's get poking!

Time for action – Poke those particles

1. Adjust the dials on your **Particle System** to match these values:

Ellipsoid Particle Emitter:

- ❏ **Emit: checked**
- ❏ **Min Size: 0.5**
- ❏ **Max Size: 0.5**
- ❏ **Min Energy: 0.05**
- ❏ **Max Energy: 0.1**
- ❏ **Min Emission: 200**
- ❏ **Max Emission: 200**

Keep all other settings in this section at their default.

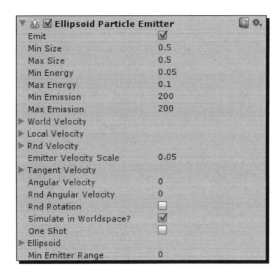

Size makes sense—that's the size of the little pictures. If you crank these settings up, you'll see big flat pictures, and the magic of particle systems will simultaneously make more sense, and will be completely ruined for you.

The energy settings govern how long it takes particles to die. We've cranked these dials way down to ensure that our particle lifespans are fast and frantic.

Emission settings govern how many little particle pictures will be spat out by the emitter. The emitter, if you haven't guessed, is an invisible ellipsoid from which the particles emanate.

Move down to the next section, the **Particle Animator**. Here, we can make the particles animated through a range of colors. We can also make the particles swirl and bend, but as sparks don't really swirl or bend, we'll leave those settings alone. With something fast and frenetic like a bunch of sparks, we can choose a bunch of hot colors to give the particles a sparky kind of look. Click on each color swatch next to the **Color Animation[x]** labels and cook up some hot, sparky colors. Here are the values I used:

Color Animation[0]: 255 / 255/ 255 (white)

Color Animation[1]: 255 / 0/ 0/ (red)

Color Animation[2]: 255 / 255/ 0 (yellow)

Color Animation[3]: 126 / 0 / 0 (dark red)

Color Animation[4]: 255 / 190 / 0 (orange)

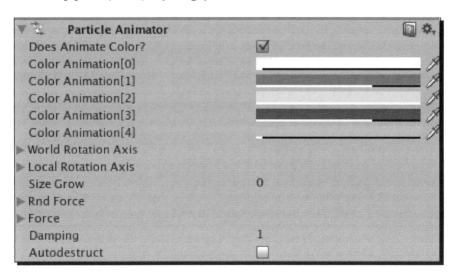

Great! That's looking more sparky already!

The last slider on the bottom of the color widget is labeled **A**, which stands for "Are we gonna be able to see through this color or not?" (It could also stand for "Alpha", which means roughly the same thing.)

Notice that there's a black and white indicator beneath each color swatch in the **Particle Animator**. This strip reflects the Alpha value of the color.

You can play around with the Alpha slider to your heart's content, adjusting the transparency of each color as you see fit.

Time for action – Creating a spark material

In order to really pull off this effect, we should add a material to the **Particle System**. We need to create that material first, so let's turn our attention to that for the moment.

1. Create a new **Material** by either right-clicking/secondary-clicking in the **Project** panel and choosing **Create | Material**, or by clicking on **Assets | Create | Material** in the menu.

2. Name the new **Material** as **Spark**. The sphere icon helps us remember that this is a **Material**. Consider dragging this new **Material** into the `Materials` folder to keep your project organized.

3. In the **Inspector** panel, choose **Particles | Additive** as the **Shader** type.

4. Click on the **Select** button in the square swatch labeled **Particle Texture** (it should say **None (Texture 2D)** inside the square), and choose the texture labeled **fire4** from the list. If you don't see it in the list, you may have forgotten to import the **Particles assets** package when you started your project. To rectify this, set your computer on fire, then go outside and enjoy the fresh air and sunshine.

5. (Or if you're bound and determined to continue, import the **Particles package** under **Assets | Import Package.**)

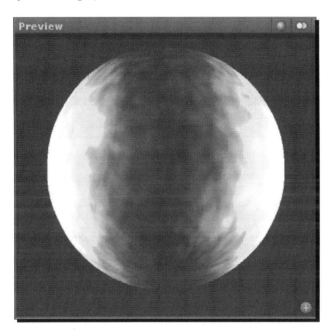

6. In the **Hierarchy** panel, click again to select your **Sparks Particle System**.

7. In the **Inspector** panel, uncheck **Cast Shadows** and **Receive Shadows** in the **Particle Renderer** section. We're not exactly going for a realistic look here, so we can spare Unity the chore of rendering fancy shadow effects that no one will notice. (Note that shadow casting is a Unity Pro feature. If you're not running Unity Pro, fuhgeddaboudit!)

8. Still in the **Particle Renderer** section in the **Inspector** panel, expand the **Materials** section by clicking on the gray arrow.

9. In the pop-up labeled **Element 0**, change the **Default-Particle** material to your newly created **Spark Material**.

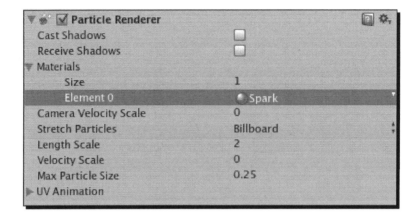

There! Now it's looking even more sparky!

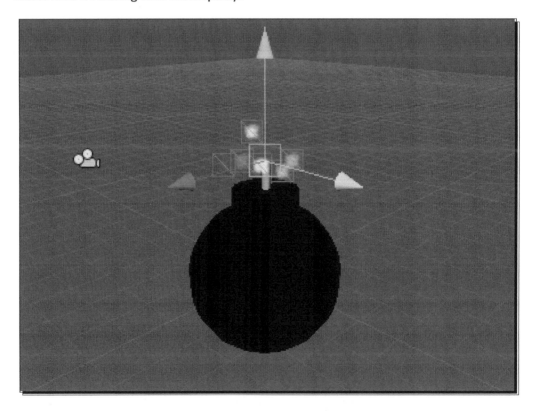

Have a go hero – Time to ignite your creative spark

Do you like fiddling with buttons and knobs? Maybe your eyes lit up when you saw all the gory bits in Unity's **Particle System**? This is a great time to put the book down and fiddle to your heart's content (with Unity that is). Maybe you can find some settings that make the sparks look even more sparky? You might try drawing your own texture that makes the sparks look sharper or pointier than the comparatively smooth and fluffy fire texture we're using. Or better yet, perhaps you could create another particle system and make a thin trail of gray smoke to flow up from your fuse? Check out the velocity settings, which give your particles direction, if you want to pull this off.

You can find a detailed explanation of every little **Particle System** setting in the Unity User Guide at this address: `http://unity3d.com/support/documentation/Manual/ Particle Systems.html`.

Time for action – Prefabulous

Our game is going to contain not one bomb, but many. As with programming, doing something more than once in Unity completely stinks, so we're going to take a shortcut. We're going to create a built-in thing called a **Prefab** that will let us create a reusable bomb, much the same way we created a programmatic function that we could call multiple times in our script.

Follow these steps to create your first **Prefab**:

1. Right-click/secondary-click on the **Project** panel and choose **Create | Prefab**, or click on **Assets | Create | Prefab** in the menu. A gray box icon appears in your **Project** panel, labeled **new prefab**. Because the box is gray, we know this **Prefab** is empty.

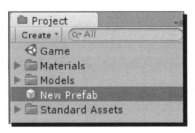

2. Rename the **Prefab** as **Bomb**. Just like the **Spark Material**, the icon helps us keep track of what type of thing it is. For further clarity, consider adding the **Bomb Prefab** to a new folder, which you should call `Prefabs`.

3. In the **Hierarchy** panel, click-and-drag the **Sparks Particle System** to the **Bomb** Game Object. You'll see that warning about losing the prefab—that's okay. Click on **Continue**.

4. In the **Hierarchy** panel, click on the gray arrow next to the **bomb** model parent, and you'll see the **Bomb** model and the **Sparks Particle System** nestled safely inside.

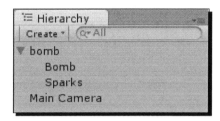

5. In the **Hierarchy** panel, click-and-drag the parent **Bomb Game Object** label, the one that the **Bomb** model and the **Sparks Particle System** are nestled beneath, onto the **Bomb Prefab** in the **Project** panel (remember, it has an empty gray cube icon next to it).

When you pull the **Bomb** Game Object into the empty **Prefab** the gray **Prefab** icon lights up blue. Filled **Prefabs** are blue, while empty **Prefabs** are gray. And 3D model icons look suspiciously like filled **Prefab** icons, except that they have a little white page on their blue boxes.

What just happened – what's a Prefab?

So what the heck is a **Prefab**, anyway? It's a container that holds stuff, and it's magically reusable. Now that the **Sparks** and the **Bomb** are stowed safely inside a **Prefab**, we can populate the **Scene** with a whole pile of bombs. If you make any changes to the **Prefab**, all other instances of the **Prefab** receive the same change. Let's see this in action:

1. Click on the **Bomb** parent in the **Hierarchy** and press the *Delete* key on your keyboard (*Command + Delete* on a Mac) to get rid of it. It's okay. The **Bomb** model and the **Sparks** are tucked inside our new **Prefab** down in the **Project** panel.

2. Click-and-drag the **Bomb Prefab** out from the **Project** panel into the **Scene** lots of times. Populate your **Scene** with five or more **Bomb Prefabs**.

3. Move the **Bombs** around the **Scene** so that they're not all stacked on top of each other.

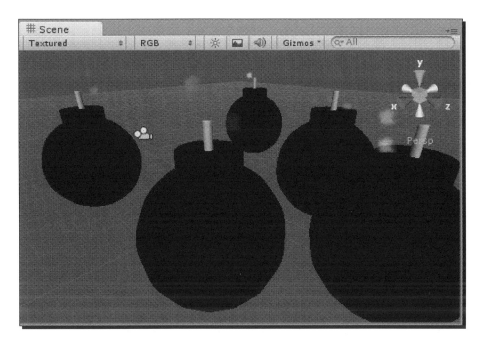

4. In the **Inspector** panel, open up the **Bomb Prefab** by clicking on its gray arrow.

5. Click on the **Sparks Particle System** inside the **Bomb Prefab**.

6. In the **Inspector** panel, scroll down to the **Particle Renderer** section.

7. Click on the **Particle Texture** swatch, where we originally chose the **fire4** texture, and choose a different texture from the list. Choose something silly, like the soapbubble texture.

8. All of the **Bomb Prefabs** in your **Scene** should update to display a soapbubble texture on their particle systems! Test your game to see this in action.

9. Be sure to change the texture back to **fire4** before continuing.

You've just proven that what happens to the master prefab happens to all prefabs. We'll come back to the bombs in a bit. For now, delete all of the **Bomb Prefab** instances from the **Hierarchy** panel to get back to an empty **Scene**.

Flashback

If you've ever used Flash, the concept of **Prefabs** may feel familiar. **Prefabs** behave very much like Flash Movieclips.

Time for action – Lights, camera, apartment

One of the models in the `Models` folder in the **Project** panel is called **brownstone**. This is the **brownstone** apartment building from which our hapless hero has been ejected. Let's set it up:

1. In the **Project** panel, click on the gray arrow to expand the **Models** folder.

2. Click-and-drag the **brownstone** model into the **Scene**.

3. In the **Inspector** panel, set the apartment building's **Transform Position** to X:0, Y:0, Z:0.

    Our camera's not exactly pointed the right way. Let's adjust the camera's **Transform** to get a nice low-angle view of the brownstone building.

4. Click to select the **Main Camera** in the **Hierarchy** panel.

5. In the **Inspector** panel, change its **Transform Position** to **35, 2.5, -38**.

6. Change its **Rotation** values to **333, 355, 0.4**.

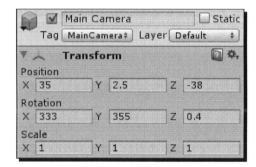

The brownstone should swing into view in your **Game** view.

Change the camera's field of view to 51, to hide the fact that the brownstone model is only two floors high. This place is rather dimly lit, so let's set up a light in our scene to simulate daytime.

7. Navigate to **GameObject | Create Other | Directional Light**.

8. In the **Inspector** panel, change the light's **Rotation** values to **X:45, Y:25, Z:0**.

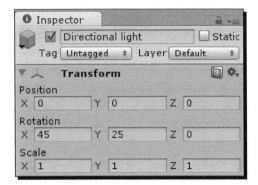

Now the building is illuminated rather nicely.

Time for action – Adding the character

The biggest missing piece at this point is the player character. Let's get him in the **Scene**.

1. Create an empty **Prefab** and name it **Character**. (Drop it into the `Prefabs` folder if you'd like to keep your project organized.)

2. In the **Project** panel, click and drag the character model from the `Models` folder into the **Character Prefab**.

3. Click-and-drag an instance of the **Character Prefab** from the **Project** panel into the **Scene**.

4. Use these settings to place the character:
   - **Position: 24, 0, -16**
   - **Rotation: 0, 90, 0**

These settings place the character at the foot of the brownstone. He looks like he's about to do some intensive aerobics with his arms out like that. This is called the "Christ pose" or the "T-pose", and it's the preferred position for a character model because it makes it easier to add a skeleton to the mesh, a process called **rigging**. A fully-rigged character is called a **character rig**.

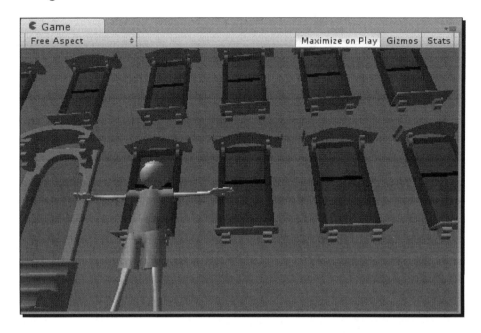

Time for action – Registering the animations

The character model that we're using has been pre-animated in Blender. It has three animations: idle, step, and catch. Before we can play these animations using a **Script**, we have to tell Unity the frame ranges the model uses.

1. In the **Project** panel, click on the character model inside the **Models** folder.

2. In the **Inspector** panel, scroll down to the **Animations** section.

3. Make sure that **Bake Animations** and **Split Animations** are both checked.

4. Click on the little plus icon at the right edge of the box three times to add three new animations.

5. Name the animations **step**, **idle**, and **catch**.

6. Use these settings for the **Start**, **End**, and **WrapMode** parameters:

    ❏ **step 1-12, Loop**

        ❑   **idle 22-47, Loop**

        ❑   **catch 12-20, Once**

7. When you are finished, click on the **Apply** button.

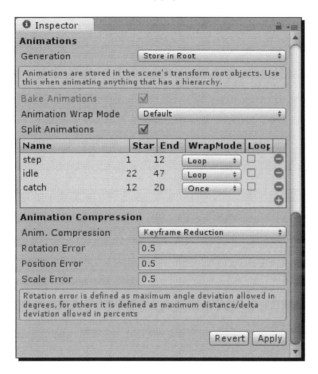

Now that these animations have been named and identified, we can call them up with code.

Time for action – Scripting the character

Let's do exactly that! We'll create a new **Script**, and use what we already know about following the mouse to snap the player character to our mouse movement. Then we'll tell the character which animation cycle to use when he's moving around.

1. Create a new **JavaScript Script**. Rename it **Character**. If you're keeping your project tidy, consider creating a new folder called `Scripts` and dropping your new script into it.

2. Open the script and type in this code:

```
var lastX:float; // this will store the last position of the
//  character
```

```
var isMoving:boolean = false; //flags whether or not the player is
//    in motion
function Start()
{
   animation.Stop();  // this stops Unity from playing the
      character's default animation.
}

function Update()
{
   var halfW:float = Screen.width / 2;
   transform.position.x = (Input.mousePosition.x)/20;
}
```

So far, this should all look very familiar. We're using the same type of commands we used with the keep-up game to make the Game Object follow the mouse around, but this time the player is locked to the X-axis, so he'll only be able to move from side to side.

Now we'll add a chunk of logic in the Update function to determine whether or not the player is moving.

3. Add the following code to your Update function:

```
function Update()
{
   var halfW:float = Screen.width / 2;
   transform.position.x = (Input.mousePosition.x)/20;
   if(lastX != transform.position.x)
   {
      // x values between this Update cycle and the last one
      // aren't the same! That means the player is moving the
      //  mouse.
      if(!isMoving)
      {
         // the player was standing still.
         // Let's flag him to "isMoving"
         isMoving = true;
         animation.Play("step");
      }
   }
   else
   {
      // The player's x position is the same this Update cycle
      // as it was the last! The player has stopped moving the
      //  mouse.
      if(isMoving)
```

```
    {
        // The player has stopped moving, so let's update the
        // flag
        isMoving = false;
        animation.Play("idle");
    }
}
lastX = transform.position.x;
}
```

4. Save the script. Now attach the script to your **Character Prefab** in the **Project** panel. I find it tricky to master the click-and-drag process when it comes to **Prefabs**. Unity always thinks I'm trying to drag my script above or below the **Prefab**. For a sure-fire way to stick that script to your character, click on the **Character Prefab** in the **Project** panel. Then, in the menu, click on **Component | Scripts | Character**. You should see the **Character** script get added as a component in the **Inspector** panel.

5. Play your game to try it out. When you move the mouse, the character loops through his "step" animation. When you stop moving the mouse, he goes back to his "idle" animation, looking for more stuff to catch.

What just happened – stepping through the "step" code

The comments should help clarify this code. This crucial line:

```
if(lastX != transform.position.x)
```

means "if the last x position of the character does not equal the character's current x position..."we base the rest of the logic on that check.

If he was moving and he just stopped, flag him as "not moving" and play the "idle" animation. If he was not moving and he just started moving since the last Update cycle, flag him as "moving" and play the "step" animation.

Why the flag?

We use the isMoving flag to determine that the player has just started or stopped moving since the last cycle. It's important that we play the "step" and "idle" animations only at a single point. If we were to issue the animation.Play command on every Update, the character would get stuck on the first frame of the animation. The animation would keep saying, "Play? Okay! Here's frame 1!" And then, a millisecond later, "Play? Okay! Here's frame 1!"

Time for action – Opening the pod bay door, Hal

I don't know about you, but I'm about ready to drop some bombs on this chump. We could do what we've done before and add a **Rigidbody Collider Component** to the **bomb**, as we did with the **ball/heart** in the keep-up game, and let Unity's physics take care of the rest. But in this case, we might like a little more control over the velocity of the bombs. So let's add **Rigidbody** and **Collider Components** to the bomb, but exclude it from Unity's gravity calculations.

1. In the **Project** panel, click on the **Bomb Prefab**.

2. Click on **Component | Physics | Rigidbody**. You should see the new **Rigidbody Component** appear in the **Inspector** panel.

3. In the **Inspector** panel, uncheck the **Use Gravity** checkbox. This will exempt the bomb from Unity's gravitational pull. PROTIP: I kind of wish I had this checkbox on my own body. That would be fun.

4. Click **Component | Physics | Sphere Collider**. We don't need any fancy poly-perfect **Mesh Collider** in this case because the **bomb** is basically a sphere anyway.

5. In the **Inspector** panel, enter a value of **2** for the **radius** of **Sphere Collider**. That should fit the bomb snugly. You can confirm this by placing a **Bomb Prefab** in your **Scene** and checking it out, or you can take my word for it.

You'll remember from the keep-up game that the **Rigidbody** and **Sphere Collider** or **Capsule Collider Components** work together to make Game Objects collide with each other.

Time for action – Collision-enable the character

Now that the bomb is all rigged up, we'll be able to determine through code when it hits the player character. However, the player character is missing its **Collider Component** too! Let's fix that.

1. Click to select the **Character Prefab** in the **Hierarchy** panel.

2. Click **Component | Physics | Box Collider** in the menu. You'll see that "Losing prefab" warning. Don't fret—just click on **Add**.

3. In the **Inspector** panel, update the **Size** and **Center** settings for your new **Box Collider** with these values:
    - **Center: -1, 8, 1**
    - **Size: 5, 16, 10**

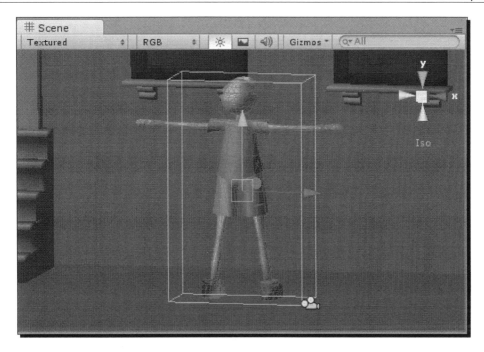

Just like we did with the bomb, we'll forego using a computationally complex **Mesh Collider** in favor of a rough-hewn primitive. We've made a big, ugly green box around the character. This will make less work for Unity, and for our game's purposes, anything fancier would be overkill.

Time for action – Re-prefab the prefab

Because we broke the **Prefab** by adding something new to it, any new instance of the **Character Prefab** we drag out of the **Project** panel won't have the **Box Collider** on it. We can tell Unity that we want this aberrant, and modify **Prefab** to actually overwrite what's in the **Prefab** container by clicking on the **Apply** button. Here's how to find it:

1. Make sure the **Character Prefab** is selected in the **Hierarchy** panel.

2. At the top of the **Inspector** panel, just beneath the **Tag** and **Layer** buttons, look for a set of three buttons that say **Select**, **Revert**, and **Apply**.

3. Click on the **Apply** button. Go on. You know you want to.

When you apply the changes you made to your broken **Prefab**, it lights up blue again in the **Hierarchy** panel. This means that the **Prefab** in the **Project** panel has been updated to include these new changes. Now, every new **Character Prefab** you place in your **Scene** will have that **Box Collider** around it.

Select and Revert

Wondering what those other two buttons are about? Click on **Select**, and Unity will highlight the source **Prefab**. That way you can make changes to it (and all its instances) without going through this change/break/apply process.

The **Revert** button will hook your broken **Prefab** back up to the source **Prefab**, discarding any changes you've made to it.

Time for action – Apocalypse now?

Enough prattle. It's bomb time!

1. Create a new JavaScript and name it **Bomb**. Drop it in the `Scripts` folder if you're keeping things tidy.

2. Open up the script and type the following code:

```
function Update()
{
    transform.position.y -= 50 * Time.deltaTime;
    if(transform.position.y < 0)
    {
        transform.position.y = 50;
        transform.position.x = Random.Range(0,60);
        transform.position.z = -16;
    }
}
```

We've seen these keywords before, so there should be no surprises here. On every update cycle, move the bomb down in the Y-axis by 50 units per second:

```
transform.position.y -= 50 * Time.deltaTime;
```

If the bomb has fallen through the floor:

```
if(transform.position.y < 0) {
```

Pop the bomb back up to the top of the apartment building:

```
transform.position.y = 50;
```

And use `Random.Range` to make it appear in a different spot along the top of the building. This will create the illusion that there are multiple bombs falling from the sky.

Save this script. Just as we did with the **Character Prefab,** click on the **Bomb Prefab** in the **Project** panel and select **Component | Scripts | Bomb Script** to add the new script to the bomb.

Drag the **Bomb Prefab** into your **Scene**, and give it the following **Transform Position: x:-9, y:36, z:-16**. Now playtest your game.

Zut alors! There are sparky, lit bombs falling from the top of that apartment building! For added amusement, try catching one on your character's face. We haven't done any collision handling yet, so our ousted friend gets a grill full of bomb.

Time for action – Go boom

I must say, there's a distinct missing element to our bomb-centric game to this point. What could it be, what could it be? Ah, yes. ASSPLOSIONS. When they hit the ground OR the player, those bombs need to blow up real good. Sounds like a particle system would do just the trick.

1. Make sure you're no longer testing the game.

2. Click on **GameObject | Create Other | Particle System**. Rename it **Explosion**.

3. Create a new **Prefab** and name it **Explosion**. (Or **Assplosion** if you want to be awesome about it.) Drop it into your `Prefabs` folder to keep the project organized.

4. From the **Hierarchy** panel, click-and-drag the **Explosion Particle System** into the **Explosion Prefab** container.

5. Re-select the **Explosion** Game Object in the **Hierarchy** panel. Point your mouse at the **Scene**, and press the *F* key to bring the new **Particle System** into focus.

6. In the **Inspector** panel, adjust the Explosion's settings thusly:
   - **Emit: checked**
   - **Min Size: 5**
   - **Max Size: 5**
   - **Min Energy: 1**

□ **Max Energy: 1**

□ **Min Emission: 150**

□ **Max Emission: 150**

□ **World Velocity: 0, 10, 0** (This will make the particles shoot upward along the Y-axis.)

□ **Local Velocity: 0, 0, 0** (Leave it at the default.)

□ **Rnd Velocity: 10, 10, 10** (Crazy random particle scattering!)

□ **Emitter velocity scale: 0.05** (Leave it at the default.)

7. Leave everything else in this section at its default value, EXCEPT the **One Shot** checkbox. This is vital and should be checked. A **One Shot** particle system gives us single splashes, splurts, and explosions.

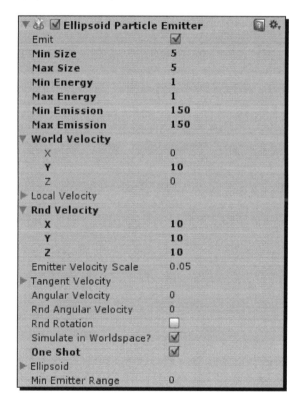

8. In the **Particle Animator** section, choose a series of colors. I used the same values as the **Spark** system, except I flipped the orange and dark red colors to fool myself into thinking I was doing something new and exciting.

□ **Color Animation[0]: 255 / 255/ 255** (white)

❏ **Color Animation[1]: 255 / 0/ 0/** (red)

❏ **Color Animation[2]: 255 / 255/ 0** (yellow)

❏ **Color Animation[3]: 255 / 190 / 0** (orange)

❏ **Color Animation[4]: 126 / 0 / 0** (dark red)

You'll find another important checkbox at the bottom of this section: it's called **Autodestruct**, and it should be checked. This means that once the particle system is finished blowing its wad, Unity will remove it from the scene.

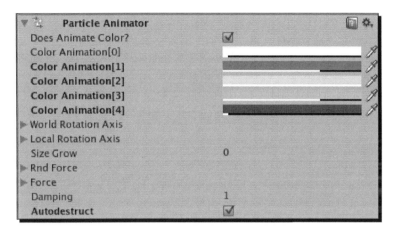

9. In the **Particle Renderer** section, uncheck **Cast Shadows** and **Receive Shadows**.

(These matter only for Unity Pro users.) In the **Materials** pop up, choose the **Spark Material** that we used for our bomb fuse.

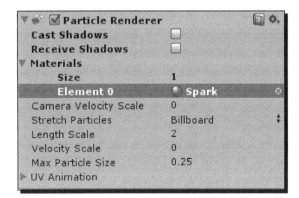

10. If you move the **Explosion** around, you'll see from the **Scene** view that this explosion is entirely too large for the screen, as it flowers violently up over the character's head. Yes, it will do nicely.

11. Change the **Transform** position of **Explosion** back to **X:0 Y:0 Z:0**, and click on the **Apply** button to commit these changes to the source **Prefab**.

Time for action – The point of impact

We're finished tweaking the explosion, so you should delete the instance of the **Explosion Prefab** from the **Scene** view. The original stays safe and sound in the **Prefab** container in your **Project** panel. Naturally, we want this explosion to appear whenever we detect that the bomb has hit the ground. We've already put the logic in place to detect a ground hit—remember that we're moving the bomb back up into the sky as soon as it drops below ground level. So it should be a reasonable hop, skip, and jump towards making that explosion happen. And luckily, it is!

1. Open up your **Bomb Script** and add the following variable at the very top:

```
var prefab:GameObject;
```

2. Then, just after the code where we detect a ground hit, add this line:

```
If(transform.position.y < 0)
{
    Instantiate(prefab, transform.position, Quaternion.identity);
```

We created a variable called `prefab` at the top of the script to store some sort of **GameObject**. Note that small-p "prefab" is not a Unity keyword—we're calling it that because calling it "monkeybutt" would make the code even more confusing.

The `Instantiate` command does exactly what you suspect it does. We need to pass it a reference to a **Game Object** (in our case, we've got one stored in the `prefab` variable), along with arguments to determine the position and the rotation of the thing. Then Unity goes looking for the **Game Object** we specified, and places it in the game.

What do we pass for the position value? The bomb's own position, before we move the bomb to the top of the apartment building. And what do we pass in for its rotation? SCARY MATH! BLAH!!

Once again, I'm not even going to pretend that I understand quaternion mathematics. What I do know is that `Quaternion.identity` means "no rotation"—the object is aligned perfectly with the world or parent axes.

Time for action – Hook up the explosion

"But wait," you say. "How do we actually tell the **Script** what we want to instantiate?" Ah, there's the magic of Unity yet again. Save the **Bomb Script**, and follow these next steps:

1. In the **Project** panel, select the **Bomb Prefab**.

2. In the **Inspector** panel, find the **Bomb (Script) Component**. Notice that the variable we called `prefab` is listed there. (If you actually did call your variable "monkeyButt", you'll see that instead.)

3. Click-and-drag the **Explosion Prefab** from the **Project** panel into the **Prefab** variable slot in the **Inspector** panel. You should see a little red, green and blue icon appear in the slot, with the label **Explosion Prefab**. I've got a good feeling about this!

Test out your game. The bomb falls from the top of the building, "hits" the ground, and calls in the **Explosion Prefab** before popping back up to the top of the building at some random **X** position. The **Explosion**, because it's set to **Autodestruct**, does its thing and then disappears from the scene. It's... *sniff*... it's a beautiful thing.

Summary

So! Do we have a game yet? Not quite. Catching a bomb with your face sounds like a great party trick, but our game is obviously missing a few things to make it playable. We still need to handle the collision of the bomb against the player, and we need to get those beer steins in there. They're apparently worth breaking up with your girlfriend, so they sound pretty important.

In the next chapter, we'll do all these things and more. Buckle your seatbelt and turn that page!

10

Game #3: The Break-Up Part 2

When last we left our put-upon protagonist, he had been kicked out of his apartment by his girlfriend, who began throwing lit bombs at him from the fourth floor. Luckily, our hero is bizarrely invulnerable to bombs, and what's more, he can defy the laws of physics by balancing them on his nose. Clearly, we've got some work ahead of us if we want this game to make any sense.

As we continue to round out The Break-Up, we'll add the beer steins and their smash animations. We'll write a collision detection script to make the character react when he catches things. We'll learn how to save time by using one script for two different objects. Then we'll add some sound effects to the game, and we'll figure out how to throw a random number to play different sounds for the same action. Let's get gaming.

Time for action – Amass some glass

If the whole point of the game is to catch mugs from the character's precious beer steins of the world collection, then adding the steins should be our next step.

1. Create a new **Prefab**. Remember, you can either right-click in the **Project** panel and choose **Create | Prefab**, or you can create one through the menu by clicking on **Assets | Create | Prefab**.

2. Name the new **Prefab** as **Stein**. Drop it into your `Prefabs` folder.

3. Locate the **Stein** model in the `Models` folder of the **Project** panel.

4. Click-and-drag the **Stein** model into the empty **Stein Prefab** container. As we saw before, the icon should light up blue to indicate that the **Prefab** has something in it.

Time for action – Creating a Particle System

We've learned these steps before—no surprises here. Now let's review how to create a **Particle System** so that we can get a shattering glass effect for when our steins hit the pavement:

1. Go to **GameObject | Create Other | Particle System** in the menu.

2. Rename the new **Particle System Glass Smash**.

3. Hover the cursor over the **Scene** view and press the *F* key to focus the camera on your **Particle System**. You may have to orbit the camera if the apartment building gets in the way (hold down the *Alt* key and click/drag to do this).

4. In the **Inspector** panel, use the following settings (keep all other settings at their default):

   In the **Ellipsoid Particle Emitter** section:

   - **Min Size: 0.2**
   - **Max Size: 0.2**
   - **Min Energy: 0.05**
   - **Max Energy: 3**
   - **Min Emission: 50**
   - **Max Emission: 100**
   - **World Velocity Y: 20**
   - **Rnd Velocity: 10 for all values**
   - **One shot: Checked**

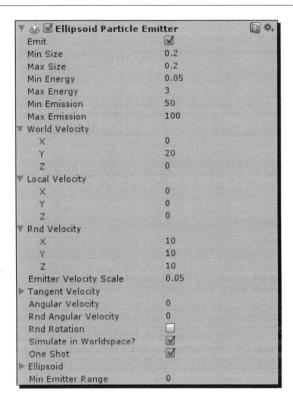

In the **Particle Animator** section:

- ❑ **Does Animate Color?**: Unchecked. We'll just keep our particles white, so there is no need to put an extra color-animating burden on Unity.

- ❑ **Force Y**: -50

- ❑ **Autodestruct**: Checked

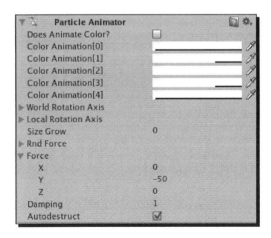

In the **Particle Renderer** section:

- ❑ **Cast Shadows**: Unchecked
- ❑ **Receive Shadows**: Unchecked

What just happened – getting smashed

After punching in these settings, you should see a reasonable approximation of a shatter. We get this splash effect by sending the particles up in the Y-axis with our **World Velocity** setting. The particles are then pulled back to Earth with a **Force** of **-50** in the Y-axis, which we set in the **Particle Animator** section. Particles go up, particles come down. (Note: you won't see this effect if you're in the top isometric view. Rotate your **Scene** into a **Perspective** view to see what's happening.)

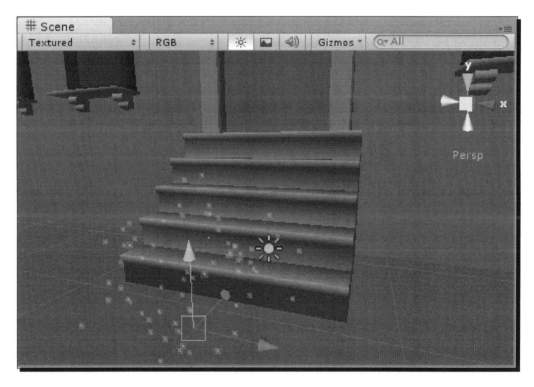

Time for action – Making it edgier!

The particles look a bit like snowflakes at the moment. We want something more like sharp glass fragments, so let's set up a new **Material** with a sharper-edged texture on it to make this effect look more convincing.

1. In the **Project** panel, right-click an empty area and choose **Create | Material**.

2. Name the **Material** as **Glass**.

3. In the **Inspector** panel, choose **Particles | Additive** in the **Shader** dropdown.

4. Click on the **Select** button in the texture swatch, and choose `glassShard.png` from the list. (This image is in the `assetsPackage` file for *Chapter 10*.)

5. Select the **Glass Smash Particle System** from the **Hierarchy** panel.

6. In the **Inspector** panel, scroll down to the **Particle Renderer** component.

7. In the **Materials** section, choose the **Glass** material from the pop-up menu.

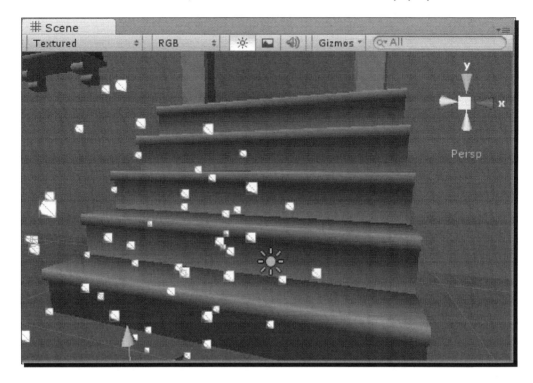

What just happened – I fall to pieces

Once we swap in these harder-edged textures, the effect is much improved! Now our **Glass Smash Particle System** looks a little more like an explosion of glass chunks than a violent headshot to *Frosty the Snowman*.

Time for action – Containing the explosion

Let's place this **Glass Smash Particle System** into a **Prefab** so that it's ready to use with our falling beer steins.

1. In the **Project** panel, right-click and choose **Create | Prefab**.

2. Rename the new **Prefab** as **Glass Smash**.

3. Click-and-drag the **Glass Smash Particle System** from the **Hierarchy** panel into the empty **Glass Smash Prefab**. The icon lights up blue. That's how you know it's working.

4. With the **Particle System** tucked safely away into the **Prefab**, delete the **Glass**.

5. **Smash Particle System** from the **Scene** (select it in the **Hierarchy** panel, and press the *Delete* key on your keyboard, or *Command + Delete* if you're using a Mac).

Clean up

I've kept my **Project** panel neat and tidy by putting all of my **Prefabs** into a folder. I've done the same thing with my scripts, my materials, my models, and my dirty sweat socks. Because there's not a lot going on in this project, it may seem like wasted effort. Still, organizing assets into folders is a good habit to get into. It can save your sanity on larger projects.

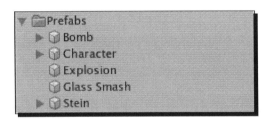

What just happened – duped?

We've almost duplicated the same process we followed to get the bomb working. Have you noticed? With both the bomb and the stein, we put an imported model into a prefab, and we created a particle system and put it in its own prefab. Then we created a script to move the bomb down the screen. We attached that script to the bomb. Then we dragged the bomb's explosion particle system into the `prefab` variable of its **Script** component.

This is all starting to sound familiar: too familiar. In fact, remember when we said earlier that programmers are always finding ways to do less work? We saw that if you type the same line of code twice, you may not be writing your code to be as maintenance-friendly as possible. The same holds true for this bomb/beer mug situation. If the bomb and the beer mug both need to do the exact same thing, why don't we use the same script for both?

Time for action – Let's get lazy

There's no need to create an entirely separate script for the stein. Follow these steps to get more bang for your buck out of a single script:

1. Find the script you called **Bomb Script** in the **Project** panel, and rename it **FallingObjectScript**. Because we'll be using the script more generically, we should give it a more generic name.

2. In the **Project** panel, select the **Stein Prefab** (not the **Stein Model**).

3. Choose **Component | Scripts | FallingObjectScript** in the menu to attach the script to the **Prefab**.

4. In the **Inspector** panel, you should see that the **FallingObjectScript** has been added as a **Script** component to the **Stein Prefab**.

5. As we did earlier with the **Bomb Prefab**, find the **Glass Smash Prefab** in the **Project** panel. Click-and-drag it into the `prefab` variable. By doing this, you're telling the **Script** which thing you want to add to the screen when the stein falls on the ground. In the bomb's case, it's the explosion. In the stein's case, it's the glass smash.

6. Add a **Capsule Collider** component to the beer stein.

7. Click to select the **Cylinder** child inside the **Stein** (click the grey arrow to expand the child list to see it). Change the **Cylinder's** X/Y/Z position values to 0.

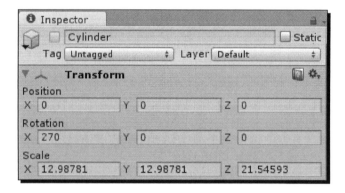

8. Jump back up to the parent **Stein** node. Change the parameters of its capsule collider:

Radius: 2

Height: 5.5

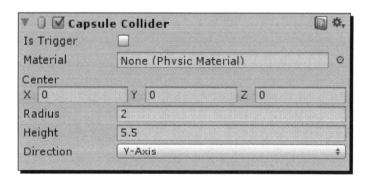

9. Add a **Rigidbody** component to the beer stein.

10. Remember to uncheck **Use Gravity** in the `Rigidbody` component settings. We're handling the beer stein's movement programmatically.

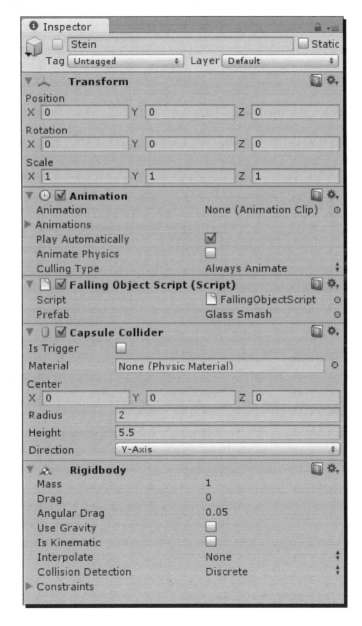

Two birds, one stone; or rather, two objects, one script! To test out the beer stein, drag the **Beer Stein Prefab** into your **Scene**, then click on the **Play** button.

What just happened – FallingObject: The PuppetMaster

Just like the bomb, the beer stein plummets from a random **X** position at the top of the screen and explodes in a shower of particles when it hits the "ground". The bomb explodes and the glass smashes, but both are controlled by an identical script. Unfortunately, they both come to a gentle stop on top of the character's face when they collide, but that's what we'll take a look at next.

Very variable?

You may already be sending up warning flags about this madcap plan to use one script for two different objects. What if we wanted the bomb to travel at a different speed than the beer stein? And don't we want two completely different reactions depending on whether the player collides with the bomb or the stein?

We'll answer the collision question a little later in the chapter, and we'll tackle the variable speed question now. But before we do, fire up your gray matter. How would you solve this problem? How would you make the objects move at two different speeds, with two different collision reactions, and still use the same script?

Terminal velocity is a myth—bombs fall faster

Ignoring the laws of physics for a second, let's look at how to make the two objects fall at different speeds using the same script. One solution is to declare a variable called `speed` at the top of the **FallingObjectScript**.

```
var speed:int;
```

Change this line:

```
transform.position.y -= 50 * Time.deltaTime;
```

to:

```
transform.position.y -= speed * Time.deltaTime;
```

Then for each object, input a different number for the speed value in the **Inspector** panel. Try 30 for the stein and 50 for the bomb. Two objects, one script, and two different speeds. Awesome? Confirmed: awesome.

Know when to double down

At some point, objects become different enough that sharing a script is no longer saving you time and effort, it's causing you grief. As a game developer, you need to decide what sort of structure best suits your game-creating goal. Programmers have all kinds of tricks to save themselves work and to logically structure their code. The object-oriented programming pillar called **inheritance** (which we've looked at briefly) is another way to get two objects to share code, while ensuring that they function as two different things.

Wait till Sunday to take your code to church

When it comes down to just getting your game finished and playable, don't ever feel foolish about making mistakes and writing your game the "wrong" way. A great rule, especially when you're starting out, is to get the game working first, and then go back to make the code elegant. TOTALLY A FACT: tuning up your code and making it as organized and pretty as possible is called **refactoring**. When you're just starting out, worry more about functional code than elegant code.

What just happened – when Game Objects collide?

Bombs plummet from the top floor of the apartment building and explode around our character, as his beloved beer steins shatter on the pavement with every step he takes. These are the origins of a competent catch game! Now, let's worry about what happens when the player catches a stein or comes in contact with a bomb.

There are a few different ways we can go about this. We can write the collision detection code into the `FallingObjectScript`, but that might get complicated. We're using the same script for both objects, and the objects need to do different things when they hit the player. It makes more sense to me to put the collision detection on the player character. We'll check to see when he gets hit by something, and then based on what hits him, he'll react in different ways.

Time for action – Tagging the objects

As we saw before with our bouncing heart, we can tag objects in the **Scene**, and then refer to objects in code using their tag names. Let's tag the bomb and the stein so that the player character can tell what hit him.

1. Select the **Bomb Prefab** in the **Project** panel. (You can actually select anything in this step. We're not actually applying a tag—just creating one. But we need to select something so that we see the **Tag** interface in the **Inspector** panel. You can also reach it by clicking **Edit | Project Settings | Tags** in the Unity menu.)

2. At the top of the **Inspector** panel, press and hold on the dropdown labeled **Tag**, and select **Add Tag....**

3. Click on the gray arrow to expand the **Tags** list near the top of the **Tag Manager**.

4. Click in the blank area to the **Element 0** label, and type the tag name **bomb**.

5. Then punch in a tag called **stein**.

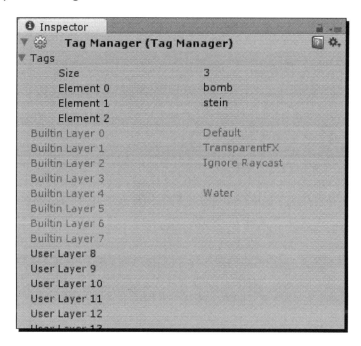

6. Select the **Bomb Prefab** again in the **Project** panel. (This is where it counts.)

7. In the **Inspector** panel, choose your new **bomb** tag from the drop-down list labeled **Tag**.

8. Follow the same process to tag the **Stein Prefab**.

With the bomb and stein properly tagged, we can write our collision detection code.

Time for action – Writing the collision detection code

Pop open the **Character Script** and let's get bizzay.

Type up the following function within the script. Be sure to follow the rules we've learned about where to properly write a new function (that is, "outside" of your other functions):

```
function OnCollisionEnter(col : Collision)
{

  if(col.gameObject.tag == "bomb")
  {
    // I got hit by a bomb!
  }
  else if (col.gameObject.tag == "stein")
  {
    animation.Play("catch"); // Ima catch that stein!
  }
  col.gameObject.transform.position.y = 50;
  col.gameObject.transform.position.y = -16;
  col.gameObject.transform.position.x = Random.Range(0,60);
}
```

Once again, our prior knowledge of useful game code serves us well. This line should already look familiar:

```
function OnCollisionEnter(col : Collision) {
```

We're declaring a function—in this case, a special built-in Unity function called `OnCollisionEnter`—and accepting a variable called `col` as an argument. The value of `col` is a collision that Unity's physics calculations detect whenever rigid bodies smack into each other.

```
if(col.gameObject.tag == "bomb")
```

`col.gameObject` refers to whatever thing hits the **Game Object** to which this script is attached (the **Character**). `gameObject.tag`, naturally, refers to whatever tag that **Game Object** has stuck to it. We stuck **bomb** and **stein** tags on the **Bomb Prefab** and **Stein Prefab**, so that's what we should get. We use a branching conditional (`if`) statement to react to either the bomb or the stein.

```
animation.Play("catch"); // Ima catch that stein!
```

If the player gets hit by a beer stein, we'll play the "catch" animation stored in the **Character** model.

```
col.gameObject.transform.position.y = 50;
col.gameObject.transform.position.z = -16;
col.gameObject.transform.position.x = Random.Range(0,60);
```

No matter what hits the player, we're going to throw it back up to the top of the screen at some random **X** position and let it fall back down. This becomes problematic if we end up having other stuff hit the player that doesn't need to respawn at the top of the building, but let's get it working simply, for the time being.

But wait! Ees problem, señor. Save the script and try the game out. Then see if you can spot the problem.

Time for action – Animation interrupts

The trouble is that we're telling the character to play his "catch" animation, but it's not happening. We see, at best, the first frame of that animation, and then it's interrupted by either the "idle" or "step" animation.

Luckily, we can add a condition to the script to prevent these glory-hog animations from playing if we're trying to catch a beer stein. Dip back into your **CharacterScript** and make these changes:

```
if(lastX != transform.position.x) {
  if(!isMoving) {
    isMoving = true;
    if(!animation.IsPlaying("catch")){
      animation.Play("step");
    }
  }
}
else {
  if(isMoving) {
    isMoving = false;
    if(!animation.IsPlaying("catch")) {
      animation.Play("idle");
    }
  }
}
```

By wrapping the `animation.Play` calls in these `animation.isPlaying` conditionals, we can ensure that the character isn't busy playing his catch animation when we determine it's time to step or idle. Remember that!

Save the script and try it out. Your player character should start catching those steins like a champ!

What just happened – the impenetrable stare

The magical properties of our character's iron-clad bomb-catching face continue to amaze: now, the bombs hit the character straight in the schnozz and wondrously disappear! I don't know how many cartoons you watch, but last time I saw someone get hit in the face with a bomb, there was a satisfying explosion, along with (possibly) a snickering mouse nearby.

How convenient. We just happen to have a reusable **Prefab** that contains a satisfying bomb explosion. Wouldn't it be great if we could trigger that explosion to happen right on top of the character's face? (The character might disagree with us, but I say let's go for it!)

Time for action – Adding facial explosions

Just as we did when our falling object hit the ground, we'll use the `Instantiate` command to make a copy of a **Prefab** appear in the game world. This time around, when we determine that the player has been hit in the face by a bomb, we'll instantiate the **Explosion Prefab** on top of his head.

1. Add the following line to the top of the code:

```
var lastX:float;
var isMoving:boolean = false;
var explosion:GameObject;
```

2. Later on, in the conditional statement that determines when the player is hit by a bomb, add the `Instantiate` command:

```
if(col.gameObject.tag == "bomb")
{
  // I got hit by a bomb!
  Instantiate(explosion, col.gameObject.transform.position,
    Quaternion.identity);
}
  else if (col.gameObject.tag == "stein") {
```

3. Save and close the **Script**.

4. In the **Project** panel, select the **Character Prefab**.

5. In the **Inspector** panel, locate the **Explosion** variable in the **Script** component.

6. Click-and-drag the **ExplosionPrefab** into the **Explosion** variable slot.

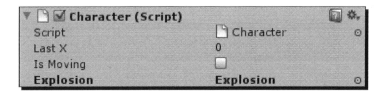

What just happened – raindrops keep 'sploding on my head

We already know how the `Instantiate` command works, so we won't dissect it again. When the bomb drops on the player's head, it appears to explode. The explosion removes itself when it's finished, because the **Particle System** is set to autodestruct. Of course, we know what's really going on: we're just moving the bomb to the top of the building and setting it to some random position along the X-axis so that the player thinks it's a new bomb. Meanwhile, we're instantiating a new copy of the **ExplosionPrefab** at the exact spot where the bomb was when it collided with the player. Sneaky!

Time for action – Making some noise

So far, the games we've made have been completely silent. I count this as a terrible tragedy; audio in a game can account for *half* of the player's emotional experience. In the case of games like *Rock Band*, there would be no game without audio (hilarious little plastic instruments notwithstanding). Audio is so important to games that even crummy little low-rent sound effects (like the ones we're about to add to this game!) can increase the game's awesomeness by a factor of WOW... to the power of GEE GOLLY—something like that. It's all very scientific.

Let's rig up our **Bomb** and **Stein Prefabs** so that they can emit sounds.

1. In the **Project** panel, click on the **Bomb Prefab**.

2. In the menu, click on **Component | Audio | Audio Source** to add the **Audio Source** component.

3. Repeat those steps to add an **Audio Source** component to your **Stein Prefab**.

Now hear this

You may have noticed that Unity also offers an **Audio Listener** component. What's the deal? Well, in the case of a 3D game, you don't necessarily want the player to hear everything that's going on all the time. You want him to hear audio fading in and out as he moves closer to or farther from the source (the **Audio Source**, to be specific). By default, an **Audio Listener** component is attached to the **Main Camera** in any **Scene**. In something like a first-person perspective game, the **Audio Listener** will only pick up sounds from **Audio Source**-enabled **Game Objects** if it's within range. If we tweak the settings just right, the player won't hear a noisy washing machine **GameObject** from the other side of the level. Each scene can only have one **Audio Listener** at a time.

Unity also offers a **Unity Reverb Zone** component. This is a spherical gizmo that lets you define an area where the sound is "pure" and unaffected, with a candy-coated craziness shell around it that lets you define echoes and other potentially oddball effects.

With the **Bomb** and **Stein Prefabs** so enabled, we can add a few lines to the **FallingObjectScript** to make them play sounds when they hit the ground.

Time for action – Adding sounds to the FallingObjectScript

Let's drop a couple of lines into the **FallingObjectScript** to fire off a few sounds:

1. Open the **FallingObjectScript**.

2. Declare a `clip1` variable at the top of the script:
    ```
    var prefab:GameObject;
    var speed:int;
    var clip1:AudioClip;
    ```

3. Just after we determine that the falling object has hit the ground, play the `clip1` sound:
    ```
    if(transform.position.y < 0)
    {
        audio.PlayOneShot(clip1);
    ```

By now, you've probably guessed that there's one more step involved. The script really has no idea what a `clip1` actually is—it's just a variable placeholder. Let's add some actual sound files to the **Bomb** and **Stein** prefabs to get this party started:

1. In the **Project** panel, click to open the SFX folder. Yay—sounds!!

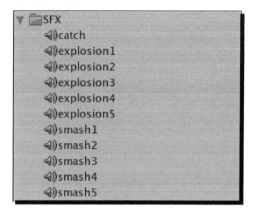

2. Again in the **Project** panel, click to select the **BombPrefab**.

3. In the **Inspector** panel, locate the `clip1` variable in the **FallingObjectScript** component.

4. Click-and-drag the sound effect labeled **explosion1** into the `clip1` variable slot.

5. Repeat the previous steps for the **Stein Prefab**, but this time, choose the **smash1** sound effect.

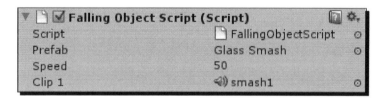

Test your game. Whenever the bomb hits the dirt, there's a satisfying (if retro) sound effect to accompany it. Likewise, there's an 8-bit approximation of glass smashing whenever the beer stein shatters.

What's the catch?

Using the same method that you used earlier, you should be able to figure out how to add that "catch" sound effect to the player character when he catches a beer stein. Likewise, you want to enable the **explosion1** sound effect if the player gets hit by a bomb. If you can't figure it out on your own, take a deep breath, and then go nag someone else to figure it out for you. That's called **delegating**, and it's a perfectly legit way to develop a game.

Perfect for smashing

Unity has all kinds of complex sound controls for playing music and other effects, but like the **One Shot** setting for **Particle Systems**, the `audio.PlayOneShot` command is perfect for collision sound effects. If you'd like to learn more about adding sounds and music to your game, look up **AudioSource** class, **AudioListener** class, and **AudioClip** class in the Unity Script Reference.

Low-fi, high fun

The sound effects that we're using for our game were created with a freeware sound effects generator called **SFXR**. The sounds are all free to use and adorable, hearkening back to a time when dragons looked like ducks and heroes had big white 4-pixel squares for heads. Download a copy of SFXR to generate your own temporary (or even final) game audio. Look for a download link for SFXR and loads of other helpful resources in the appendix at the back of this book.

Have a go hero – Sound off

If you're not a big fan of the retro sounds, it's possible that you may have missed out on the cavalcade of cheese we now know as the 1980s. Feel free to create and import your own sound effects for the game. There are a few different ways you can go about this:

- Get bizzay with a microphone and record your own effects. This is the only way you can truly be happy with the results and get exactly what's in your head into the game. The industry term for sound effect scores is called "foley". You could use the method acting approach and actually smash glass and detonate high-powered explosives next to your computer (not recommended), or you could say "boom!" and "smash!" into the microphone. It's a style thing.

♦ There are a number of companies that sell royalty-free sound effects for film, television, and movies. I'll give you two warnings about using these: the first is that royalty-free sound effect collections can be very expensive on a hobbyists' budget. The second is that once you get enough experience with these popular collections under your belt, movies and teevee shows will be forever ruined for you. You'll hear these same sound effects everywhere! It's tough to stay immersed in a tense film when all you're thinking is "Hey, that's track #58 from disc 2 of the Explosive Ballistics Collection."

There are less expensive royalty-free sound effect websites online, but I've found that a good number of them contain pirated sound effects from the pricy collections that are passed off as legit effects. *Caveat emptor*, which is Latin for "You probably won't get sued, but do the right thing anyway."

Time for action – Mixing it up a bit

One of my personal beefs about sound design in games is when the sound effects are too samey. In our game, hearing the same two sound effects over and over again is wearying. One of the things I like to do is to create a bunch of slightly different sound effects for the same event, and when the time comes to play a sound, I just choose one of them at random. This can really vary the soundscape of the game and keep your player from overdosing on the same sound effects.

You probably noticed that the SFX folder contained five versions of the **smash** and **explosion** sound effects. Let's learn how to set them up to play randomly:

1. Open the **FallingObjectScript**.

2. Delete the line where you define the `clip1` variable, and replace it with an array declaration:

    ```
    var prefab:GameObject;
    var audioClips : AudioClip[];
    ```

3. Modify the line where you play the sound:

    ```
    audio.PlayOneShot(audioClips[Random.Range(0,audioClips.length)]);
    ```

4. Let's take a closer look at this new code:

    ```
    var audioClips : AudioClip[];
    ```

This is a special built-in array; it is statically typed, which means we're telling Unity what kind of thing it's going to contain. In this case, it's going to be a list of **AudioClip** types. A normal array (`var myArray = new Array()`) won't show up in the **Inspector** panel, but a built-in array will.

```
audio.PlayOneShot(audioClips[Random.Range(0,audioClips.length)]);
```

What we're doing here is picking a random number from 0 to the built-in array's length. We're using the resulting number as the index of the `audioClip` in the array that we want to play.

The last step is to click-and-drag the **explosion** and **smash** sound effects into the new built-in array in the **Inspector** panel:

1. Select the **Bomb Prefab** in the **Project** panel.

2. In the **Inspector** panel, locate the **FallingObjectScript** component.

3. Click to expand the **AudioClips** array.

4. Enter a value of **5** in the **Size** label. The list expands even further to accommodate five empty slots for **AudioClip** objects.

5. Click-and-drag the five explosion sound effects into the various indices of the array.

6. Repeat these steps for the **Stein Prefab** using the **smash** sound effects.

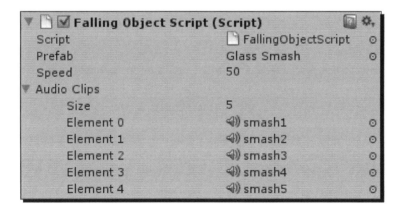

7. Run the game.

Now the falling objects make different-ish noises when they hit the ground. Variety is the spice of life. Paprika is also reasonably delicious.

Have a go hero – Filling in the gaps

Consider this the jumping-off point for your catch game. With the basics roughed in, there are a number of finer elements missing from the experience:

- Title screen with **Play** button
- Instructions page
- Credits screen
- Endgame
- **Play Again** button
- Onscreen scoring (counting the number of steins the player has collected)

We already know how to do a lot of this stuff. We've built a **Title** screen with a **Play** button for **Robot Repair**, and it's the same process to build in the other screens, like **Credits** and **Instructions**. We've created an onscreen counter for **Ticker Taker**. We've built a timer for use in our games as well.

If you imagine all of these elements as ingredients in a cake, you should know how to bake a pretty scrumptious dessert by now. There are a few different decisions you can make about how the game plays:

Score points

Let the player catch beer steins. Count up each one he catches. End the game when he gets hit by a bomb. Show the player his last and best scores, and add a message when he beats his best score, exactly as we did with the Ticker Taker.

Survive

Add a timer to the screen. The player has to keep collecting beer steins until the timer runs out. He's allowed to miss only three beer steins—if he drops his third stein, or gets hit by a bomb, the game ends. This is different from the last scenario because there's a definite win scenario, whereas the other method kept the player playing until he inevitably lost. This win scenario doesn't lend itself as well to adding a high score board, and it doesn't have as much replay value. But certain players (myself included) just can't get excited about games they can't win.

Quota

Clocks are a great and frequently used gameplay tool, but sometimes they just give players the jitters. Another way you can determine a player's success is by defining a quota: "You must catch x beer steins to finish the game."

Levels

One possibility that a "win" scenario opens up is a multi-level structure for your game. If the player makes it through the first level, you increase the number of bombs (or the falling speed of the objects). Maybe a bus periodically drives through the screen, and the player has to jump down a manhole to avoid it? Maybe the mugs get smaller and harder to catch, or the bombs get larger and harder to avoid? If you are using a timer for a survival mode, increase the length of time the player has to spend to survive. If you're using a quota system, increase the number of steins the player has to catch to finish the level.

In this way, you combine the best of both worlds: the game has finite successes because the player can finish and feel accomplished. But the player is also guaranteed to lose because the quota keeps getting larger and more impossible to fill. You could even loop it right back around and put a level cap on the game; after finishing level 10, the player wins once and for all. Perhaps his high score is the lowest time it took him to complete all ten levels?

Health points

You could create some *Legend of Zelda*-style heart graphics and display them at the top-right of the screen. Every time the player gets hit by a bomb, remove a heart. If the player loses all his health, the game ends. This feature works with both the "score points" and "survive" ideas, and helps to give the player much more of a fighting chance. The player is usually more willing to play your game if he perceives that the rules are "fair" and if he can own any mistakes he makes. He should never feel like the game "made him die". Keep in mind that "fair" can sometimes mean "unfairly advantageous to the player"—as long as the computer doesn't "cheat", it's fair in the player's eyes.

Catch unlit bombs

You could create another **bomb Prefab** that doesn't have the sparking fuse, and ask that the player catch both beer steins AND unlit bombs. The objects would probably need to fall more slowly, and you may need to increase the size of the fuse sparks to help the player differentiate a lit bomb from an unlit one. Better yet, to make it even more "fair", you could put a bright red texture on the lit bombs.

Vary the landscape

Doesn't this guy have anything in his apartment other than cartoon bombs and Oktoberfest souvenirs? In order to make the game more visually interesting, you could import a few new models and chuck those out the window. Tighty whities and naughty magazines might make nice additions to the fiction.

Summary

The savings don't stop there! We've already been able to take a scant knowledge of programming and a few simple Unity concepts and turn them into three capable beginner games, with a lot of potential. In the next chapter, we'll actually milk even more mileage out of our blossoming game development skills by applying a graphics re-skin to *The Break-Up* to turn it into a completely different game! Join us, won't you?

11

Game #4: Shoot the Moon

Way back in Chapter 2, we talked about the difference between a game's mechanics and its skin. We've used Unity to create some very simple games with funny, strange, or interesting skins. In this chapter, we'll investigate the enormous difference a new skin can make to our games.

We're going to re-skin The Break-Up from the last few chapters as a completely different game: a sci-fi space shooter (think Galaga, Space Invaders, Centipede, and so on). We're going to leverage the work we've already done on The Break-Up to create a game with a very different feel, but the guts will be the same. In the industry, we call this getting more product for less effort, and it's a very good plan.

When you break it down, there's not much difference between a catch game and a space shooter. In both games, you're moving your character back and forth across the screen. In a catch game, you're trying to collide with valuable objects, while in a space shooter; you're trying to avoid dangerous objects—namely, enemy ships. Luckily, our catch game includes both colliding AND avoiding objects, so we're all set. The only other real difference is that a space shooter, by definition, requires shooting. You may be surprised to see how easy it is to include a new shooting feature based on techniques you've already learned!

Here's a preview of the game we'll build in this chapter:

Time for action – Duplicating your game project

Unity does not provide us with a **Save as** option to duplicate a project. You have to do it through your computer's operating system.

1. Close Unity.

2. Navigate to the folder where you saved your finished The *Break-Up* game from the last two chapters.

3. Copy the folder.

4. Paste the folder wherever you'd like your new **Shoot the Moon** game to live.

5. Rename the copied folder Shoot the Moon (or ShootTheMoon if you're picky about spaces).

Unity copies over our whole `Assets` folder and everything in it, so you should have an exact duplicate of The *Break-Up*, with a different project name. Let's open the new project:

1. Open up Unity, and then select **File | Open Project...**.

 Protip: If you hold down the *Alt* key on your keyboard after double-clicking to open Unity, the project picker prompt will appear, enabling you to choose a project without opening the most recent one.

2. Navigate to your new `Shoot the Moon` project folder and open it.

3. Your project may open on a blank scene. Find the **Game Scene** in the **Project** panel and double-click it. You should see the brownstone apartment building, the bomb, the stein, and all the other game goodies as you left them at the end of the last chapter.

4. Import the new assets for this chapter, which includes two spaceship models and their materials, a new sound effect, and a new background texture. Tuck all of the new stuff into appropriate folders to keep everything organized.

Time for action – Spacing this sucker up a bit

I've never known a space shooter to take place in front of an apartment building, so let's get rid of our old backdrop. Then we'll pull a fun trick with multiple cameras to add a space backdrop to our game.

1. Click on the brownstone apartment building Game Object and delete it from the **Scene**.

2. Click on **GameObject | Create Other | Camera** to add a second camera to the scene.

3. Rename the camera as **SpaceCam**.

4. In the **Project** panel, select the **starfield** texture.

5. Click on **GameObject | Create Other | GUI Texture**.

Suddenly, the **starfield** image appears in the **Game** view, but it completely takes over! Let's fix this.

6. In the **Hierarchy** panel, click on the **starfield GUITexture** that you just created.

7. In the **Inspector** panel, we'll create a new layer. Click on the **Layer** drop-down and select **Add Layer...**.

8. Look down the list, past all the built-in layers. The next available slot is going to be **User Layer 8**. Click on the empty field beside that label and type **starfield**. Press the *Enter* key when you're finished to commit the layer name.

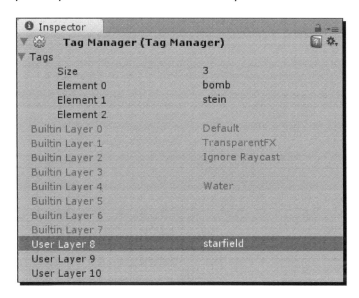

9. In the **Hierarchy** panel, click again to select the **starfield GUITexture**.

10. In the **Inspector** panel, click on the **Layer** drop-down and choose the new **starfield** layer you just created.

With the **starfield GUITexture** placed in a layer, we'll modify the **SpaceCam** camera so that it only ever "sees" that **GUITexture**.

11. In the **Hierarchy** panel, click to select the **SpaceCam**.

12. In the **Inspector** panel, remove the **Flare Layer** and **Audio Listener Components** (right-click/secondary-click on the names of the **Components** and choose **Remove Component**, or pick this option by clicking on the small black gear icon to the right of the **Component** label, next to the blue book icon). We can have only one **Audio Listener** in the **Scene**, so let's leave that job up to the **Main Camera** by getting rid of this extraneous listener. Likewise, we don't need this secondary camera to render any lens flare effects, which is why we're nixing the **Flare Layer**.

13. Find the **Clear Flags** drop-down at the top of the **Camera Component**. It defaults to **Skybox**. Instead, set it to **Solid Color**.

14. Change the **Depth** to **-1**.

15. In the **Culling Mask** drop-down, choose **Nothing**. This deselects all other options in the list, and the little **Camera Preview** window in the **Scene** view is cleared.

16. Again in the **Culling Mask** drop-down, select the **starfield** layer.

We've now told our **SpaceCam** to only render (draw, look at) stuff that's on the **starfield** layer. Currently, the only thing on the **starfield** layer is our **starfield GUITexture**. We changed the **SpaceCam** depth to a low number because we want whatever it sees to appear behind everything our **Main Camera** sees. Let's make a few changes to the **Main Camera** to blend the two cameras' views.

17. In the **Hierarchy** panel, select the **Main Camera**.

18. In the **Inspector** panel, set its **Clear Flags** to **Depth only**.

19. In the **Culling Mask** drop-down, click to uncheck the **starfield** layer. When you do this, the value of **Culling Mask** changes to **Mixed**, and the character model pops into view.

20. Ensure that the **Depth** value of the **Main Camera** is set to **1**.

Because the **Main Camera**'s depth is 1 and the SpaceCam's depth is -1, the **Main Camera**'s imagery gets layered in front of the SpaceCam's picture. You should now see the jilted lover character from **The Break-Up** floating in the vacuum of space. As if the poor guy wasn't having a bad enough day already!

Resizing a GUI texture

If you're running a very high resolution on your monitor, the 1024x768 pixel **starfield** image may not be large enough to cover your screen's real estate. You can always select the **GUI Texture** in the **Hierarchy** panel, and adjust its **Width** and **Height** properties under the **Pixel Inset** heading. Keep in mind, though, that scaling up a bitmap image will lead to an increasingly poorer-quality picture. The very best thing, as we've learned in other chapters, is to choose your target resolution and to build all of your texture assets to work with that resolution.

Clear Flags

The **Clear Flags** setting we just used determines what a camera renders in all the empty space that isn't *stuff* (models, particle effects, and so on). The default is to render the skybox, which is an inverted cube to which you can map, among other things, a sky texture, to provide the illusion that the open world continues on for miles in any direction (which it does not).

The **Clear Flags** drop-down lets us fill that empty space with a skybox, a solid color, or depth only. With depth only, the camera just draws the stuff in its **Culling Mask** list. Any empty areas are gaping holes that get filled with whatever the camera at a lower depth is showing. The final **Clear Flags** option is **Don't Clear**, which Unity doesn't recommend because of the resulting "smear-looking effect".

Time for action – Enter the hero

Because the hero from our last game does a lot of the same stuff we want our spaceship to do, we really only have to replace the dude with the ship for fast, fun results.

1. In the **Project** panel, find the **HeroShip** model and drag it into the **Scene**.

2. In the **Hierarchy** panel, click on the gray arrow to expand the **Character Prefab**.

3. Click on the child object called **Armature**, and press the *Delete* key on your keyboard (*Command + Delete* on a Mac) to get rid of it.

4. Click on **Continue** if Unity warns you about losing the connection to the **Prefab**. Aaand... poof! No more dude.

5. In the **Hierarchy** panel, drag the **HeroShip** into the recently gutted **Character Prefab**. (Do this all within the **Hierarchy** panel—not in the **Project** panel.)

6. In the **Inspector** panel, punch in all of the default transform values (or choose **Reset Position** by clicking on the little black gear icon) for the **HeroShip**. Then tweak the rotation:

   Position: X:0, Y:0, Z:0

   Rotation: X:0, Y:-180, Z:-180

   Scale: X:1, Y:1, Z:1

7. In the fbx importer for the model, change the scale factor to 0.02.

8. In the **Hierarchy** panel, click to select the parent, the **Character Prefab**.

9. In the **Inspector** panel, position the **Character Prefab** thusly:

   Position: X:25, Y:5, Z:0

Set all **Rotation** values to 0 and all **Scale** values to 1. The **HeroShip** swings into view near the bottom of the **Game** view. I changed the **Main Camera**'s **Field of View** setting to 60 to pull it back out a smidge.

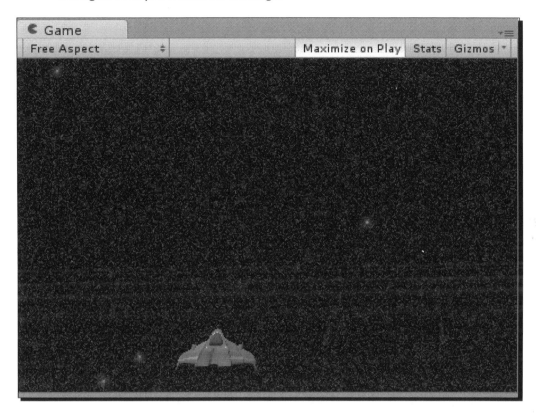

The **HeroShip Game Object** becomes a child of the **Character Prefab**, instead of the human model and armature bones. This means that it keeps all of the components we tacked onto our character—the **Box Collider**, the **Script**, the **Audio Source**, and so on. This is way faster than recreating this **Prefab** from the ground up!

Save the project and play the game. Some wacky things may be going on with the bomb and stein, but notice that the spaceship controls beautifully.

Time for action – It's a hit!

Now we'll do a little fiddling to bring the **Character Prefab** in line with its new, smaller spaceship model. You remember when we added that gigantic green box collider to the human character? Well it's still there, and it's not going to cut it for this game. We fix!

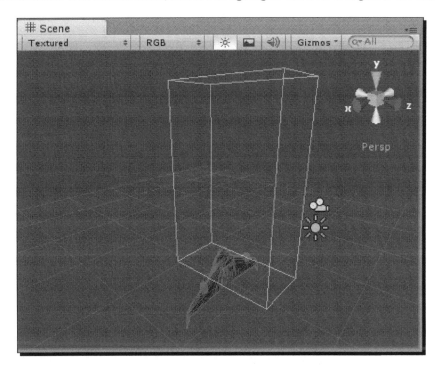

1. In the **Hierarchy** panel, click to select the **Character Prefab**.

2. Point your mouse cursor over the **Scene** view, and press the *F* key on your keyboard to focus in on the ship.

3. In the **Inspector** panel, find the **Box Collider** component.

4. In the menu, go to **Component | Physics | Mesh Collider**. A prompt asks us whether we want to **Replace** or **Add** the new collider. Click on **Replace** to knock out the oversized collider and replace it with the new one.

5. In the **Project** panel, find the **HeroShipCollisionCage** model.

6. Click on the gray arrow to expand the list of goodies inside **HeroShipCollisionCage**. One of these goodies should be a mesh called **CollisionCage** (remember that a mesh has a black grid pattern icon beside its name).

7. In the **Hierarchy** panel, click again to select the **Character Prefab**.

8. Click-and-drag the **CollisionCage** mesh into the **Inspector** panel, in the **Mesh** drop-down of the **Mesh Collider** component.

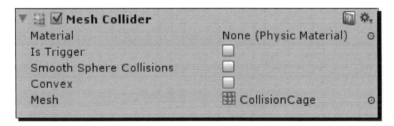

9. At the top of the **Inspector** panel, click on the **Apply** button to commit all of these changes to the **Prefab**.

Instead of a coarse, bulky box collider around our ship, we've used a special, separate model to determine its collision contours. Now, objects won't hit the empty space above the wings, on either side of the nose cone, as they would if we kept using a box collider.

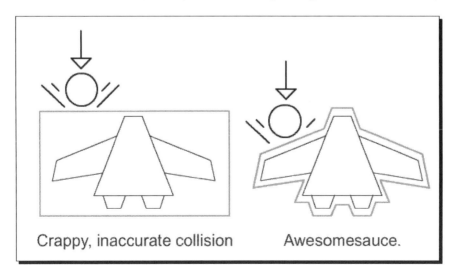

Crappy, inaccurate collision   Awesomesauce.

Custom colliders

You may have guessed that we could have used the **HeroShip's** own mesh as its **Mesh Collider**. The trouble with that plan is that the **HeroShip** mesh is too complex. If you're making a game where you're trying to squeeze every last ounce of performance out of Unity, you might consider modeling a separate, simpler mesh to use as the **Mesh Collider** for your spaceship—one that roughly approximates the ship's shape, but with less detail, which is what we've done here. Unity can chew through its calculations faster if you use optimized mesh colliders. If you want Unity to turn your **Mesh Collider** into a convex **Mesh Collider**, like we did with the hands and tray models in **Ticker Taker**, the mesh has to have fewer than 256 triangles. You'll recall that convex mesh colliders give us better results when testing collisions between moving objects. An unoptimized mesh, like a poorly constructed wall, can actually let other colliders pass right through it which is called "tunneling". Be sure to optimize your collider meshes to prevent tunneling.

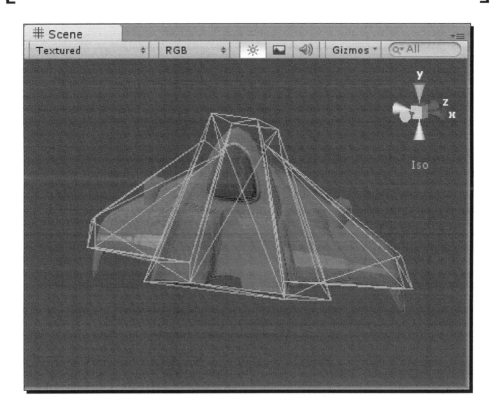

Time for action – Bring on the bad guys

Unlike **The Break-Up**, where we had good items and bad items, we'll have only bad items in our space shooter. Those bad items will be evil enemy spaceships that are hell-bent on destroying the universe, or whatever. Let's nix the beer steins, and leverage the work we've already done on our **Bomb Prefab** to swap them out for our enemy spacecraft.

1. In the **Hierarchy** panel, click on the **Stein Prefab** and delete it. So much for space beer. You can get rid of the stein model and the stein **Game Object** while you're at it.

2. Drag the **EnemyShip** model from the **Project** panel into the **Scene**.

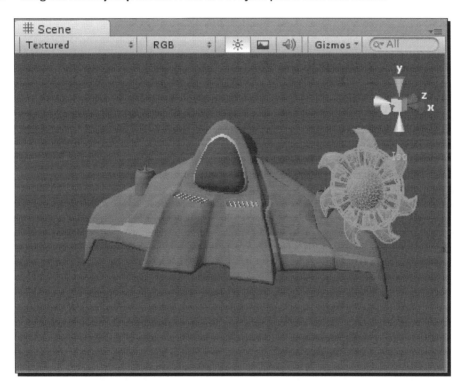

3. In the **Hierarchy** panel, click on the gray arrow to expand the **Bomb Prefab** contents.

4. Delete the **Bomb** child. Once again, you'll get the **Losing prefab** prompt—click on **Continue**.

5. Delete the **Sparks** child.

6. Drag the **EnemyShip** Game Object into the **Bomb Prefab** (all within the **Hierarchy** panel). As before, the **EnemyShip** becomes a child of the **Bomb Prefab**.

7. Ensure that the transform of the **EnemyShip** is set to default (the **Reset** option under the gear icon will handle this quickly):

Position: X:0, Y:0, Z:0

Rotation: X:0, Y:0, Z:0

Scale: X:1, Y:1, Z:1

8. In the **Hierarchy** panel, click on the **Bomb Prefab**. In the **Inspector** panel, position it like so:

Position: X:25, Y:71, Z:0

9. In the **Inspector** panel, within the **Rigidbody** component, check the **Freeze Rotation X Y** and **Z** boxes under the **Constraints** fly-out. This will prevent the enemy ship from spinning all over the place after a collision.

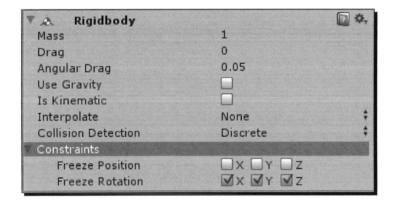

10. Click on the **Apply** button at the top of the **Inspector** panel to commit these changes to the **Prefab**.

11. Try out the game.

Positions are still nutty, but check it out—we've got a "good" spaceship that we can move across the screen, and a "bad" spaceship that uses the old **FallingObject Script** to slither down the screen.

Time for action – Do some housekeeping

We're most of the way to a brand new game, and we barely broke a sweat! Let's take a moment to rename a few things before we make some script adjustments.

1. Rename the **Bomb** and **Character Prefabs EnemyShip** and **HeroShip**, respectively. You should make this change in both the **Hierarchy** and **Project** panels.

2. In the **Project** panel, rename the **Character** script as **HeroShip**.

3. Likewise, rename the **FallingObject** script as **EnemyShip**.

4. In the **Hierarchy** panel, click to select the **EnemyShip Prefab** (formerly the **Bomb Prefab**).

5. Hover your mouse cursor over the **Scene** view and press the *F* key to focus in on the **EnemyShip**. You may notice that the **Sphere Collider** is too large. Let's fix that.

6. In the **Inspector** panel, change the **radius** of the **Sphere Collider** to **1.7**.

7. Click on the **Apply** button to apply these changes to the source **Prefab** when you're finished. It's safe to delete the **Bomb** and **Stein** models from the **Project** panel if you like.

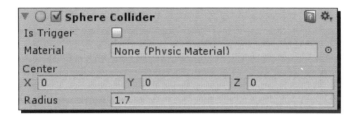

Time for action – Fixing the fall

In **The Break-Up**, our falling objects were larger, and they fell through a smaller vertical range. Now that there's no ground to hit and the sky's the limit, we should tweak a few lines of code in our **EnemyShip** script (formerly the **FallingObject** script). Double-click the **EnemyShip** script and roll up your sleeves:

◆ Change:

```
if (transform.position.y < 0)
```

to:

```
if (transform.position.y < -4)
```

This allows the enemy ship to reposition itself when it moves off the bottom edge of the screen, instead of when it hits the non-existent ground plane at y : 0.

◆ Change:

```
transform.position.y = 50;
```

to:

```
transform.position.y = 71;
```

When the **EnemyShip** is repositioned, cranking up its y value will start it just above the top edge of the screen.

♦ Change:

```
transform.position.x = Random.Range(0, 60);
```

to:

```
transform.position.x = Random.Range(-11, 68);
```

This gives the **EnemyShip** a corrected horizontal range at which to spawn—somewhere between -11 and 68 along the X-axis. You can either delete or comment out these two lines (remember, to turn a line into a comment, you just add a double slash // to the beginning of the line):

```
//audio.PlayOneShot(audioClips[Random.Range(0,audioClips.length)]);
//Instantiate(prefab, transform.position, Quaternion.identity);
```

We're commenting out/deleting these lines because we don't really want the **EnemyShip** to explode and make a noise when it moves off the bottom of the screen. In space, no one can hear you getting all blowed up.

♦ Change the value in this line:

```
transform.position.z = 0;
```

♦ Just below the position.z line, add this line:

```
transform.position.z = 0;
rigidbody.velocity = Vector3.zero;
```

Here's how the complete Update function should look:

```
function Update(){
  transform.position.y -= speed * Time.deltaTime;
  if(transform.position.y < -4) {

    //audio.PlayOneShot(audioClips[Random.Range(0,audioClips.length)]);
    //Instantiate(prefab, transform.position, Quaternion.identity);
    transform.position.y = 71;
    transform.position.x = Random.Range(-11,68);
    transform.position.z = 0;
    rigidbody.velocity = Vector3.zero;
  }
}
```

What's with that `rigidbody.velocity` reset? Well, when Game Objects smack into each other, it's possible for them to get knocked out of orbit, or for the physics engine to apply a velocity to the Game Object's `rigidbody`. We'll just use those two lines to flatten everything to zero when the ship starts a new descent down the screen.

The **EnemyShip** looks like a pretty cool buzzsaw thing. In a single line, we can throw a rotation on there that'll make the ship spin and look all scary-cool.

◆ Add this line within the `Update` function:

```
function Update () {
    transform.position.y -= speed * Time.deltaTime;
    transform.Rotate(0,0,Time.deltaTime * -500); // buzzsaw!!
```

You'll remember from earlier chapters that multiplying by `Time.deltaTime` sets things to the tempo of time, rather than updates. This way, an enemy ship takes two seconds to travel across the screen, regardless of how fast or slow the player's computer is. It's hardly fair to give players with slow computers a twitch advantage.

Save the **EnemyShip** script and play your game. The angry-looking enemy ship bent on universal annihilation or something like that, now makes a complete trip from the top to the bottom of the screen. It respawns properly at the top, at some random **X** position. And it spins just like a sharp, pointy bad guy should.

Time for action – Tweak the hero

There are a few changes we should make to the **HeroShip** script (formerly the **Character** script) to suit our new game. Let's do it:

1. Open the **HeroShip** script.

2. Delete the `else if` condition handling the steins. Get rid of everything in this snippet in bold:

```
if(col.gameObject.tag == "bomb")
{
    audio.PlayOneShot(explosionSound);
    Instantiate(explosion, col.gameObject.transform.position,
        Quaternion.identity);
}
  else if (col.gameObject.tag == "stein") {
      animation.Play("catch"); // Ima catch that stein!
  }
```

Shoot the Moon doesn't have beer steins, so we can safely kill this chunk.

3. Delete all of the code controlling the character model animation. Get rid of this whole section in bold:

```
if(lastX != transform.position.x) {
    // x values between this Update cycle and the last one
    // aren't the same! That means the player is moving the mouse.
    if(!isMoving) {
        // the player was standing still.
        // Let's flag him to "isMoving"
        isMoving = true;
        if(!animation.IsPlaying("catch")){
            animation.Play("step");
        }
    }
}
else
{
    // The player's x position is the same this Update cycle
    // as it was the last! The player has stopped moving the
        mouse.
    if(isMoving) {
        // The player has stopped moving, so let's update the flag.
        isMoving = false;
        if(!animation.IsPlaying("catch")){
            animation.Play("idle");
        }
    }
}
lastX = transform.position.x;
```

4. Delete the `isMoving` variable from the top of the script:

```
var isMoving:boolean = false; // flags whether or not the player
    is in motion
```

5. Delete the `lastX` variable definition from the top of the script:

```
var lastX:float; // this will store the last position of the
    character
```

6. Delete the entire `Start` function:

```
function Start() {
    animation.Stop();  // this stops Unity from playing the
        character's default animation.
}
```

The hero ship doesn't have any default animation, so this code is unnecessary.

Here's how the complete, freshly preened script should look. Notice that we've updated the reset position values at the bottom of the script:

```
var explosion:GameObject;

function Update() {
    var halfW:float = Screen.width/2;
    transform.position.x = (Input.mousePosition.x)/20;
}

function OnCollisionEnter(col : Collision) {
    if(col.gameObject.tag == "bomb")
    {
        // I got hit by a bomb!
        Instantiate(explosion, col.gameObject.transform.position,
          Quaternion.identity);
    }
    col.gameObject.transform.position.y = 50;
    col.gameObject.transform.position.x = Random.Range(0,60);
    col.gameObject.transform.z = -16;
}
```

Our human character in *The Break-Up* had animation cycles that we tapped into, but the **HeroShip** model doesn't. Unity will keep throwing complaints that it can't find these animations unless we tidy up the code as described above.

What just happened – hooray for lazy!

Take a look at these three lines in our **HeroShip** script:

```
col.gameObject.transform.position.y = 50;
col.gameObject.transform.position.x = Random.Range(0,60);
col.gameObject.transform.z = -16;
```

Those are the lines we used to reposition the falling object when it hit the player. We have similar lines in our **EnemyShip** script that we just updated with new values. Should we do the same thing here? What if the values have to change again later? Then we'll have to update the code in two different scripts. And that, in professional parlance, sucks.

It makes sense to fold this code into some kind of ResetPosition function that both scripts can call, yes? Then we'll only ever have to update the values in one place. BUT can you really call a function on one script from a completely different script? Yes, Virginia, there is a Santa Claus.

Time for action – Give up the func

Let's get that function set up in the **EnemyShip** script first. Double-click to open the **EnemyShip** script, and get typing.

1. Write this new function outside of and apart from the other functions in the script:

```
function ResetPosition(){
    transform.position.y = 71;
    transform.position.x = Random.Range(-11, 68);
    transform.position.z = 0;
    rigidbody.velocity = Vector3.zero;
}
```

These are the very same repositioning lines we already have. You can even just type the shell of the function, and copy/paste those lines right in there. Either way, you need to go back and eradicate those lines from the Update function and replace them with a ResetPosition() function call.

2. Erase these bolded lines:

```
if(transform.position.y < -4) {
    transform.position.z = 0;
    transform.position.y = 71;
    transform.position.x = Random.Range(0, 60);
    rigidbody.velocity = Vector3.zero;
}
```

And replace them with the ResetPosition() function call:

```
if(transform.position.y < -4) {
    ResetPosition();
}
```

When the interpreter hits that ResetPosition() function call, it'll jump into the ResetPosition function and run those repositioning lines.

3. Save the **EnemyShip** script. Next, hop over to the **HeroShip** script to make some changes.

4. Get rid of those old repositioning lines from the **HeroShip** script. Delete the lines in bold:

```
function OnCollisionEnter(col : Collision) {
    // (a few lines omitted here for brevity)
    col.gameObject.transform.position.y = 50;
    col.gameObject.transform.position.z = -16;
    col.gameObject.transform.position.x = Random.Range(0,60);
```

5. Replace those lines with these ones:

```
function OnCollisionEnter(col : Collision) {
    // (a few lines omitted here for brevity)
    if(col.gameObject.GetComponent(EnemyShip))
    {
        col.gameObject.GetComponent(EnemyShip).ResetPosition();
    }
}
```

Here's how the whole `OnCollisionEnter` function should look:

```
function OnCollisionEnter(col : Collision) {
    if(col.gameObject.tag == "bomb")
    {
        // I got hit by a bomb!
        Instantiate(explosion, col.gameObject.transform.position,
            Quaternion.identity);
    }

    if(col.gameObject.GetComponent(EnemyShip))
    {
        col.gameObject.GetComponent(EnemyShip).ResetPosition();
    }
}
```

Let's break those new lines down.

```
if(col.gameObject.GetComponent(EnemyShip)){
```

The value of `col` is something of type **Collision**. The **Collision** class has a variable called `gameObject`, which refers to the **Game Object** involved in the collision. The **Game Object** class has a function called `GetComponent`. You can pass the name of the script you want to access as an argument.

In this case, we're referring to the **EnemyShip** script attached to whatever hit the **HeroShip**. By wrapping it in an `if` statement, we're effectively saying "if whatever just hit the **HeroShip** has a component called **EnemyShip** attached to it..."

```
col.gameObject.GetComponent(EnemyShip).ResetPosition();
```

... then call the `ResetPosition()` function on that script.

Our conditional check confirms that such a script even exists on the colliding object. Later, if a **FallingStar** GameObject hits the ship, and it doesn't have a script called **EnemyShip** attached to it, we would get an error when trying to refer to the **EnemyShip** script. The conditional statement protects us from getting that error.

The end result of all this is that when the **EnemyShip** hits the bottom of the screen, it calls the `ResetPosition()` function and pops back up to the top. When the **EnemyShip** (or any **Game Object** with the **EnemyShip** script component attached) hits the **HeroShip**, it calls the **EnemyShip** script's `ResetPosition()` function, and the **EnemyShip** pops back to the top of the screen.

6. Save the script and give your game a try! The enemy ship resets its position in both of these cases. Success!

Optimization

Here's one example of how we could optimize our code to make it more efficient. The `GetComponent` function is an "expensive" operation, which means that it takes longer for the computer to execute than other built-in functions. You'll notice that we're calling the function here twice. We could store the results of the `GetComponent` function in a variable. Then we'd have to call that function only once. Look here:

```
var other = col.gameObject.GetComponent(EnemyShip);
if (other) {
    other.ResetPosition();
}
```

As with refactoring (making the code pretty), we should focus on getting our code to work first. Then we can go back to make it faster and cleaner.

Time for action – Itchy trigger finger

This is a whole lot of nerd-talk and not enough shooting. Let's build a bullet so that we can take these alien bad boys down.

1. In the menu, click on **GameObject | Create Other | Sphere**. Rename the resulting sphere **bullet**.

2. In the **Hierarchy** panel, click to select your newly minted bullet.

3. In the **Inspector** panel, reset the bullet's **Transform** values, and then punch in **0.5** for all three scale values:

   Position: X:0, Y:0, Z:0

   Rotation: X:0, Y:0, Z:0

   Scale: X:0.5, Y:0.5, Z:0.5

4. Hover over the **Scene** view and press the *F* key to focus it within the **Scene**.

Time for action – Futurize the bullet

A dull, gray bullet just won't cut it in a sci-fi game. Let's make a neon-green **Material** and apply it to the bullet, because in the distant future, bullets are obviously neon-green (I have this crazy hunch).

1. In the **Project** panel, create a new **Material**. Rename the new **Material** as **Bullet**.

2. Click to select the new **Bullet Material**.

3. In the **Inspector** panel, click on the **Material**'s color swatch and choose a neon space-bullet green. I chose these values:

   R: 9

   G: 255

   B: 0

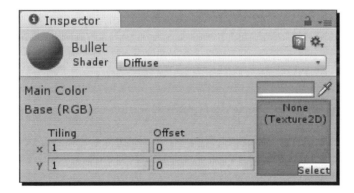

4. In the **Hierarchy** panel, select the **bullet Game Object**.

5. In the **Inspector** panel, find the **Mesh Renderer** component.

6. Apply the **Bullet Material** to the **bullet**. You can either do this by choosing the **Bullet Material** in the **Element 0** pop-up of the **Materials** section, or by clicking-and-dragging the **Bullet Material** into the slot. (You may have to click on the gray arrow to open the **Material** list first.) You can also drag the **Material** onto the Game Object in either the **Hierarchy** or the **Scene** view.

7. Uncheck **Cast Shadows** and **Receive Shadows** in the **Mesh Renderer** component.

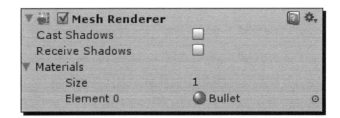

Time for action – Building Halo

OK, don't get too excited. We're not actually going to build *Halo*... we're going to build *a* halo to make our bullet look all glowy and awesome.

1. Ensure that the **bullet Game Object** is still selected.

2. In the menu, select **Component | Rendering | Halo**. This adds a cool halo effect to the bullet.

3. In the **Inspector** panel, click on the color swatch for the **Halo Component**. Enter the same neon-green color values as before:

   R: 9

   G: 255

   B: 0

4. Change the halo's **Size** value to **0.5**.

Now let's get the bullet ready to move around in the physics engine.

5. Make sure the **bullet Game Object** is still selected.

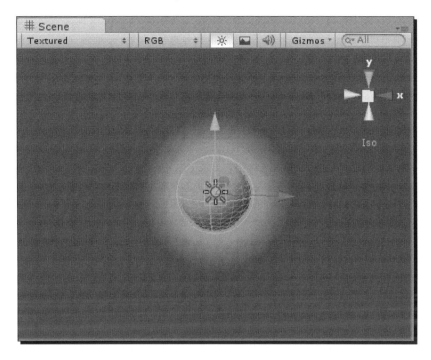

6. In the menu, click on **Component | Physics | Rigidbody**.

7. In the **Inspector** panel, uncheck **Use gravity**.

8. At the top of the **Inspector** panel, click on **Add Tag...** in the **Tag** drop down.

9. Create a new tag called **bullet**. (If you want to keep your file tidy, you can delete the old **bomb** and **stein** tags left over from the previous project, and shrink the list size down to 2.)

10. Click again to select the **bullet Game Object**.

11. In the **Inspector** panel, choose the new **bullet** tag from the **Tag** drop-down to apply the new bullet tag to the **bullet Game Object**.

We'll create a very simple script and hook it up to the bullet.

12. In the **Project** panel, create a new **JavaScript**.

13. Rename the new script **Bullet**.

14. Give the **Bullet** script this `Start` function:

```
function Start() {
    rigidbody.velocity.y = 100;
}
```

This gives the bullet some oomph to get it moving along the Y-axis.

15. Add the following lines to the `Update` function:

```
function Update () {
  if(transform.position.y > 62) {
    Destroy(gameObject);
  }
}
```

16. In the **Hierarchy** panel, click to select the **bullet GameObject**.

17. Attach the script to the bullet by clicking-and-dragging the script on top of the **bullet GameObject**, or choosing **Component | Scripts | Bullet | BulletScript** from the menu.

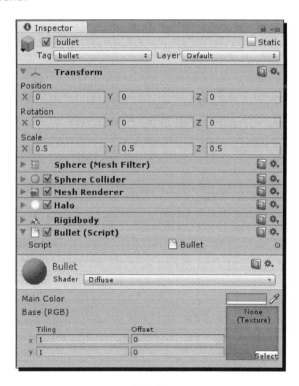

Finally, we'll create a new **Prefab** to house the **bullet GameObject**.

18. In the **Project** panel, create a new **Prefab** and call it **Bullet**. (Remember to keep your project organized by dropping your assets into their respective folders.)

19. Drag the **bullet Game Object** from the **Hierarchy** panel into the empty **Bullet Prefab** container. The gray icon lights up blue to indicate that the **Prefab** is full.

20. Select and delete the **bullet Game Object** from the **Hierarchy** panel. It's safe inside the **Prefab** now.

Put your toys away

If you've been keeping all of your assets organized in folders up to this point, things should be humming along nicely. If not, you may be facing a growing mess of similarly named assets and disused pieces from the previous project. Take some time to go through the **Project** panel and clean the house. We don't need the bomb, brownstone, stein, or character models any more, and their **Materials** can get chucked as well. A clean project is a happy project.

Time for action – Fire!

Let's add a few lines of code to the **HeroShip** script to make the bullet fire when you click on the mouse button, because shooting is cool.

```
function Update ()
{
  var halfW:float = Screen.width/2;
  transform.position.x = (Input.mousePosition.x )/20;
  if(Input.GetMouseButtonDown(0)){
     Instantiate(bullet, transform.position + new Vector3(-3,2,0),
        Quaternion.identity);
     Instantiate(bullet, transform.position + new Vector3(3,2,0),
        Quaternion.identity);
  }
}
```

Let's review.

```
if(Input.GetMouseButtonDown(0)){
```

This line returns `true` if the left (or primary) mouse button (which has an ID of 0) has been pushed down within this `Update` cycle.

```
Instantiate(bullet, transform.position+new Vector3(-3,2,0),

    Quaternion.identity);

Instantiate(bullet, transform.position+new Vector3(3,2,0),

    Quaternion.identity);
```

We've used the `Instantiate` command before—this time, we're creating two new **Bullet Prefab** instances in the same position as the **HeroShip**, with the same rotation. In the same statement, we're moving the bullets two units along the Y-axis, which places them at the wings of our hero ship. The left bullet gets nudged `-3` units along the x axis, while the right bullet is nudged `3` pixels the other direction, which places the bullets right around the ship's wing-mounted cannons. The bullets start moving up the screen because of the `rigidbody.velocity` we applied in the bullet script's `Start` function.

Before this will work, we have to create a variable at the top of the script called **bullet**, and then click-and-drag the **Bullet Prefab** into the variable slot in the **Inspector** panel. Otherwise, the script will have no idea what we're talking about when we try to instantiate something called **bullet**.

Follow these steps:

1. Add the variable declaration at the top of the **HeroShip** script:

    ```
    var bullet:GameObject;
    ```

2. Save the script.

3. In the **Hierarchy** panel, select the **HeroShip Prefab**.

4. In the **Inspector** panel, find the **HeroShip** script component.

5. Hook up the **Bullet Prefab** to the **bullet** variable.

Now test your game. When you click on the left mouse button, two new instances of the **Bullet Prefab** are added to the **Scene**. A force is applied to their **Rigidbody** components that will eventually send them careening up to the top of the screen. Then they're positioned at the wing cannons of the **HeroShip**. The script attached to each bullet detects when the bullet has passed the top edge of the play area, and destroys the **BulletPrefab** instance and everything in it.

Put more simply: CLICK MOUSE. MAKE SHOOT.

Time for action – Code do-si-do

Because the needs of our game have changed, we might reconsider how and where our code is written. In *The Break-Up*, it made sense for the player character to detect all collisions. But in *Shoot the Moon*, all the significant collisions actually happen on the enemy ship. The enemy ship needs know when it hits the hero ship, and it needs to know when it hits a bullet. So we can actually localize all of the collision code on the enemy ship. This makes a lot of sense, so let's make that change by transplanting some code.

1. In the **HeroShip** script, delete the `OnCollisionEnter` function.

2. Delete the explosion variable declaration from the top of the script.

3. Save the **HeroShip** script.

   As we did with the `ResetPosition()` function, let's build a reusable `Explode()` function, and fold the explosion-related code into it.

4. In the **EnemyShip** script, create an `Explode()` function outside and apart from the other functions:

   ```
   function Explode()
   {
     audio.PlayOneShot(audioClips[Random.Range(0,audioClips.length)]);
     Instantiate(prefab, transform.position, Quaternion.identity);
   }
   ```

5. Give the **EnemyShip** an `OnCollisionEnter` function, and call the `Explode` and `ResetPosition` functions. The enemy ship will explode regardless of what it hits:

   ```
   function OnCollisionEnter(col : Collision) {
     Explode();
     ResetPosition();
   }
   ```

6. Next, we'll set up a conditional statement in the `OnCollisionEnter` function to determine whether the enemy ship has hit a bullet, or the hero ship:

```
function OnCollisionEnter(col : Collision) {
    Explode();
    ResetPosition();
    if(col.gameObject.tag == "bullet") {
      Destroy(col.gameObject);
    }
    else if (col.gameObject.tag == "heroShip") {
    // This enemy ship hit the player!
    }
}
```

7. At the very top of the **EnemyShip** script, rename the `prefab` variable `explosion`:

```
var explosion:GameObject;
```

8. Change the `Explode()` function to call the new variable:

```
Instantiate(explosion, transform.position, Quaternion.
identity);
```

9. Save the script.

Since we changed the name of our prefab variable to "explosion", we should duck out to the **Inspector** panel and make sure that the **Explosion** prefab is still set as the proper value. Changing variable names like this can sometimes cause Unity to lose track of things. In my case, I had to drag-and-drop the **Explosion** prefab into the **Explosion** variable's slot.

What just happened – eat lead

Try out the game. When the enemy ship hits either a bullet or the hero ship, it runs the `Explode()` function and repositions itself at the top of the screen. Specifically, if it hits a bullet, the bullet gets destroyed. If it hits the hero ship, it looks like it's behaving properly. But if you try putting a `print` command inside the conditional that says "//This enemy ship hit the player!" you'll realize that the code isn't getting executed.

This is because we haven't tagged the **HeroShip**. Without that tag, our **EnemyShip** script has no idea that it's hit the hero ship. It just knows that it's hit *something*, so it shows an explosion and bounces back up to the top of the screen.

You may notice a small but unwanted side effect of our code. Because we're instantiating the explosion using the enemy ship's `transform.position`, the explosion appears exactly where the enemy ship used to be. This makes sense when a bullet hits the enemy ship, but it doesn't quite make sense when the enemy ship hits the hero. It makes it seem as though the hero ship is impenetrable—that anything that crashes into it will burst into flames. It's actually the HERO ship's position that we need for that explosion.

Thankfully, there is a quick fix using the maaaagic of aaarguments.

Time for action – The maaagic of aaaarguments

To make the explosion happen on the thing that hits the enemy ship, rather than on the enemy ship itself, we'll pass the position of the colliding **Game Object** to the `Explode()` function.

1. Open the **EnemyShip** script, and make these changes:

2. In the `OnCollisionEnter` function, pass the `transform.position` of the colliding object's **Game Object** to the `Explode()` function:

    ```
    Explode(col.gameObject.transform.position);
    ```

3. Now make sure that the `Explode` function accepts this argument:

    ```
    function Explode(pos:Vector3){
    ```

4. And finally, position the instantiated explosion to the `pos` variable that receives the argument value:

    ```
    function Explode(pos:Vector3){
    audio.PlayOneShot(audioClips[Random.Range(0,audioClips.
    length)]);
    Instantiate(explosion, pos, Quaternion.identity);
    }
    ```

5. Save the script and try it out. The explosions go off at the site of the collision, and it makes a lot more visual sense.

Time for action – Adding the most important part of any space shooter

We're almost ready to close the book on the main functionality of our space shooter game. We can fire bullets and explodify enemy ships. Although it may well defy the laws of physics, a satisfying fiery explosion occurs in the oxygen-free vacuum of space. But there's just something... missing, yes?

Numerous studies have been conducted to determine the most scientifically accurate sound for a badass neon-green irradiated bullet being fired through space, and the results have settled unanimously on the onomatopoeic "pew". Luckily, we have just such a sound effect in our Assets folder, so let's get it going.

1. At the top of the **HeroShip** script, declare a variable to hold the "pew" sound effect:

   ```
   var pew:AudioClip;
   ```

2. In the left mouse button firing section of the code, play the "pew" sound effect:

   ```
   if(Input.GetMouseButtonDown(0)){
       audio.PlayOneShot(pew);
   ```

3. Save and close the script.

4. Find the "pew" sound effect in the **Project** panel.

5. In the **Hierarchy** panel, click to select the **HeroShip**.

6. Click-and-drag the "pew" sound effect into the **HeroShip** script component in the **Inspector** panel, in the slot labeled "pew".

7. Click on **Apply** to apply the changes to the source **Prefab**.

Now when you fire, the spaceship goes "pew". And lo, all becomes right with the world!

Last year's model

We've taken a game about a guy who gets kicked out of his apartment and turned it into a game about destroying an onslaught of alien spacecrafts. That's the difference theme makes. The underlying bones of both games are quite similar, and it wasn't an enormous effort to make these changes. It's the rough equivalent of throwing a new coat of paint and some seat warmers on last year's model and selling it as a brand new car.

And I say "why not"? The beautiful thing about game development is that you don't have to reinvent the wheel every time. You should absolutely build things with a mind towards reusing them in future projects. The momentum you build up will make you an unstoppable game development machine.

Have a go hero – Filling in the empty space

This game, like *The Break-Up*, has a number of missing elements that I'll let you fill in, based on what you've learned in previous chapters. But in addition to the title screen, instructions, credits, win/lose conditions, and the player's health that we discussed earlier, here are a few ideas to strive for if you decide to develop **Shoot the Moon** further:

- Build a couple of neat-looking jet trail particle systems and hook them up to the exhaust pipes sticking out the back of your hero ship.

- Make the ship angle as it moves left and right. You might try repurposing some of your paddle code from *Ticker Taker* to do this.

- Add some power-ups that appear randomly in the void of space. If the player collides with them, you can give him awesome skillz... maybe he becomes invincible for a short period of time? Or you could crank up the number of bullets that he can fire, for a triple-shot effect. That's a very easy change to make based on the code you've already written.

- Duplicate and reupholster an enemy ship to paint it purple or something. Give that type of ship some hit points so that it doesn't explode until it's been hit by three bullets.

- Mess around with the enemy ship's movement script. Using mathemagic, can you make the ships travel diagonally, or even in spirals or waves? Can you do it without math?

- Make it so that when you hold down the mouse button, you charge up a super shot, and when you let go, some crazy-huge bullet blasts out of your ship's nose cone.

- Make the enemy ships fire back!

- After the player has shot down x enemy ships, introduce the big boss: THE MOON. Give the moon a big pile of hit points and some missiles. Then, and only then, will the title of the game make sense... which I'm sure has been keeping you up at night.

Summary

We've learned something today: the value of friendship, the importance of kayak safety, and the dangers of eating mysterious red berries you find in the forest. But most of all, we've learned how to:

- Set up a 2-camera system to composite two different views together
- Change existing prefabs to use different models
- Apply a mesh collider
- Use the Halo component
- Fire bullets
- Completely re-skin a game in a single chapter

More hospitality

The last chapter is nigh! In our final hurrah, we'll leverage our newfound dual-camera technique to add environmental ambience to the *Ticker Taker* game. Then we'll explore the animation tools, and learn how to publish our games so that anyone can play them.

12
Action!

When last we left Ticker Taker, our slightly demented hospital-themed keep-up game, we had two hands bouncing a heart on a dinner tray. The game mechanic was pretty functional, but we hadn't fully delivered on the skin. If Ticker Taker is about a nurse rushing a heart to the transplant ward, then where is the hospital?

In this final chapter we'll:

◆ Use the dual-camera technique from *Shoot the Moon* to render a fully-3D environment

◆ Set up a movable lighting rig for our **Scene**

◆ Dive into Unity's animation tools to animate Game Objects

◆ Publish a Unity game so that we can unleash our masterpieces on an unsuspecting public

Open heart surgery

To get started, open the last version of the *Ticker Taker* game. You can also copy the game files to another folder, as we did with *The Break-Up* and *Shoot the Moon*.

Once the project is open, find the **Game Scene** in the **Project** panel and double-click to open it (if it doesn't open by default). You should see the **Scene** just as we left it: heart, hands, and tray.

I took the time to organize the different assets into folders to tidy up the project. Recall that as your projects become more complex, neatness saves sanity.

Once that's all in order, download and import the assets package for this chapter. Now we're ready to dig in.

Time for action – Haul in the hallway

The assets package contains a hallway model. Created in the free 3D software package Blender, it's essentially a square donut with the normals flipped so that it appears inside out.

We're going to set up one camera to bounce up and down, as if the character is running, and send it flying through the hallway. Then we'll set that view as the background for our **Main Camera**, which is aimed at the heart-and-tray action. By using **Depth** as our **Clear Flags** setting on the foreground camera, the background camera will show through the empty space to make it appear as though the player is running through the hallway.

Find the hallway model in the **Project** panel. It's the one with the blue cubic "model" icon next to it—not to be confused with the model *texture*, which uses a little image thumbnail as its icon. (I placed my models in the folder called `Models`, and dropped my textures into a `Textures` folder to keep them sorted.)

1. Drag the hallway model into the **Scene**.

2. Adjust the hallway's **Transform** properties in the **Inspector** panel:

   ❑ **Position: X:0, Y:2, Z:-25**

   ❑ **Rotation: X:0, Y:0, Z:180**

   These settings place the hallway behind the **Main Camera** in our **Scene** so that it's out of the way while we work with it. In the **Hierarchy** panel, select the hallway Game Object and press *F* to frame the selected object.

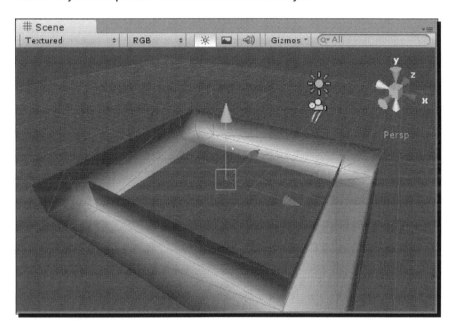

3. In the **Inspector** panel, add a new layer called **hallway**, as we did when we created the **starfield** layer in our **Shoot the Moon** project. Be sure that you're adding a new layer, not a new tag.

4. In the **Hierarchy** panel, select the **hallway**. Choose the new **hallway** layer in the **Layer** drop-down. Unity will pop up a dialog asking you whether you want to put the hallway's child objects in the **hallway** layer as well. Answer **Yes, change children**.

Time for action – Meet me at camera two

In order to pull off this foreground/background effect, we'll need two cameras. Let's create the second camera and set it up to look at the hallway.

1. In the menu, select **GameObject | Create Other | Camera**.

2. Rename the new camera as **hallwayCam**.

3. Change the **Transform** settings of **hallwayCam** to:

   ❑ **Position: X:6.5, Y:1.2, Z: -31.5**

The **hallwayCam** jumps to one corner of the hallway model.

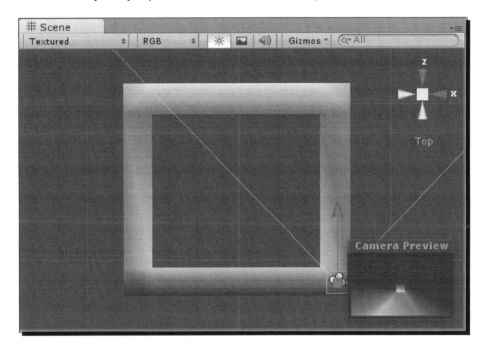

4. Select the **hallwayCam** in the **Hierarchy** panel.

5. In the **Inspector** panel, adjust the following settings:

   ❑ **Clear Flags: Solid Color**

   ❑ **Culling Mask: nothing** (This deselects everything in the culling mask list.)

   ❑ **Culling Mask: hallway** (This selects only the hallway layer, which contains our hallway model.)

   ❑ **Depth: -1**

☐ **Flare Layer**: unchecked/removed

☐ **Audio Listener**: unchecked/removed

No surprises here—these are the very same settings we used for the background camera in *Shoot the Moon*.

Time for action – Adjusting the Main Camera

As before, we'll nudge a few settings on the **Main Camera** in order to composite the two views together.

1. In the **Hierarchy** panel, select the **Main Camera**.

2. In the **Inspector** panel, adjust the following settings:

☐ **Clear Flags: Depth only**

☐ **Culling Mask**—uncheck hallway (it now says **Mixed...**)

☐ **Depth: 1**

The two cameras' views are now layered together in the **Game** view. That's a good start!

Time for action – Deck the halls

This bland gray hallway model looks less like a hospital and more like the white light patients see when they quit the mortal coil. Luckily, there's a quick fix: the **Project** panel contains a texture that we'll apply to the model to make it look more—you know—hospitable.

1. In the **Hierarchy** panel, click on the gray arrow next to the hallway to expand its list of children.

2. The hallway contains one child, also called **Hallway**, which contains the **Mesh Renderer** and **Mesh Filter** components. Select the **Hallway** child.

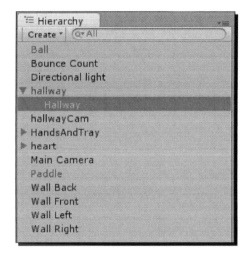

3. Find the **hallway** texture in the **Project** panel, and click-and-drag it into the texture swatch in the **Inspector** panel, under the hallway's **Material**.

Wonderfully, the **hallway** texture wraps itself around the hallway model. In a twinkling, we're inside a hospital!

Time for action – Turn on the lights

This hospital texture is great and all, but our level looks like something straight out of a survival horror game. Every hospital that I've ever visited has been bright and shiny. Let's add some lights to the level to perk it up some.

1. Click on the green Y-axis cone in the axis gizmo at the top-right of the **Scene** view. This swings us around to a top view, looking down on our **Scene**.

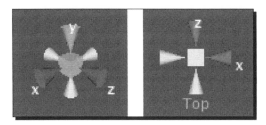

2. Pan and zoom the **Scene** view to center the hallway model.

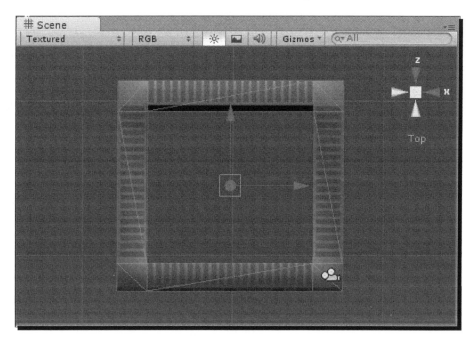

3. In the menu, select **GameObject | Create Other | Point Light**.

4. Create a new prefab and call it **hallwayLight**.

5. In the **Hierarchy** panel, click to select the **Point Light**, and reset its **Transform** in the **Inspector** panel.

6. Drag the **Point Light** into the **hallwayLight Prefab**.

7. Delete the **Point Light** from the **Hierarchy** panel.

8. Drag an instance of the **hallwayLight Prefab** from the **Project** panel into your **Scene**. Position it at the top-right corner of the hallway—around x: 6.3 y:1 z:-19.7.

 Note: We could have kept the **Point Light** in there, as it's connected to the **hallwayLight Prefab**, but I think it's easier to work with the project when **Prefab** instances are named consistently.

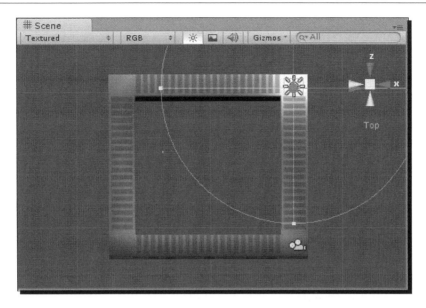

9. Create an empty **GameObject** and call it **LightingRig**. This Game Object will hold all of our lights, so we can keep them organized. Move the lighting rig to x:0 y:0 z:-25.

10. In the **Hierarchy** panel, click-and-drag the **hallwayLight** instance onto the **LightingRig** Game Object. This makes the light a child of the rig, and we see that familiar gray arrow appear indicating a parent/child relationship.

11. Select and then duplicate the **hallwayLight** instance by pressing *Ctrl + D* (*Command + D* on a Mac). Notice that the second light is also a child of the **LightingRig** Game Object.

12. Move the duplicated light to the top-middle of the **hallway** model.

13. Duplicate a third light, and move it to the top-left corner of the level.

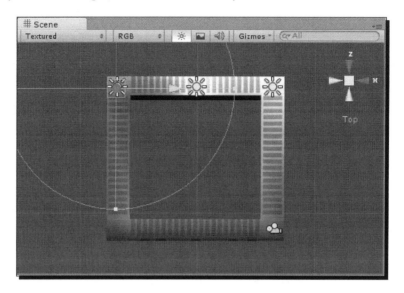

14. Hold down the *Shift* key on your keyboard and click on the other two lights, until all three lights are selected at once. (It may be easier to shift-select the three lights in the **Hierarchy** panel instead of the **Scene** view.)

15. Duplicate the trio of lights, and move them down across the middle of the level. You may need to zoom out slightly to see the transformed gizmo handles.

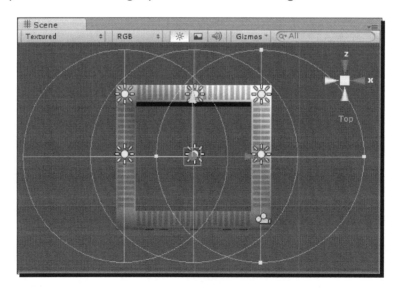

16. Duplicate the set of three lights again, and move them down to the bottom of the level. You should now have an array of nine lights.

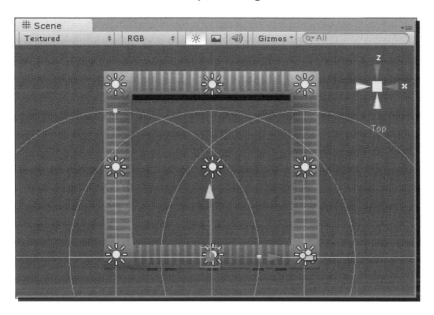

17. Click on a blank area in the **Scene** view to deselect all the lights.

18. Click to select the light in the middle of the level and delete it. Now there's a light in each corner, and a light in the middle of each hallway section.

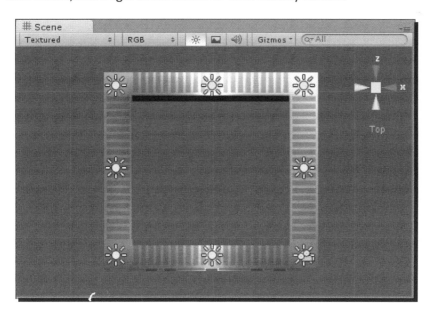

19. Unity 3D supports "expensive" pixel lighting and less "expensive" vertex lighting. Pixel lighting is more taxing on the player's computer, but it's more believable and it can pull off fancier tricks like cookies (think of the "bat symbol" from the *Batman* comics) and normal-mapping, which creates the illusion of detail on a flat polygon. In trying to preserve performance, Unity only lets us have two active pixel lights and drops the other lights down to vertex quality, which interpolates (makes a calculated guess) at the light levels between the light source and an object.

In order for our lighting rig to light the hallway well, we need to tell Unity that it can use all of our lights as pixel lights. This is sort of a lazy solution, but we can get away with it because our geometry is so simple. In more complex games, you may need to employ real ingenuity to present your scene in the best possible "light" with minimal performance trade-off.

Follow these steps to increase the number of pixel lights Unity will allow:

20. In the menus, click **Edit | Project Settings | Quality**. Unity allows us to create different quality profiles, and to apply those profiles to different scenarios: playing a game standalone, using the web player, deploying to a mobile, and viewing a game in the editor. Note that all of these scenarios default to using the "Good" profile.

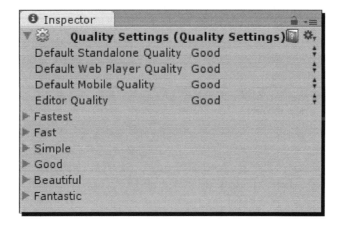

21. Open the "Good" profile by clicking the grey arrow next to its label. Punch in "8" to increase the number of pixel lights Unity will allow.

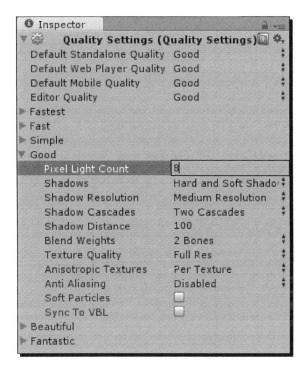

22. Once you make this change, you should see the light levels in your scene punch up. Now Unity is rendering proper lighting effects for every pixel on the screen based on all eight lights, rather than calculating only two lights and fudging the others.

The light! It bliiiiiiiinds! Luckily, these eight lights are all instances of the same **Prefab**, so by adjusting one of them, we'll affect the rest.

23. Click to select the **hallwayLight Prefab** in the **Project** panel.

24. In the **Inspector** panel, change the intensity to 0.5 and the range to 20.

That should mute all the lights to the point where they look like they belong in a hospital, and not like a hospital built on the surface of the sun.

When you rotate your **Scene** view, you should see all eight lights nestled within the hallway model. If they ended up far above or below the level, just move the **LightingRig** Game Object around to move all eight lights as a single unit.

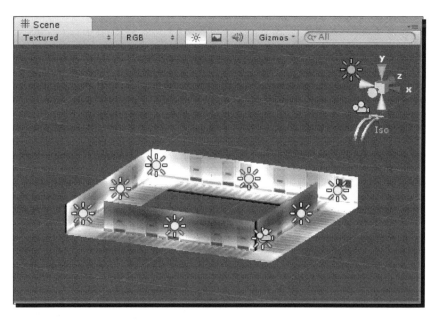

Time for action – Setting up the camera rig

We want to depict the player running through these hallways. There are at least two ways we can handle the **HallwayCam**'s animation. We can use a **Script** to control the camera motion, or we can use Unity's built-in animation tools to record some camera motion that we'll play back during gameplay. We've already done a bunch of scripting, so let's see what the Unity IDE can do to help us pull off our running-through-the-hallway effect without writing any code.

We're going to build a camera rig, where the camera is a child of a Game Object that bounces up and down, and that Game Object is a child of another Game Object that runs through the hallways.

Order of operations

Because of the way Unity's built-in animations work, it's super important to set up your objects' parent-child relationships before you animate. The values we set in our animation clips become relative to an object's parent. In short, that means "bad news" if you animate first before setting up your rig. Existing animations can swing wildly out of position. Because redoing work is for chumps, let's get it right the first time.

1. Create an empty Game Object and name it **bouncer**.

2. Set its **Transform** using these values:

    ❑ **Position: X: 6.5, Y:1.2, Z:-31.5**

    These are the same values as for the **hallwayCam**.

3. Duplicate the **bouncer** Game Object and call it **runner**.

4. In the **Hierarchy** panel, make the **hallwayCam** a child of the **bouncer** by clicking and dragging **hallwayCam** onto **bouncer**.

5.   Make the **bouncer** a child of the runner by clicking - and - dragging the bouncer onto the **runner**.

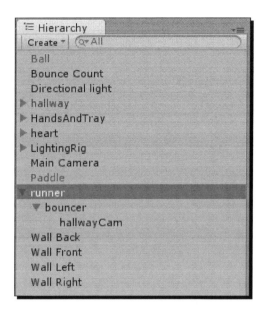

Time for action – Animating the bouncer

We'll use the Unity animation tool to create an animation clip for our **bouncer** Game Object.

1.   In the **Hierarchy** panel, click to select the **bouncer** Game Object.

2.   In the menu, select **Window | Animation** to bring up the **Animation** window. If you so choose, you can dock it within the interface like the **Hierarchy** and **Project** panels. I prefer not to because I like having a lot of space for this window. I resize the window so that it covers most of the right half of my screen. You can drag the middle line that splits the **Animation** window (dividing the dark and light parts of the window) to give more or less real estate to the key view (dark side).

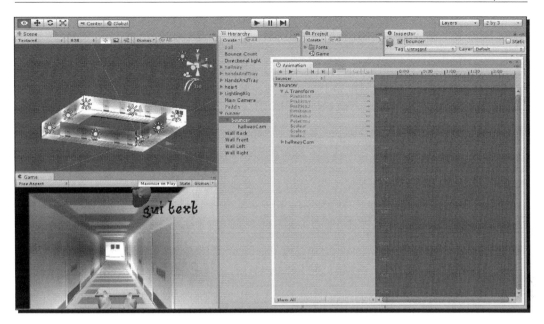

3. Click the round reddish-pink **Record** button near the top-left of the window.

4. Unity asks you to name your new **Animation** clip. Save it as **animBounce**.

What just happened – red and raging

When you save your animation clip, two things happen: the clip becomes a tangible, reusable asset in your **Project** panel, and the **Record** button and **Play**, **Pause**, and **Step** buttons all light up red to notify you that you're in animation mode.

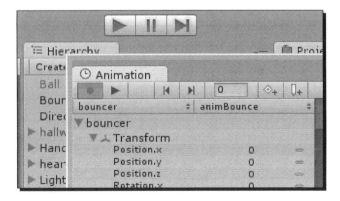

Why make such a big, noticeable deal out of it? Because whenever you move your recorded **GameObject** around, Unity is going to remember its position, rotation, and scale in a keyframe. **Keyframe** is a term borrowed from classical animation. Animation software packages store the position, rotation, and scale values of objects in keyframes, and use a process called **interpolation** to figure out how to animate an object between those keys. In classical animation, this is called **in-betweening**.

If you create a keyframe for a Game Object on frame 1 and another on frame 10 where the Game Object is moved across the screen, Unity will interpolate between those two keyframes, filling in the blanks to make the Game Object move from one side of the screen to the other.

Time for action – I like to move it, move it

In the case of our **bouncer** Game Object, we'll set up three keyframes: one for the up position, one for the down position, and a third to bring it back to the top of the bounce.

1. Click on the X cone in the **Scene** view's axis gizmo to view the level from the side.

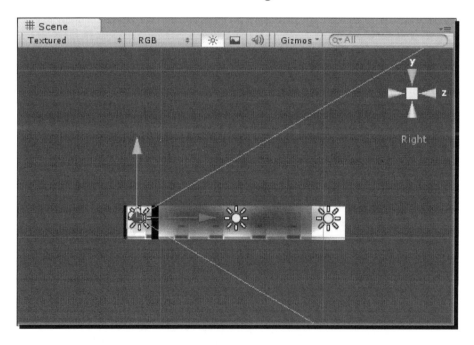

2. In the **Animation** view, enter an initial value of **-0.5** for the bouncer's **Position.y** value. A little, diamond-shaped keyframe symbol appears on frame 1 at the top of the **Animation** view. This means that Unity is remembering the position, rotation, and scale of the Game Object on that frame.

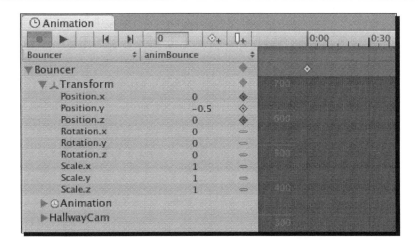

3. Click-and-drag the vertical red line (not the keyframe diamond) to frame 10, or enter the number **10** into the frame field at the top of the **Animation** window (next to the playback controls). It's very important not to mistake frame 10 with the 10:00 second mark!

4. On frame 10, punch in a **Position.y** value of **-0.1**. A second keyframe is created for us on frame 10, storing the new values.

5. Go to frame 20.

6. Enter the initial **Position.y** value of **-0.5** to bring the bouncer back to the top of its bounce. A third diamond keyframe icon appears.

7. At the bottom of the **Animation** view, click the drop-down labeled **Default** and choose **Loop** instead.

8. The animation arc between keyframes for the bouncer's y position spans into infinity to indicate that the animation loops. (You may have to pan and zoom around the **Animation** view to see this using the same controls that you use to pan and zoom around your 3D **Scene**.)

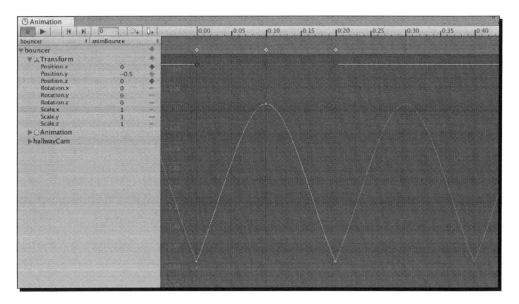

9. Click on the **Record** button to stop recording.

10. Test the game.

Now, Nurse Slipperfoot bounces the heart on the tray while running on the spot! That's great for her personal calisthenics routine, but not so hot for her poor transplant patient.

 Note: If it doesn't work, check to make sure that the **animBounce** animation component is attached to the **bouncer** Game Object.

Have a go hero – Bounce your brains out

You can click-and-drag animations onto any Game Objects you like. Try removing the **animBounce** animation from the **bounce** Game Object and applying it to the **hallway**.

When you test your game, you should see the hallway snap to the X and Z position defined in our **animBounce** animation keyframes. The entire hallway model bounces up and down just like our **bounce** Game Object did. You can apply the same animation to the heart or the tray. Just as you can apply one script to many different Game Objects, a single animation can go a long way.

Time for action – Animating the runner

Let's get that RN RuNning!

1. Click on the green Y-axis cone to switch into top view. Pan and zoom so that the hallway fills the **Scene** view, like it did when we were building our lighting rig.

2. In the **Hierarchy** panel, select the **runner** Game Object.

3. In the **Animation** window, click on the **Record** button.

4. Name the new animation **animRun**. A new, reusable animation appears in the **Project** panel.

5. Punch in the following values on frame 0:

   ❑ **Position.x: 6.5**

   ❑ **Position.y: 1.2**

   ❑ **Position.z: -31.5**

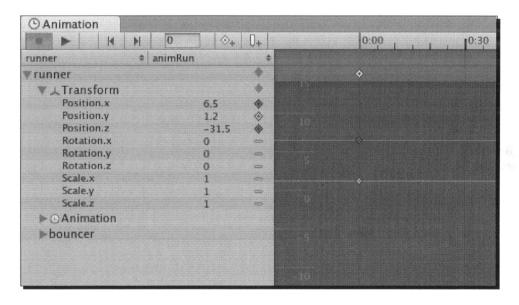

6. If those values are already punched in when you create the animation, click on one of them and press the *Enter* key to make sure Unity registers a diamond-shaped keyframe to remember those settings.

7. Click on the little, gray dash symbol to the right of the **Rotation.x** value. You'll find a small drop-down menu. Choose **Add Curves** from that list. We're adding curves to the rotation values because we'll need to modify them later.

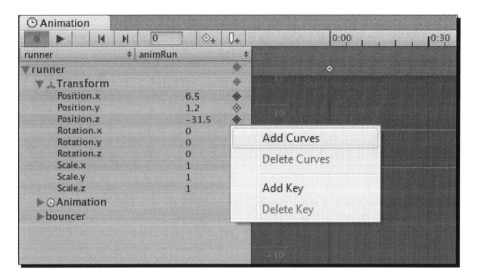

8. Go to frame 120.

9. Move the **runner** up along the Z-axis to the top-right corner of the building, or type in **-19.4** for its **Position.z** value. Note: you'll have to press the *Enter* key on all three x, y and z values to make them "stick" on this keyframe if you decide to key in the values by hand.

10. Go to frame 240.

11. Move the **runner** along the X-axis to the top-left corner of the level, or key in **-6.5** for **Position.x**.

12. Move to frame 360.

13. Move the **runner** down in the Z-axis to **-31.5** to the bottom-left corner of the hallway.

14. Go to frame 480.

15. Move the **runner** along the X-axis back to the bottom-right corner where it started. Use these values:

- ❏ **Position.x: 6.5**
- ❏ **Position.y: 1.2**
- ❏ **Position.z: -31.5**

16. Set this **Animation** clip to **Loop**, just like the **bounce**.

17. Uncheck the pink round **Animate** button to stop recording, and then test your game!

What just happened – holy hospital rampage, Batman!

At this point, it looks like Nurse Slipperfoot herself may be in serious need of medical attention. True, we haven't rotated her to look down the hallways, but even so, she flies through the emergency ward like a banshee, busting through walls and generally freaking me out.

That's because like other 3D programs, Unity gives us **Bezier** control over our keyframe values. A **Bezier** is a line that you can bend with little handles, which can either work separately or in tandem to create smooth motion. This enables us to ease animations in and out so that they look less robotic (or not, depending on our needs).

Time for action – How to "handle" Nurse Slipperfoot

You can mess around with each node's Bezier handles by clicking on the dots in the **Animation** window, selecting a handle style from the right-click menu, and pulling the little gray handles around, provided the keyframes are set to **Flat**, **Broken**, or **Free Smooth**. To correct this animation simply, we're going to apply a boring straight line between all of the key points.

1. In the **Animation** window, press *Ctrl/Command + A* to select all of the nodes in the animation.

2. Right-click/secondary-click on any one of the nodes.

3. Select **Both Tangents | Linear** to flatten the curves between the nodes.

4. Test your game.

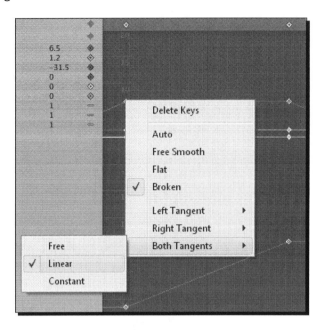

That's better! Nurse Slipperfoot's still not facing the right direction as she runs, but at least she's no longer in need of an exorcism.

> Note: If Nurse Slipperfoot is still phasing through walls, you may need to revisit your keyframes and make sure she's positioned correctly at each corner of the hallway on frames 0 (bottom-right), 120 (top-right), 240 (top-left), 360 (bottom-left), and 480 (bottom-right). If she's not ending up where you think she should be, you may have forgotten to punch *Enter* to confirm all three position axes—x, y and z—on all of the frames we just modified.

Time for action – You spin me right round

Let's correct that little issue of the nurse careening sideways and backwards through the hallway by adding rotation values for the **Runner** Game Object, to make her face the proper direction.

1. In the **Animation** window, go to frame 100. This is 20 frames before our next keyframe.

2. Click on the little button with the white diamond and plus symbol—the "add keyframe" button—to tell Unity to remember the Runner's position/rotation/scale on this frame.

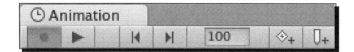

3. Go to frame 120.

4. Enter a **Rotation.y** value of **-90** to face the camera down the next hallway.

5. Move the **Runner** down the second hallway just a bit, maybe to **Position.x 6.0**, to make the motion slightly less robotic.

6. Go to frame 220 and add a new keyframe.

7. On frame 240, rotate the **Runner** to **Rotation.y**: **-180** to aim it down the third hallway.

8. Keep repeating these steps through the rest of the animation. Set a keyframe 20 frames before the existing one, and then move to the corner keyframe and set the Y rotation. Use -270 and -360 for the next two Y rotation values.

9. Select all of the keyframes and set their curves to linear.

10. Stop recording animation, and test your game.

The runner tears down the hallways, turning the corners and facing the proper direction. Having a hospital background cranks up the credibility and polishes of this game so much! It's like a doctor-prescribed injection of awesomeness.

Anticipating the turns

Are you wondering why we dropped a keyframe 20 frames before turning the corner? If we had simply rotated the **Runner** at each corner, Unity would have tweened towards that new rotation the entire time the nurse was running down the hallway. We want the rotation to stay constant almost to the end of the hallway, so we set a keyframe as a sort of break point to tell Unity "okay, you can start tweening the rotation right here."

Have a go hero – Give Robo-Nurse a soul

With straight Bezier curves connecting our nodes, our **Runner** animation tends to look a little artificial or robotic. Now that you've seen the right-click menu to adjust the smoothness of those Beziers, why not spend some time fiddling with the handles to see if you can eke out a more natural motion through the hallway? But first, a warning: adjusting Bezier handles for 3D animation can be very time-consuming! If you get bogged down, or lose heart, just select the nodes and slap "Linear" on them to be done with it. That's the equivalent of blowing up a building and walking away in slow motion like a badass while a giant fireball ignites the sky. Aw yeah.

Have a go hero – Use your new-found powers for good

Just as we did with our other games, let's whip up a quick list of modifications and improvements we could make to *Ticker Taker* to make it a complete game.

◆ Title Screen, Instructions, Credits—these all go without saying.

◆ Sound Effects—you know how to hook these in, so why dontcha? The Ticker Taker cries out for a big wet *squish* whenever the heart hits the tray. You could also add the frantic clippity-clop sounds of Nurse Slipperfoot's Doc Martens slapping the linoleum as she makes her mad dash down the hallway.

◆ Returning to the debate of creating an endless, always-lose game versus one the player can finish, what if you built a GUI element that depicted a 2D nurse icon running from point A to point B? All the player has to do is keep the heart aloft until the nurse icon reaches the end of the progress bar.

◆ To add a bit of difficulty, you could add a little ECG heart monitor to the corner of the screen that beeps every time the player bounces the heart with enough force. Add a timer so that if x seconds elapse without the player bouncing the heart hard enough, the heart stops beating and the player loses the game. This will ensure that the player doesn't simply let the heart roll around on the tray until the nurse reaches the transplant ward.

◆ The player's going to catch on pretty quickly that Nurse Slipperfoot is running in a circle! How about building two connected hallways, and making her run a figure-8 course for added visual variety?

◆ The hallway is pretty flat and bland at the moment. Perhaps you could add spice to the environment by placing gurneys, IV stands, and even other patients in the level.

Time for action – Deploying your game

You may be wondering why the section on deploying your game has been squeezed into a tiny section at the very end of the book. That's because Unity makes it so darned simple to package up your game, that we don't need any more space. Here's how to do it:

1. In the menu, select **File | Build Settings...**.

2. We need to add **Scenes** to this list that we want bundled into our **game** file. The first **Scene** we add to the list will be the first one Unity displays to our player, so that's where our preloader or title screen should normally go.

   Because we have only one **Scene** in this game so far, click on the **Add Current** button to pop it into the list. In games with multiple **Scenes**, you can simply click-and-drag those **Scenes** into the list to add them to the build. Be sure to choose "Web Player" as your deployment preference if you'd like a file that can be played in a browser.

3. Click on the **Build and Run** button.

4. Unity asks where you want to save the `.unity3d` game file. Choose a folder and click on the **Save** button.

5. In the background, Unity cranks out a `.unity3d` file and an `.html` file to house it. Then Unity throws us to our default web browser and opens the HTML file. And there's our game, running beautifully within the browser.

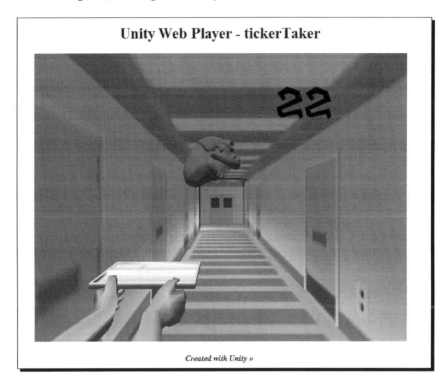

6. To publish the game live to the world, just upload the `.unity3d` file and the `.html` file to your web host, or pop it onto one of the Unity game portals we looked at off the top of the book. Unity support grows on a daily basis, so there are bound to be many more places hosting Unity games by the time you read this paragraph.

Note that you can also deploy your game as a standalone version to run on the Mac and PC platforms. And if you spring for additional Unity licenses and development kits, you can deploy your content to a growing list of platforms, including iOS, the Xbox 360, the Playstation 3, the Wii, and Android.

Time to grow

The theme in all of this is "growth." While only a few years old, Unity has made a huge splash in the game development world by offering a suite of tools that blew the lid off of 3D browser-based gaming, while making it easier for people without serious C-based programming knowledge to develop for once-unfathomable devices.

It's a complete cliché, but practice really is the one thin line separating you from developing those big projects you put up in jars on the shelf at the beginning of the book. Start building a game with what you know. With each project, set a new attainable challenge for yourself. This book has taught you how to set lights in a flat-looking hallway environment. But you've heard this term "lightmap" when reading about 3D games and models. What's that all about? Well, why not build a new game using the skills you've already developed, and commit to incorporating one lightmapped object in it? When you finish the game, you'll have added one extra tool to your tool belt, and you'll have a new, finished game for your portfolio.

How do you make a skybox so that the corner seams are invisible? How do you make your player appear damaged when he steps in lava? What's normal mapping? How do you program an enemy to follow and shoot at the player? How do you create your own models, textures, and animations? How do you put a different hat, gun, or pair of pants on a character model? How do you detect when one Game Object is near another, without colliding?

With each new thing you want your game to do, you'll come up with a question. Too many questions could discourage you and sink your ship before it even gets out to sea. Pick one thing and lock onto it with your laser scope. Do whatever it takes to discover the answer to your question, the solution to your problem, and build that solution into your game. Problem solved. Dragon slain. Checkbox checked. You will slay many dragons/cuddle many kittens in your journey as a game developer, but there's no need to take on the entire dragon/kitten army all at once.

Be sure to check out the resources listed at the end of the book for places to turn to when you're stuck. You can also use that section to source new information when you're ready to add new tools to your tool belt.

Beyond the book

If you're starting from scratch and you made it this far, I hope you've found Unity to be well within your ability to develop your own 3D and 2D games. If you're sidling over from another development tool like Flash, GameMaker Pro, or Unreal Engine, I hope this book has provided you with a sampling of the slick pipeline and process that Unity makes possible. A book like this can only ever scratch the surface of such an enormously powerful tool as Unity; if you've enjoyed what you've done with Unity so far, a fantastically supportive community and a deliciously deep development tool awaits you beyond the back cover of this book.

References

Online resources

Here's a list of websites where you can tap into the Unity development community to find answers and to ask questions. Please remember to be courteous and respectful of more experienced developers' time. As with any online forum, be sure to search existing content for an answer before you ask a question.

Unity Manual: When you're new to a technology and you ask naive or poorly researched questions, you may hear "RTFM" a lot, which stands for "would you please be so kind as to review the product manual?" Well, here's the link to the product manual, which covers both beginner and advanced topics, including examples on writing your own custom Shaders:

```
http://unity3d.com/support/documentation/Manual/index.html
```

Google: A search engine should be the first place you look for answers. If the solution is plainly available with a simple query, you'll quickly exhaust the goodwill of the real-live people you petition for help online.

```
http://lmgtfy.com/
```

Unity Answers: This Unity sub-domain bills itself as "The best place to ask and answer questions about development with Unity", and it's not lying. Many of your Google searches will lead you here.

```
http://answers.unity3d.com/
```

Internet Relay Chat (IRC) is a chat system. You can download an IRC client to reach one of its many servers. IRC users split themselves into channels by topic. The very best channel that I've found for Unity discussion is *#unity3d* on the server group `irc.freenode.net`. Wikipedia hosts this list of IRC client programs:

```
http://en.wikipedia.org/wiki/Comparison_of_Internet_Relay_Chat_
clients
```

Unity for Flash Developers: *The Ethical Games Blog* has a great collection of tutorials for Flash developers looking to make the jump.

```
http://ethicalgames.wordpress.com/2009/01/14/unity-for-flash-
developers-tutorial-1/
```

Unity 3D Tutorials: The creators of Unity host a growing number of tutorials on the program's official site.

```
http://unity3d.com/support/resources/tutorials/
```

YouTube: The Internet's most popular video sharing site has tons of Unity 3D tutorials. Just search "Unity 3D" to get started.

```
http://www.youtube.com
```

Twitter: The best place to get up-to-the-minute news and information about practically everything is on Twitter. Follow as many Unity developers as you can find, and keep a watch on the `#unity3D` hash tag to become the smartest kid on your block. Twitter: it's not just about what your friends are having for lunch.

```
http://www.twitter.com
```

Untold Entertainment: It's shameless, I know, but I'll add a plug for my own corporate site. I'll be posting tutorials and articles about my own adventures with Unity 3D and my ongoing exploits as an independent game developer. If you liked this book, but felt that it needed more rude jokes and ridiculous animal pictures swiped from a Google Image Search, join me over at *Untold* and I'll give you the cure for what ails you.

```
http://www.untoldentertainment.com/blog
```

Offline resources

Local User Groups: Lots of Unity developers are banding together to form user groups, which usually meet monthly. Boston has launched **Boston Unity Group (BUG)**, and many other cities are following suit. If your town doesn't already have a user group, why don't you start one?

Unite: This annual Unity 3D conference is the premiere event and is the best place to go to meet the planet's top Unity developers, and to hear exciting announcements about the future of the product. See you there!

```
http://unity3d.com/unite/
```

Free development tools

There are a number of great development tools that integrate well with Unity 3D, like 3D Studio Max and Maya. However, many of these programs can cost thousands of dollars (like 3D Studio Max and Maya). Here are some links to free tools that may help you to develop your games:

Graphics

Blender: A 3D modeling and animation program, with its own built-in game engine. Blender has a steep, often infuriating, learning curve, but if you buy a book you'll be fine. I recommend *Blender for Dummies*.

```
http://www.blender.org/download/get-blender/
```

GIMP: A 2D photo manipulation program, somewhat like Photoshop.

```
http://www.gimp.org/downloads/
```

Paint.NET: Another 2D photo manipulation program, with perhaps a simpler interface than GIMP.

```
http://www.getpaint.net/
```

Sound

SFXR: For lo-fi sound effects creation. The sounds in this book were created with SFXR.

```
http://www.drpetter.se/project_sfxr.html
```

This Flash port of SFXR works right in your browser!

```
http://www.superflashbros.net/as3sfxr/
```

Audacity: For audio editing and processing.

```
http://audacity.sourceforge.net/
```

Content sites

There are many different companies that offer packages of Unity-ready materials and models that you can license for use in your games. Licensing prices vary, but using these kits may be less expensive than hiring an artist or spending time creating these components yourself.

Unity Prefabs: These folks have built Twitter and Facebook integration kits, and host their own great collection of free tutorials to sweeten the deal. Use the coupon code "UntoldSavings" for 10% off all purchases!

    http://www.untoldentertainment.com/gamePrefabs

ActiveDen: This network of sites offers tons of user-submitted prefab content. The great news is that you can build and submit your own turn-key Unity 3D kits and split the revenue with ActiveDen when visitors buy your stuff.

    http://www.untoldentertainment.com/activeden

Frogames: This gorgeous site hosts some good-looking and wonderfully inexpensive content packs for your Unity 3D games, including buildings for real-time strategy games, spaceships, dungeons, and warriors. Use the coupon code "UntoldFrogames" for a 15% discount!

    http://www.untoldentertainment.com/frogames

Unity Technologies has put together an Asset Store packed with assets like the ones above, along with more scripts and shaders and time-saving wizwangs than you can shake a 300-poly-count stick at. I strongly urge you to use whatever help you can to get your game finished. Paying $30 to save yourself months of work isn't cheating—it's just using your head. If it comes down to a choice between paying a few bucks and never finishing your game, it's time to break open your piggy bank.

    http://unity3d.com/unity/editor/asset-store.html

Game portals

We kicked off the book by looking at some Unity games. As Unity gains support among developers, you can expect to see more sites devoted to hosting Unity-created content. Here are some of the portals and distribution services specializing in Unity 3D games:

    http://musegames.com/

    http://www.wooglie.com/

    http://dimerocker.com/

    http://blurst.com/

    http://www.kongregate.com/unity-games

Index

Symbols

3D games
  siren song 35
+= operator 207

A

aCards array 167
ActiveDen 380
aGrid array 168
ambient light 71
Anal Retentive 146
AngryBots Demo
  URL 19
animation.isPlaying, Break-Up game 300
animation.Play command 277
Animation view 364, 365
animBounce animation 366
animBounce animation keyframes 366
Application.LoadLevel call 142
Apply button 201
Armature 318
aRobotParts array 166
Array class 166
ArrayList class 179
Artillery Live!
  about 40, 44
  core mechanic 41
  feature set 42
  multilayer, features 43
  skin 41
  skinny on multiplayer 43

  Worms series 44
asterisk ("star") 83
Audacity 379
Awake function 196, 210

B

Bake Animations 274
Ball and Paddle, Ticker Taker game 239
Bezier 369
Big Fun Racing 16
billboarding 263
Blender 379
Blurst 15
bomb Prefab, Break-Up game 309
Bomb Script, Break-Up game 293
boolean 109
Boom Blox 49
Boston Unity Group (BUG) 378
bouncer
  animating 362
Break-Up game
  about 259, 260
  animation.Play command 277
  animations, registering 274, 275
  Bake Animations 274
  Bomb Script, renaming 293-295
  brownstone apartment, setting up 272, 273
  cartoon bomb model, setting up 261-263
  catch sound effect, adding 305
  character, adding 273, 274
  Character Prefab 273
  character rig 274

character, scripting 275-277
Collider Component 278, 279
Collider Components, adding to bomb 278
collision detection code, writing 299, 300
color, selecting 282
explosion sound effect 307
Explosion's settings, adjusting 281
facial explosions, adding 301
FallingObjectScript 296, 297
glass, adding 287
Glass Smash Particle System, placing into Prefab
292, 293
health points 309
Inspector panel 266
Instantiate command 285, 302
isMoving flag 277
landscape, varying 309
levels 309
new material, creating 291
objects, tagging 297, 298
Particle Animator 265
Particle Effect 264
Particle Renderer section 290
Particle System 264-266
Particle System, creating 288, 289
particle system effect, adding 261-263
Particle Systems 264
Particle System setting, URL 269
prefab 285
Prefab creating, steps 269, 270
Prefab, modifying 270, 271
prefab, re-prefabbing 279, 280
quota 308
Reconnect button 280
rigging 274
Rigidbody, adding to bomb 278
Rock Band 302
score points 308
smash sound effect 307
sound, adding 302, 303
sound, adding to FallingObjectScript 303, 304
sound effects, importing 305
sound effects, playing randomly 306, 307
spark, igniting 269
spark material, creating 266-268
Sparks Particle System 267
Split Animations 274

stein model 287
survive 308
testing 286
unlit bombs, catching 309
Update function 276
Browser-based 3D
about 10
Unity Web Player, installing 10, 11
BuildDeck function 163-165, 174, 180
BuildGrid function 152, 172, 182
BuildGrid() function 168
bullet, Shoot the Moon game
building 332
Bump Map 242

C

camera rig
setting up 361, 362
Capsule Collider, Ticker Taker game 238, 239
Card class 167
Cascading Style Sheets (CSS) 128
centerPoint value 223
centerPoint variable 224
Character Prefab 273
character rig 274
Clear Flags dropdown 318
clockFG graphic 210
clockFG texture 209, 211
clockIsPaused flag 202
code, volleyball game
about 81
animating with 100
ball, reappearing 88, 89
best practices 86
examining 86
hiding 84
Mesh Renderer component, finding 87, 88
paddle, animating 100
Unity Script Reference 89, 90
Unity script, writing 81, 82
update function 85, 86
viewing 83
content
versus features 36
content sites
about 380

ActiveDen 380
Frogames 380
Unity Prefabs 380
Culling Mask dropdown 316
customSkin variable 129

D

Dance Dance Revolution 49
Debug.Log() call 106
Debug.Log() function 104
Debug.Log() statement 104, 107, 171
Debug statements 203
delegating 305
development tools
Blender 379
GIMP 379
Paint.NET 379
Diceworks 16, 17
directional light 71
DisappearMe script 84, 96
DoCountdown function 209
DoCountdown() function 202, 204

E

Ellipsoid Particle Emitter section, Break-Up game
288
else if condition 327
enabled property 87, 89
enabled variable 93
EnemyShip Script 325
Euler function 117
Explode function 339
Explode() function 339-341

F

FallingObjectScript, Break-Up game 294
FBXImporter 231
FBXImporter, Ticker Taker game 233
features
versus content 36
File | New Project 123
FlexibleSpace() 158
FlexibleSpace elements 161
FlexibleSpace function 160
FlexibleSpace() function call 160

FlexibleSpace() method 157
FlipCardFaceUp function 174, 175, 181
flip n match memory game
bits, dissecting 166, 167
BuildDeck function 163
card-flipping function, buidling 174-177
deck, building 163-165
flip, dissecting 178
game grid, centering horizontally 160
game grid, centering vertically 157-160
GameScript script 188-192
Golly-GDD 156
grid, building 162
ID number for cards, providing 180, 181
IDs, comparing 181, 182
img argument, modifying 167, 168
playerCanClick flag 163
Random.Range() method 170
requisites 156
Start function 163
this 169
this.img = img; 169, 170
two-sided cards, making 172-174
victory, checking for 184, 185
float 109
for keyword 148
Frogames 380
FusionFall 12, 13

G

Game Design Document (GDD) 156
GameObject
adding, to scene 55
Game Portals 380
games
featureless game 36
redesigning 48
re-skinning 311
game scene 142
Game view 84
Game window, Scene window 22
Generate Mip Maps checkbox 137
GetComponent function 332
GIMP 379
Glass Smash Particle System, Break-Up game
292

Golly-GDD 156
Google 377
Graphical User Interfaces. *See* GUI
GUI 121
GUI.BeginGroup() function 213
GUI.Button method 132
GUI.EndGroup() function 213
GUILayout.BeginVertical() call 157
GUILayout class 150, 157
GUILayout commands 185
GUILayout.EndVertical() call 157
GUILayout.FlexibleSpace() call 157
GUILayout.Width method 153
GUI Texture 136
GUIUtility class 220

H

halfH (half height) 111
halfW variable 109
hallwayLight Prefab 354, 359
Halo, Shoot the Moon game
    building 334-337
HandsAndTray Game Object, Ticker Taker game 248
handsAndTray model, Ticker Taker game 232
handsAndTray parent, Ticker Taker game 230
Hand tool (Q) 29
hardcoded numbers 105
hasLost flag, Ticker Taker game 253
Head-up display (HUD) 40
HeartBounce script, Ticker Taker game 248
HeroShipCollisionCage model 320
HeroShip model, Shoot the Moon game 318
Hierarchy panel, Scene window
    about 23, 24
    inspector panel 25, 26
    layers dropdowns 28
    layout dropdowns 28
    playback controls 28
    project panel 24, 25
    scene controls 29

I

img variable 145, 174
ImportinghandsAndTray model, Ticker Taker game 229

in-betweening 364
IndexOf() method 179
inheritance 297
Input.mousePosition entry 102
inspector panel 84, 89, 130, 142, 266, 352
Inspector panel, Break-Up game 296
Instantiate command 285, 302, 338
Instantiate command, Break-Up game 301
int 109
internet games 37
Internet Relay Chat (IRC) 378
interpolation 364
int.ToString() method 206
isFaceUp Boolean flag 174
isFaceUp variable 174
isMoving flag 277
isMoving variable 328
isPastHalfway variable 217
isVisible variable 92
iterator 148

K

Katamari Damacy 49
Keyframe 364

L

lastX variable 328
light
    ambient light 71
    directional light 71
    moving 69, 70
    point light 71
    rotating 69, 70
    spotlight 71
    turning on 353-360
lightbulb 34
LightingRig Game Object 355
Local User Groups 378

M

Massively Multiplayer Online Role-Playing Game (MMORPG) 12
matchesMade variable 184
matchesNeededToWin variable 184

Material parameter, Sphere Collider Component 78

Materials 197

materials, Ticker Taker game
adding, to models 242, 244
papier-mâché coating 241
UV mapping 242

Maximize on Play button 74, 84

mechanic
versus skin 36

mesh 65-67

Mesh Collider 322

Mesh Collider component 321

Mesh Collider Component, Ticker Taker game 235

mesh filter component 56

mesh renderer compoennt 56

Mesh Renderer component
finding 87, 88

Metal Gear Solid 49

minutes variable 206

mip-mapping 137

Models 348

Monodevelop 82

motherload
about 38
core mechanic 39
features 39
front-of-house 39
skin 39

MouseFollow script
about 100
creating 97, 98

MouseFollow script, Ticker Taker game 235

Move tool (W) 29

MyGUI custom GUI skin 143

N

nested loop 149

new keyword 149

numHits variable, Ticker Taker game 253

nurse slipperfoot, handling 369, 370

O

offline resources
local user groups 378

unite 379

Off-Road Velociraptor Safari 14, 15

OnCollisionEnter function 248, 331, 339-341

OnGUI function 130, 132, 134, 151, 184, 210, 217

online resources
about 377
Google 377
Internet Relay Chat (IRC) 378
Twitter 378
Unity 3D Tutorials 378
Unity answers 377
Unity, for Flash Developers 378
Unity manual 377
Untold Entertainment 378
YouTube 378

origin 58

P

paddle
about 66
adding 62-64

Paint.NET 379

Particle Animator 265

Particle Animator section, Break-Up game 289

Particle Effect 264

Particle Systems 264

Peggle
about 46
lessons 47

physic material 78

physics
adding, to game 74, 75

pie clock, robot repair game
clock uut 224
code, preparing 201
countdown logic, creating 202-204
font texture, creating 197-200
half-circle pieces, rotating 220, 221
impact font 200, 201
material, creating 197-200
picture clock graphics 207-209
pie chart script, writing 217-219
script, preparing 194
shrinking clock 213
text color, changing 196

text, preparing 195, 196
textures, drawing 216
time on-screen, displaying 204, 205
Pixel Inset heading 317
Play Again button, Ticker Taker game
adding 256
Play button 79
playerCanClick flag 163, 178
playerHasWon variable 184
Play Game button 132
point light 71
polygon 66
polygon count 66
Pong
about 44
feature set 46
mechanic 44
skin 45, 46
Powerup class 99
print 133
print command 340
print() statement 133, 171
print statements 152
Project panel 348, 352
Pseudocode 106

Q

quaternion 115, 116
Quaternion class 117
Quaternion.Euler function 118

R

Random.Range() method 170
Range() method 166
raster images 201
Reconnect button 280
RemoveAt() method 166
Renderer class
about 91, 92, 144
enabled variable 93
ResetPosition function 329, 339
ResetPosition() function 330-332, 339
Resources.Load call 153
Return-On-Investment (ROI) 193
rigging 274
Rigidbody 75

Rigidbody component, Break-Up game 295
robot repair game, example
about 123
aCards buckets 147
aCardsFlipped buckets 147
aGrid array 148
aGrid buckets 147
Application.LoadLevel call 141
area, creating to store grid 151
assets package 136
button, centering 138
button UI control, creating 130-133
clock code, preparing 201
clock script, preparing 194
clock, shrinking 213, 214
clock text color, changing 196
clock text, preparing 195, 196
clock uut 224
code, grokking 152
code, investigating 138-140
countdown logic, creating 202, 203
custom GUI skin, creating 128-130
custom GUI skin, linking 128-130
essentials, storing 145, 146
font texture, creating 197-200
for keyword 148
game, planning 143, 144
game scene, preparing 142, 143
GameScript script 144, 145
grid, building 151, 152
GUICam 127
GUILayout.Width method 153
GUI muscles 209-212
GUI, preparing 126, 127
half-circle pieces, rotating 220, 221
impact font 200, 201
iterative loop 148
iterator 148
material, creating 197-200
mip-mapping 137
nested loop 149, 150
OnGUI function 134, 135
OnGUI function, building 150
operation pie clock, commencing 220-222
picture clock graphics, grabbing 207-209
pie chart script, writing 217-219
pie chart-style clock, building 214

pie chart-style clock, building steps 214-216
pie clock, positioning 223, 224
pie clock, scaling 223, 224
Play Game button 140, 142, 147
Resources.Load call 153
scenes, adding to build list 141, 142
scene, setting 124, 125
stage, setting 142
textures, drawing 216
TimeIsUp() method 224
time on-screen, displaying 204, 205
ToString() method 206, 207
Rotate tool (E) 29
rotation variable 219
runner
  animating 367-369

S

Scale tool (R) 29
scene
  saving 62
Scene window
  about 22
  Game window 22
  Hierarchy panel 23
  inspector panel 25, 26
  inspector panel, using 26-28
  layers dropdown 28
  layout dropdown 28
  playback controls 28
  Project panel 24, 25
  scene controls 29
screen coordinates
  versus world coordinates 102, 103
Screen.width property 139
SFXR 305, 379
Shoot the Moon game
  Apply button 325
  Bomb child, deleting 323
  Bomb, renaming 324
  bullet 333
  bullet, building 332
  Character Prefab 320
  Character Prefabs EnemyShip, renaming 324
  clear flags, setting 318
  CollisionCage 321

  custom colliders 322
  EnemyShip 327
  EnemyShip Game Object 323
  EnemyShip Script 325, 326
  Explode function 339
  Explode() function 339, 340, 341
  GetComponent function 332
  GUI texture, resizing 317
  Halo, building 334-337
  HeroShip Game Object 319
  HeroShip model 318, 319
  HeroShip, renaming 324
  HeroShip Script 329
  HeroShip script, code adding to 337-339
  HeroShip Script, modifying 327-329
  Mesh Collider component 321
  OnCollisionEnter function 331-340
  print command 340
  project, duplicating 312, 313
  ResetPosition function 339
  ResetPosition() function 330, 331, 339
  sound effect, in Assets folder 342, 343
  space backdrop, adding 313-316
  Stein Prefab 323
  Update function 326
ShowTime() function 202, 205
singular piece of joy 37
skin
  versus mechanic 36
Slerp 117
Slerp() function 117, 118
solitaire flip n' match game 122
someNum (ssome crazy old random number)
  166
space backdrop, Shoot the Moon game
  adding 313-315
Sparks child 323
Sparks Particle System 267
sphere collider component 56
Spherical linear interpolation 117
Split Animations 274
spotlight 71
Start function 163, 168, 328
startMatrix variable 220
startTime variable 202
statements 81
Stein model, Break-Up game 288

Stein Prefab container, Break-Up game **288**
string **109**
Super Monkey Ball 49
System.Object 144
System.Object class 144

T

target **117**
Texture2D variables **209, 217**
this.img = img; **169, 170**
three-dimensional intersecting planes **110**
Ticker Taker game
  about **227, 228**
  animBounce animation **366**
  ball and paddle **239**
  Bezier **369**
  bouncer, animating **362**
  bouncer Game Object **364**
  bounces, tracking **252, 253**
  bounce, tweaking **251, 252**
  camera rig, setting up **361**
  colliders, auto-generating **234**
  deploying **373, 374**
  FBXImporter **231**
  FBX import scale settings, changing **233, 234**
  font texture, creating **247**
  halls, checking **352, 353**
  hallway model **348, 349**
  HeartBounce script, creating **248**
  heart, creating **236-239**
  in-betweening **364**
  interpolation **364**
  invisible walls, erecting **244, 246**
  Keyframe **364**
  lights, turning on **353-360**
  lose condition, adding **254, 255**
  main camera, adjusting **351**
  materials, adding to models **242, 244**
  materials, creating **240**
  mesh colliders, convexing **234, 235**
  model behavior **228, 229**
  models, exploring **229, 230**
  MouseFollow script, attaching to HandsAndTray
    game object **235**
  nurse slipperfoot, handling **369, 370**
  OnCollisionEnter function **248**

open heart surgery **347, 348**
Play Again button, adding **256**
runner, animating **367-369**
Runner Game Object **370, 371**
scene **232**
second camera, creating **350, 351**
tray, tagging **248-251**
velocity, storing **252**
velocityWasStored flag **252**
tiltAngle variables 118
Time.deltaTime 117
TimeIsUp() function 202, 203
TimeIsUp() method 224
timeRemaining values 209
TitleGUI script 138
TitleGUI script component 129
ToString() method 207
transform component 56, 98, 99
Transform.rotation page 113
Twitter 378
two-dimensional plane 110

U

Unite 379
Unity 3D
  about **9**
  Big Fun Racing **16**
  Bootcamp, exploring **19, 20**
  Browser-based 3D **10, 11**
  Diceworks **16, 17**
  FusionFall **12, 13**
  Off-Road Velociraptor Safari **14, 15**
  Off-Road Velociraptor Safari, building **15**
  URL, for downloading **18**
  Wooglie **15**
Unity 3D Tutorials 378
Unity answers 377
Unity, for Flash Developers 378
Unity manual 377
Unity Prefabs 380
Unity project
  creating **51, 52**
  volleyball game **53, 54**
  volleyball game, features **54**
Unity script
  unsticking **95**

Unity Web Player
  installing 10, 11
Untold Entertainment 378
update function 85, 86, 113, 130, 151, 276, 326, 336
Update() function 196
Update function, Ticker Taker game 253
UV mapping 242

V

var keyword 108
velocityWasStored flag, Ticker Taker game 252
volleyball game
  ambient light 71
  ball, creating 55-57
  ball, making bouncy 76, 77
  ball, moving into sky 60
  ball, renaming 57
  ball, shrinking 61, 62
  camera, effects 73
  Debug.Log() function 104
  deep, three-dimensional intersecting planes 110
  directional light 71
  DIY physics materials 77, 78
  flat, two-dimensional plane 110
  hardcoded numbers 105
  hitter, creating 55-57
  light, adding 68, 69
  light, moving 69, 70
  light, rotating 69, 70
  matrix, viewing 104
  mesh 65-67
  new number, adding 106, 107
  numbers, tracking 105
  origin story 58, 59
  paddle, adding 62-64
  paddle, listening to 104
  paddle, moving 103
  performance, cracking 67
  physics, adding 74, 75
  point light 71
  quaternion 115
  sample code, adding to script 113-115
  scene, saving 62
  spotlight 71
  testing 73, 74
  Unity Language Reference, revisiting 112
  variable, declaring to store screen midpoint 108
  var keyword 108
  word, picking 101, 102
  XYZ/RGB 59
  Y position of mouse, following 111

W

walls, Ticker Taker game
  erecting 244, 246
Wooglie 15
world coordinates
  versus screen coordinates 102, 103
World of Warcraft (WoW) 47

X

XYZ/RGB 59

Y

YouTube 378

Thank you for buying
Unity 3.x Game Development by Example
Beginner's Guide

About Packt Publishing

Packt, pronounced 'packed', published its first book "Mastering phpMyAdmin for Effective MySQL Management" in April 2004 and subsequently continued to specialize in publishing highly focused books on specific technologies and solutions.

Our books and publications share the experiences of your fellow IT professionals in adapting and customizing today's systems, applications, and frameworks. Our solution-based books give you the knowledge and power to customize the software and technologies you're using to get the job done. Packt books are more specific and less general than the IT books you have seen in the past. Our unique business model allows us to bring you more focused information, giving you more of what you need to know, and less of what you don't.

Packt is a modern, yet unique publishing company, which focuses on producing quality, cutting-edge books for communities of developers, administrators, and newbies alike. For more information, please visit our website: www.PacktPub.com.

Writing for Packt

We welcome all inquiries from people who are interested in authoring. Book proposals should be sent to author@packtpub.com. If your book idea is still at an early stage and you would like to discuss it first before writing a formal book proposal, contact us; one of our commissioning editors will get in touch with you.

We're not just looking for published authors; if you have strong technical skills but no writing experience, our experienced editors can help you develop a writing career, or simply get some additional reward for your expertise.

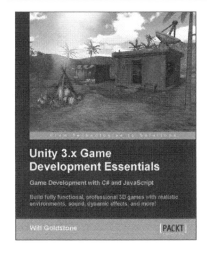